Lecture Notes in Computer Science 4746

Commenced Publication in 1973
Founding and Former Series Editors:
Gerhard Goos, Juris Hartmanis, and Jan van Leeuwen

T0223234

Andrea Bondavalli   Francisco Brasileiro
Sergio Rajsbaum (Eds.)

Dependable Computing

Third Latin-American Symposium, LADC 2007
Morelia, Mexico, September 26-28, 2007
Proceedings

 Springer

Volume Editors

Andrea Bondavalli
Università di Firenze, DSI
Viale Morgagni 65, 50134 Firenze, Italy
E-mail: bondavalli@unifi.it

Francisco Brasileiro
Universidade Federal de Campina Grande
Departamento de Sistemas e Computação, Laboratório de Sistemas Distribuídos
Av. Aprígio Veloso, 882 - 58.109-970, Campina Grande, PB, Brazil
E-mail: fubica@dsc.ufcg.edu.br

Sergio Rajsbaum
Universidad Nacional Autónoma de México (UNAM), Instituto de Matemáticas
Ciudad Univesitaria, D.F. 04510, México
E-mail: rajsbaum@math.unam.mx

Library of Congress Control Number: Applied for

CR Subject Classification (1998): C.3, C.4, B.1.3, B.2.3, B.3.4, B.4.5, D.2.4, D.2.8,
D.4.5, E.4, J.7

LNCS Sublibrary: SL 1 – Theoretical Computer Science and General Issues

ISSN   0302-9743
ISBN-10   3-540-75293-5 Springer Berlin Heidelberg New York
ISBN-13   978-3-540-75293-6 Springer Berlin Heidelberg New York

Springer is a part of Springer Science+Business Media

springer.com

© Springer-Verlag Berlin Heidelberg 2007
Printed in Germany

Typesetting: Camera-ready by author, data conversion by Scientific Publishing Services, Chennai, India
Printed on acid-free paper   SPIN: 12167449   06/3180   5 4 3 2 1 0

Foreword

The Latin-American Symposium on Dependable Computing, LADC, is the main Latin-American event dedicated to the discussion of the many issues related to dependability in computer systems and networks. It is a forum for researchers and practitioners from all over the world to present and discuss their latest results and experiences in this field. LADC 2007, the third edition of this event, followed on the success of LADC 2005, which took place in Salvador, Bahia, Brazil, and LADC 2003, which took place at the Polytechnic School of the University of São Paulo.

LADC 2007 was co-located with the Mexican Annual Computing Conference (ENC), and AdHoc NOW 2007. It was organized by Universidad Autónoma Metropolitana (UAM) and Universidad Nacional Autónoma de México (UNAM). It was co-sponsored by the Brazilian Computer Society (SBC), the Mexican Society for Computer Science (SMCC), and IEEE TC on Dependable Computing and Fault Tolerance. It was organized in cooperation with IFIP Working Group 10.4 'Dependable Computing and Fault Tolerance,' the Chilean Computer Science Society (SCCC), and the Argentine Society for Informatics and Operations Research (SADIO). LADC 2007 included the following activities:

- Five Technical sessions: Fault-Tolerant Algorithms, Software Engineering of Dependable Systems, Networking and Mobile Computing, Experimental Dependability Evaluation, Intrusion Tolerance and Security
- Two keynote speeches: Philip Koopman (CMU, USA), Jean Arlat (LAAS-CNRS, France)
- Three tutorials: Lorenzo Alvisi (UT Austin, USA), Eduardo B. Fernandez (FAU, USA), Marco Vieira and Henrique Madeira (U Coimbra, Portugal)
- Two panels, chaired by: Henrique Madeira (U Coimbra, Portugal), Rogério de Lemos (U Kent, UK). The latter was a joint panel with AdHoc NOW 2007.

We would like to thank the LADC 2007 Organizing Committee and the support staff of ENC 2007 for having helped us with the organizational tasks, the Steering Committee for their advice, and the Program Committee Co-chairs for their cooperation. Special thanks go to Rogério de Lemos, who was a source of constant support and suggestions. Additionally, we would like to thank the invited guests, all the authors of submitted papers, the sponsoring partners, and Springer for accepting to publish the LADC proceedings in the LNCS series.

We hope all present at LADC 2007 enjoyed the symposium and their stay in Morelia.

September 2007   Sergio Rajsbaum

Preface

The Latin-American Dependable Computing Conference is in its third edition. LADC is the major Latin-American event dedicated to discussing the many issues related to computer system dependability. This symposium succeeded the well-established Brazilian Symposium on Fault-Tolerant Computers. Its objective is to provide a forum for international and Latin-American scientists and engineers to present their latest research results and application experience in this very dynamic field. The first LADC was held in São Paulo, Brazil, in October 2003, while the second was held in Salvador, Brazil, in October 2005. In its third edition the symposium took place in Morelia, Mexico.

This edition of LADC was co-organized by the Universidad Nacional Autónoma de México (UNAM) and the Universidad Autónoma Metropolitana (UAM). It was co-sponsored by SBC—Brazilian Computer Society, SMCC—Mexican Society for Computer Science, and IEEE TC on Dependable Computing and Fault Tolerance. Furthermore, committees of several global professional organizations, such as IFIP Working Group 10.4 'Dependable Computing and Fault-Tolerance', SCCC—Chilean Computer Science Society and SADIO—Argentine Society for Informatics and Operations Research, supported the symposium. LADC is thus the forum for Latin-American researchers in dependability and is extending towards a world-wide dimension as researchers from all over the world show their interest by choosing LADC to submit their manuscripts and present their work.

The selection process was very careful. Each manuscript was sent out for review to three PC members plus two external reviewers. Thirty-seven submissions from 17 countries were received and the 32 members of the Program Committee and 29 external reviewers returned on time a total of 150 reviews. This made the selection process very comprehensive. The committee met in cyberspace to arrange the technical program. A total of 14 papers were selected to appear in the proceedings. The rest of the technical program was defined to include two panels, a forum for 'Fast Abstracts' to report on very recent work and two invited talks by two distinguished scholars: Phil Koopman and Jean Arlat.

We would like to thank the Program Committee members for their help in putting together the final program. They helped us in many ways, right from the beginning, including topic identification, suggestion of external reviewers, refereeing and attending the virtual PC meeting in large numbers. We also thank all of the external reviewers for making available their time and their technical knowledge and the authors of all the manuscripts for their contributions and the timely submissions. Special thanks go to Sergio Rajsbaum, LADC 2007 General Chair, Fabíola Greve, the Fast Abstract Chair, Rogério de Lemos, and Henrique

Madeira, who took leadership in organizing two panels. Finally, we would like to acknowledge the support of the Steering Committee.

We hope you find these conference Proceedings interesting and stimulating.

September 2007   Andrea Bondavalli
                                                       Francisco Brasileiro

Organizing Committee

General Chair	Sergio Rajsbaum (Universidad Nacional Autónoma de México, Mexico)
Program Co-chairs	Andrea Bondavalli (Università degli Studi di Firenze, Italy) Francisco Brasileiro (Universidade Federal de Campina Grande, Brazil)
Publication Co-chairs	Fernando Luís Dotti (Pontifícia Universidade Católica do Rio Grande do Sul, Brazil) Imelda Paredes (Universidad Nacional Autónoma de México, Mexico)
Publicity Chair	Fernando Pedone (University of Lugano, Switzerland)
Finance Chair	Elizabeth Pérez (Universidad Autónoma Metropolitana, Mexico)
Local Arrangements Chair	Ricardo Marcelin-Jiménez (Universidad Autónoma Metropolitana, Mexico)
Tutorials Chair	Marcos K. Aguilera (HP Labs,USA)
Fast Abstracts Chair	Fabíola Greve (Universidade Federal da Bahia, Brazil)

Steering Committee

Carlos Maziero	Pontifícia Universidade Católica do Paraná, Brazil
Fabiola Greve	Universidade Federal da Bahia, Brazil
Jean Arlat	Laboratoire d'Analyse et d'Architecture des Systèmes-Centre National de la Recherche Scientifique, France
João Gabriel Silva	Universidade de Coimbra, Portugal
Rogério de Lemos	University of Kent, UK
Sergio Rajsbaum	Universidad Nacional Autónoma de México, Mexico
Taisy Silva Weber (Chair)	Universidade Federal do Rio Grande do Sul, Brazil

LADC Program Committee

Jean Arlat	Laboratoire d'Analyse et d'Architecture des Systèmes - Centre National de la Recherche Scientifique, France
Saurabh Bagchi	Purdue University, USA
Hector Cancela	Universidad de la República, Uruguay
Jose Contreras	Universidad Técnica Federico Santa María, Chile
Bojan Cukic	West Virginia University, USA
Pedro D'Argenio	Universidad Nacional de Córdoba, Argentina
Xavier Defago	Japan Advanced Institute of Science and Technology, Japan
Elias Procópio Duarte Jr.	Universidade Federal do Paraná, Brazil
Christof Fetzer	Technische Universität Dresden, Germany
Joni Fraga	Universidade Federal de Santa Catarina, Brazil
Roy Friedman	Technion - Israel Institute of Technology, Israel
Fabíola Greve	Universidade Federal da Bahia, Brazil
Farnam Jahanian	University of Michigan, USA
Ingrid Jansch-Pôrto	Universidade Federal do Rio Grande do Sul, Brazil
Ricardo Jimenez-Peris	Universidad Politécnica de Madrid, Spain
Henrique Madeira	Universidade de Coimbra, Portugal
Ricardo Marcelín-Jiménez	Universidad Autónoma Metropolitana, Mexico
Magnos Martinello	Fundação Instituto Capixaba de Pesquisas em Contabilidade, Economia e Finanças, Brazil
Eliane Martins	Universidade Estadual de Campinas, Brazil
Keith Marzullo	University of California, San Diego, USA
Carlos Maziero	Pontifícia Universidade Católica do Paraná, Brazil
Pedro Mejia-Alvarez	Instituto Politécnico Nacional, Mexico
Takashi Nanya	University of Tokyo, Japan
Edgar Nett	Otto-von-Guericke-Universität Magdeburg, Germany
Rui Oliveira	Universidade do Minho, Portugal
William Sanders	University of Illinois at Urbana Champaign, USA
André Schiper	Ecole Polytechnique Federale de Lausanne, Switzerland
Richard Schlichting	AT&T Research, USA
Jie Xu	Leeds University, UK
Avelino Zorzo	Pontifícia Universidade Católica do Rio Grande do Sul, Brazil

LADC Referees

Araceli Acosta
Nazareno Aguirre
Pedro Mejia-Alvarez
Jean Arlat
Saurabh Bagchi
Andrea Bondavalli
Francisco Brasileiro
Alcides Calsavara
Hector Cancela
Silvano Chiaradonna
Walfredo Cirne
Victor Costa
Bojan Cukic
Alessandro Daidone
Pedro D'Argenio
Xavier Defago
Felicita Di Giandomenico
Elias Procópio Duarte Jr.
João Durães
Lorenzo Falai
Christof Fetzer
Pablo Florentino
Mauro Fonseca
Joni da Silva Fraga
Roy Friedman
Fabíola Greve
Farnam Jahanian
Ingrid Jansch-Pôrto
Ricardo Jimenez-Peris
Piotr Karwaczynski

Luiz Lento
Paolo Lollini
Pablo Martinez Lopez
Lau Lung
Henrique Madeira
Paulo Mafra
José Maldonado
Ricardo Marcelín-Jiménez
Magnos Martinello
Eliane Martins
Carlos Maziero
Wagner Meira Jr.
Takashi Nanya
Edgar Nett
Rafael Obelheiro
Rui Oliveira
Manoel Camillo de O. Penna Neto
David Powell
José Ferreira de Rezende
Luigi Romano
Jacques Sauvé
André Schiper
Richard Schlichting
Ana Paula da Silva
Neeraj Suri
Andre Gustavo Degraf Uchoa
Nicolas Wolovick
Avelino Zorzo

Co-organizers

Universidad Nacional Autónoma de México (UNAM)
Universidad Autónoma Metropolitana (UAM)

Co-sponsors

SBC—Brazilian Computer Society
SMCC—Mexican Society for Computer Science
IEEE TC on Dependable Computing and Fault Tolerance

In Co-operation with

IFIP Working Group 10.4 'Dependable Computing and Fault-Tolerance'
SCCC—Chilean Computer Science Society
SADIO—Argentine Society for Informatics and Operations Research

Table of Contents

Experimental Dependability Evaluation

Intrusion Tolerance and Security

Tutorials

Panels

Reliability, Safety, and Security in Everyday Embedded Systems
(Extended Abstract)

Philip Koopman

Carnegie Mellon University
Pittsburgh, PA 15213, USA
koopman@cmu.edu

Embedded systems permeate our everyday lives. From automobiles to elevators, kitchen appliances to televisions, and water heaters to cell phones, we increasingly depend upon embedded systems to operate as expected. A few obviously critical embedded application domains, such as aviation, have traditionally benefited from extraordinary care during development to ensure that everything is done correctly. But increasingly, everyday embedded applications are becoming "mission critical," with little fanfare and perhaps without the full attention to dependability properties that they truly deserve.

Consider the following potentially significant failure modes for embedded systems: A cell phone that doesn't work when the owner needs to call for emergency medical attention. A domestic hot water heater that overheats water, causing scalding burns on a child. A thermostat that doesn't turn on heat when needed, causing household water pipes to freeze and burst. A microwave oven that turns on with the door open. An automobile that unintendedly accelerates. Today, hardware interlocks mitigate many of these hazards. But, software is playing a bigger role as both a vulnerability and a mitigation mechanism for critical failures. Because most embedded systems have actuators that influence the environment, and because people count on them to operate as expected, special care must be taken to ensure that they are safe, reliable, and secure.

Safety in the context of embedded systems deals with minimizing the frequency of mishaps (especially loss of life, injuries, and damage to property). In many ways this is the most mature of the areas we are discussing, because there are several industry-specific standards that can be followed to create safe systems (e.g., IEC 61508). There are, however, some significant research challenges outstanding in this area, including:

- How can we be sure that following a given system development process actually results in the hoped-for level of safety?
- How can we make it easy for small, non-specialist teams of domain experts to follow complex, "heavy-weight" safety standards and actually get it right?
- How can we simplify the representation and specification of safety properties to make it easier to design safe systems?

Reliability in embedded systems has been studied for many years, and has to do with ensuring that once an embedded system starts a "mission," it has a high probability of completing that mission without experiencing a failure. Traditional high-reliability systems have used hardware redundancy (for example, two engines on an airplane instead of one). But, cost-sensitive everyday embedded systems often do not have a price structure that permits redundancy. An even bigger problem is

A. Bondavalli, F. Brasileiro, and S. Rajsbaum (Eds.): LADC 2007, LNCS 4746, pp. 1–2, 2007.

creating highly reliable software, especially with quick time-to-market and low development budget constraints. Some current research challenges in this area are:

- How can we make it easy for small, non-specialist teams of domain experts to create highly reliable software?
- How can we quantify software reliability to support testing for design requirements such as "software crashes no more than once per month"?
- Achieving absolute software perfection seems unrealistic. How can we create embedded systems that survive the activation of latent software defects?

Security is, of course, a hot topic. But currently, it seems to be getting less attention in embedded systems than in enterprise systems. While embedded systems have not yet experienced as many widely publicized security problems as enterprise systems have, the potential for widespread, significant impact to society is certainly there. What happens if malicious attackers gain control of many embedded systems with the ability to release energy (or hazardous substances) into the environment? What if some critical infrastructure, such as energy distribution, traffic flow control, building environmental services, or telecommunications, suddenly stops working? While there are no easy answers to security in any environment, embedded systems present unique challenges that require research beyond the scope of enterprise security research, including:

- How can we make it easy for small, non-specialist teams of domain experts to get security right, even on a small product?
- What unique security challenges arise when interconnecting embedded systems (for example, coordinating actuators across many systems)?
- What novel vulnerabilities arise in Internet-connected embedded systems?
- What security concerns arise due to threats unique to embedded systems (for example, when the system owner is the attacker).

Embedded systems have historically been simple, often non-critical, and usually very reliable, safe, and secure. Newer systems are becoming more complex, and starting to cross the fuzzy line from non-critical to criticality. Unfortunately, the techniques and culture of developers for newly critical applications often do not take into account this major shift. While improving developer literacy in the areas of reliability, safety, and security will help, significant research challenges remain.

A common, underlying challenge has to do with the central role of domain experts in embedded system design. It is common for embedded system development teams to be relatively small, and staffed more with domain experts than computing experts. This is often appropriate, because expert domain knowledge is crucial to success. However, small teams and companies that are concerned mostly with an application domain rather than computer technology often don't have access to expertise in dependability. So, even if researchers can solve the many outstanding research problems, there is still the issue of finding ways to deploy that knowledge to everyday working engineers whose training is often not primarily in computing. We must not only solve the research questions, but also find a way to deploy that knowledge.

This work was supported in part by the General Motors Collaborative Research Center at Carnegie Mellon University.

Nanoscale Technologies: Prospect or Hazard to Dependable and Secure Computing?

Jean Arlat

LAAS-CNRS, Université de Toulouse, 7 Avenue du Colonel Roche
31077 Toulouse Cedex 04, France
jean.arlat@laas.fr

1 Introduction

The continuous advances and progress made in hardware technologies makes it possible to foresee a realm of unprecedented performance levels and of new application-driven architectural designs, e. g., see [1]. One of the main drivers is the reduction of the size of the elementary devices. Nevertheless, the evolution of nanoscale technologies raises serious challenges with respect to both dependability and security viewpoints. Issues at stake encompass three main types of concerns i) unreliability and variability that will characterize the production of emerging nanoscale devices, ii) accidental disturbances that affect the operation of the systems, iii) malicious threats targeting vulnerabilities of hardware circuits. However, on the other hand, thanks to the large scale integration, one may expect the fault tolerance techniques to come to the rescue of the limitations of the currently dominating fault avoidance approaches. After a brief review of each of these issues, we will provide a few hints concerning a proposal for resilient multicore processor chips.

2 Chips Featuring Massively Defective Devices

Thanks to the advances of hardware technologies, one can envision in a near future chips that will incorporate several hundred billions of transistor devices. However, extreme downsizing results in atomic range dimensions, thus in inter- and intra-device variability. This means that nanoscale electronic devices are becoming inherently unreliable and moreover, unpredictable [2]. While it is expected that the defect density currently observed for microprocessors ($1{,}395$ defects/m^2) will remain in the same order of magnitude for the next 15 years [3], this may nevertheless have an impact on the production yield for large scale chips.

Significant progress has been made already for memory chips. Most advanced techniques consist in providing spare elements (lines, rows or words) in order to dynamically replace some defective element. Indeed, techniques have been proposed that not only cope with production defects, but also with faults occurring at run time. Such techniques are primarily meant to achieve a high yield, which may require a significant overhead. For example, in [4], it was shown that for a 1Mb chip and a cell defect ratio of 3%, a near 100% yield can be achieved, but with a close to 100% overhead.

Efficient fault tolerance techniques have been proposed also for processor chips. For example, the technique being recently proposed in [5] features a set of fragmented

A. Bondavalli, F. Brasileiro, and S. Rajsbaum (Eds.): LADC 2007, LNCS 4746, pp. 3–6, 2007.

MPUs, for which redundant fragments are available. Another important issue concerns control logic in processors, which is growing in size and complexity, and is basically unprotected. The generalization of multicore architectures, and potentially another layer of control, could well exacerbate this problem.

3 Transient Faults in Operation

One classical issue concerns mitigating the impact of disturbances (e.g., the so called "soft errors") that are increasingly affecting computing systems [6]. Such a problem, well known in aerospace applications, is expected to affect also medical electronics, cell phones and automotive systems, due to the impact of ground-based radiation. Indeed, this problem will only worsen and create substantial challenges for designers of automotive electronics who are considering turning to programmable logic devices, such as FPGAs, as a flexible, low-cost solution for their next-generation designs. A significant impact is to be expected already when considering current technologies [7]: Let us consider a 22μm SRAM-based FPGA technology featuring 1M-gate chips; then, a simulation run using SpaceRad 4.5[1] and assuming an operation at 5,000 feet altitude (e.g., Denver, CO), would lead to a prediction of 1.05 x 10^{-4} upsets/day. Then considering a fleet of 500,000 vehicles, each featuring an airbag control system using this technology, would lead to 52.5 upsets/day (on a continuous usage basis). Even assuming a more modest usage profile of 1 h per day would still lead to about 2 upsets/day. A figure that cannot be ignored by car developers!

Solutions for hardened technologies exist and have been intensively used in the past. However, the high (and often excessive) cost attached to the fabrication lines for such realizations have restricted their usage and obstructed their continuation. Hence, the increasingly need to rely on various forms of fault tolerance techniques [8]. For example, [9] proposes a low-cost time redundancy scheme to cope with soft errors and timing faults. It consists in duplicating the functional flip-flops, driving the duplicate flip-flops by delayed clocks, and then comparing the results of functional and duplicate flip-flops. The Razor architecture [10] uses a similar approach also featuring redundant flip-flops (referred to as "shadow latches") and extends it to achieve lower power dissipation. More recently, novel design solutions were proposed to cope with these issues in the case of programmable logic arrays [11].

An increasingly important issue, that is addressed into [12], is the impact of power, current and voltage fluctuations.

4 Hardware Vulnerabilities and Security Threats

Besides accidental faults, one should consider the risks faced by modern integrated circuits with respect to hacking and malicious threats. Of course, smart chips and crypto-processors are the most sensitive targets.

---

[1] http://www.spacerad.com

Intrusions may be performed via a wide variety of side channel attacks (e.g., differential power analysis or electromagnetic analysis). Embedded testing devices (such as scan-chains), that are meant to obtain high controllability and observability for test engineers, constitute also a weakness from the security viewpoint; indeed, the properties of the scan chain architecture can be used for other kinds of side channel attacks via malevolent "fault injections" exploiting the related "leakage". Indeed, the likelihood of a successful attack depends on both the information leakage of the implementation and the strength/skill of the hacker to make the most of it [13].

To circumvent such attacks, enhanced mechanisms have been proposed beyond the more classical tamper resistant designs or irreversible disconnections; they are either based on asynchronous logic designs [14], signature checks [15] or a mix of reliability and security mechanisms (e.g., see [16]). Still, there might be some goods new attached to the fact that technology shrinks [17]: i) attacks get more difficult to perform, ii) while some skills in built-in security are definitely needed, the hardware security features available can be easily transposed to nanoscale technologies.

5 Towards Resilient Multicore Processor Chips?

The recent announcement by Intel for a 80-core chip [1] already paves the way forward about the future multicore multiprocessor architectures. It is also expected that this trend will influence the software techniques so as to take advantage of such architectures. This means also that it will be possible and cost effective to consider and exploit novel resilience solutions. The goal goes beyond simply avoiding the delivery of defective chips (i.e., chips with defective cores). Alone, such an approach would require increasingly — perhaps prohibitively — high effort and cost in manufacturing and testing.

An alternative more pragmatic approach could be to maximize the capacity to exploit the valid cores available on a chip. Indeed, along the same line of what is currently the case where processors batches are sorted according to their frequency (1.6 Ghz, 1.8 Ghz or 2 Ghz), the manufactured chips could be sorted according to the achieved MIPS performance level, e.g., as a function of the number of valid cores. Such a principle is already applied by some manufacturers: e.g., Intel Core Duo chips featuring a defective device are "recycled" as Core Solo chips[2].

As reported in [18], a more ambitious would be to apply such a (re)configuration dynamically at run-time rather than simply at production time. This way, it would be possible to keep using the cores available on a multicore chip, even when operational faults would impair some additional cores.

Acknowledgments. The views expressed herein benefited from the discussions during the *Workshop on Dependable and Secure Nanocomputing* held at DSN-2007 (www.laas.fr/WDSN07). In particular, the author would like to thank the two co-organizers Ravishankar K. Iyer and Michael Nicolaïdis. This work was supported in part by the ReSIST Network of Excellence of the EU FP6 IST Program (contract: 026764).

---

[2] http://en.wikipedia.org/wiki/Intel_Core

References

1. Vangal, S., Howard, J., Ruhl, G., Dighe, S., Wilson, H., Tschanz, J., Finan, D., Iyer, P., Singh, A., Jacob, T., Jain, S., Venkataraman, S., Hoskote, Y., Borkar, N.: An 80-Tile 1.28TFLOPS Network-on-Chip in 65nm CMOS. In: Proc. IEEE ISSCC-2007, San Francisco, CA, USA, pp. 98–99, 589 (2007)
2. Haensch, W., Nowak, E.J., Dennard, R.H., Solomon, P.M., Bryant, A., Dokumaci, O.H., Kumar, A., Wang, X., Johnson, J.B., Fischetti, M.V.: Silicon CMOS Devices Beyond Scaling. IBM J. Research and Development 50, 339–361A (2006)
3. Patel, J.H.: Manufacturing Process Variations and Dependability - A Contrarian View. In: Proc. IEEE/IFIP DSN-2007 (Supplemental Volume), Edinburgh, UK, p. 235 (2007)
4. Nicolaïdis, M., Achouri, N., Anghel, L.: A Diversified Memory Built-In Self-Repair Approach for Nanotechnologies. In: Proc. IEEE VTS-2004, Napa Valley, CA, USA, pp. 313–318 (2004)
5. Nakura, T., Nose, K., Mizuno, M.: Fine-Grain Redundant Logic Using Defect-Prediction Flip-Flops. In: Proc. IEEE ISSCC-2007, San Francisco, CA, USA, pp. 402–403, 611 (2007)
6. Li, X., Adve, S.V., Bose, P., Rivers, J.A.: Architecture-Level Soft Error Analysis: Examining the Limits of Common Assumptions. In: Proc. IEEE/IFIP DSN-2007, Edinburgh, UK, pp. 266–275 (2007)
7. Mason, M.: Cosmic Rays Damage Automotive Electronics. Automotive DesignLine Newsletter (2006)
8. Iyer, R.K., Nakka, N.M., Kalbarczyk, Z.T., Mitra, S.: Recent Advances and New Avenues in Hardware-level Reliability Support. IEEE Micro 25, 18–29 (2005)
9. Nicolaïdis, M.: Time Redundancy Based Soft-Error Tolerance to Rescue Nanometer Technologies. In: Proc. IEEE VTS'99, San Diego, CA, USA, pp. 86–94 (1999)
10. Ernst, D., Das, S., Lee, S., Blaauw, D., Austin, T., Mudge, T., Kim, N.S., Flautner, K.: Razor: Circuit-Level Correction of Timing Errors for Low-Power Operation. IEEE Micro 24, 10–20 (2004)
11. Rao, W., Orailoglu, A., Karri, R.: Fault Tolerant Approaches to Nanoelectronic Programmable Logic Arrays. In: Proc. IEEE/IFIP DSN-2007, Edinburgh, UK, pp. 216–223 (2007)
12. Constantinescu, C.: Impact of Intermittent Faults on Nanocomputing Devices. In: Proc. IEEE/IFIP DSN-2007 (Supplemental Volume), Edinburgh, UK, pp. 238–241 (2007)
13. Standaert, F.-X., Peeters, E., Archambeau, C., Quisquater, J.-J.: Towards Security Limits in Side-Channel Attacks (With an Application to Block Ciphers). In: Goubin, L., Matsui, M. (eds.) CHES 2006. LNCS, vol. 4249, pp. 30–45. Springer, Heidelberg (2006)
14. Monnet, Y., Renaudin, M., Leveugle, R.: Designing Resistant Circuits against Malicious Faults Injection Using Asynchronous Logic. IEEE Trans. on Computers 55, 1104–1115 (2006)
15. Lee, J., Tehranipoor, M., Patel, C., Plusquellic, J.: Securing Designs Against Scan-Based Side-Channel Attacks. IEEE Trans. on Dependable and Secure Computing (to appear, 2007)
16. Nakka, N., Kalbarczyk, Z.T., Iyer, R.K., Xu, J.: An Architectural Framework for Providing Reliability and Security Support. In: Proc. IEEE/IFIP DSN-2004, Florence, Italy, pp. 585–594 (2004)
17. Handschuh, H.: Security Challenges for High Density Smart Cards. In: Proc. IEEE/IFIP DSN-2007 (Supplemental Volume), Edinburgh, UK, p. 285 (2007)
18. Zając, P., Collet, J.H., Arlat, J., Crouzet, Y.: Resilience through Self-Configuration in Future Massively Defective Nanochips. In: Proc. IEEE/IFIP DSN-2007 (Supplemental Volume), Edinburgh, UK, pp. 266–271 (2007)

Fault-Tolerant Dynamic Routing Based on Maximum Flow Evaluation

Jonatan Schroeder and Elias Procópio Duarte Jr.

Federal University of Paraná (UFPR)
Dept. of Informatics – P.O. Box 19018
81531-990 Curitiba - Brazil
{jonatan,elias}@inf.ufpr.br

Abstract. This work proposes a fault-tolerant dynamic routing algorithm that employs maximum flow evaluation for route selection, increasing the number of disjoint paths to the destination, enhancing the path redundancy, and so extending the possibility of using detours, or alternative paths if needed. Route distance is employed as a secondary criterion. Routes may be dynamically changed by intermediate routers, which usually have more recent information about topology changes. Formal proofs for correctness of the algorithm are also presented. The proposed algorithm was implemented in a simulation environment and experimental results are presented.

1 Introduction

Most routing algorithms employ the distance in number of hops as the main, if not the only, criterion for selecting routes. Nevertheless, for critical applications a robust route is not necessarily the shortest route.

This work proposes a novel approach for route selection based on route *robustness*. A robust route improves the probability that if faults occur along the route it is feasible and efficient to find another route, or *detour*, to the destination. A robust route improves the ability of finding detours to the destination in case of faults.

The proposed routing algorithm chooses an edge for the route of a given destination using maximum flow evaluation. This evaluation is employed in order to increase the number of disjoint paths to the destination, enhancing the path redundancy, and so improving the probability of quickly finding short detours, or alternative paths, after faults are detected. Route distance is employed as a secondary metric for route selection.

The proposed routing algorithm is dynamic in the sense that each node along the route only selects the next hop of the route, based on its current information. In other words, no route is pre-selected at the source, so that intermediate routers dynamically determine the route as they process the packet. This behavior exploits the fact that topology changes are quickly discovered by nodes that are closer to the change itself. This concept can be also extended to traffic information, i.e. information about congested or heavily/lightly used links.

A. Bondavalli, F. Brasileiro, and S. Rajsbaum (Eds.): LADC 2007, LNCS 4746, pp. 7–24, 2007.

The dynamicity of the algorithm has a potential impact on the behavior of routing during the *convergence latency* interval. Routing protocols present a convergence latency after the network topology changes [1] due to router or link failures. During the convergence latency interval all routing tables are updated in order to compute the new paths to be employed. For some protocols the convergence latency is quite large. For instance, the average latency for the Internet's BGP, (*Border Gateway Protocol*), is about 3 minutes, but intervals of up to 15 minutes [2] have also been reported. During the convergence latency interval, packets may be lost, and connections may be broken.

The proposed algorithm does not require that routers be initialized with the complete network topology, routers are initialized only with information about their neighbors. Nodes keep a local topology representation that is updated with periodic messages exchanged with neighbors. The algorithm is able to successfully route messages even when the local representation of the topology is out-of-date, or does not represent the complete network topology.

Figure 1 shows an example network topology and the route selected by the proposed algorithm to send a packet from s to t. Initially s chooses to send the packet through node a, from which there are two edge-disjoint paths to reach the destination t. As from node b there is only one available path, the edge to node a receives a better evaluation by the routing algorithm. Now, node a sends the packet to node e, because in comparison to node c both have the same number of edge-disjoint paths but the distance from e to t is shorter. However consider that the link from node e to node t has failed, and so far only node e has this information. Executing the algorithm, node e sends the packet back to node a, which then forwards the packet through c and d to the destination t. Details about the criteria employed and the formal specification of the algorithm are presented in section 2.

The algorithm was implemented, and the implementation is available on the Internet, created with Java [3]. Implementation details, as well as experimental results obtained with Internet-like networks on a simulation environment, are presented in section 4. A running applet is available at http://www.inf.ufpr.br/jonatan/mfrp.

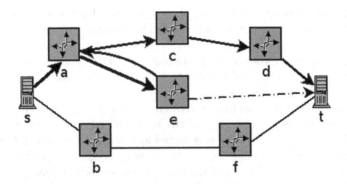

Fig. 1. An example topology and the route chosen by the algorithm

This work is organized as follows. Section 2 presents the algorithm specification. Section 3 presents the proofs of correctness of the algorithm. Section 4 presents experimental results. Section 5 points to related work. Finally, section 6 concludes the paper.

2   The Proposed Algorithm

The proposed routing algorithm is executed for each packet that is sent from a given source to a given destination. The algorithm is run initially by the source node, which chooses the next node of the route, among its neighbors. When the packet arrives at the next node, this node runs the algorithm to choose the following node, and so on, until the packet reaches the destination.

The approach used by this algorithm is similar to that of Bellman-Ford algorithm [1], in the sense that each node does not need a previous knowledge of the topology. A node running the algorithm chooses the next node of the route, instead of the complete route. Furthermore, the algorithm works even if the most recent topology changes are not known by all nodes.

The proposed algorithm chooses the next node of the route through an evaluation of each adjacent edge. This evaluation is based on a trade-off between redundancy and the distance of the paths to the destination from the evaluated edge. After the evaluation, the best edge is chosen.

The formulae and equations for the computation of the metrics used in this work assert that each node has a local representation of the network topology. The topology is learnt and updated by each node through periodic messages exchanged with neighbors, as described below. This topology update messages are sets of tuples <*edge,state,timestamp*>, where *state* is either faulty or fault-free and *timestamp* is a counter of state changes. This timestamp allows nodes to determine whether the information is newer than the one it already has. The local representation, however, does not need to be complete and up-to-date. The topology is represented through a directed graph structure, with a set of vertices, corresponding to the network nodes, and a set of edges, corresponding to the network links.

This work considers crash faults, and the system is considered to be partially synchronous, i.e., there is a finite time limit, not necessarily known, for the delay on the communication between any pair of nodes.

2.1   Algorithm Specification

This section initially presents some preliminary definitions used in the algorithm specification.

A *directed graph* (or *digraph*) G is a pair (V, E) of sets, in which V is a set of nodes (or vertices) and E is a set of edges (or links). Each edge is a pair of exactly two different nodes.

Let $G = (V, E)$ be a digraph; let $c : E \rightarrow \Re$ be a function corresponding to the capacity of the digraph edges; let $u, v \in V$ be nodes of the digraph G. A *flow* between u and v is a function $f : E \rightarrow \Re$ where:

$$\forall e \in E, f(e) \leq c(e)$$

$$\forall t \in V - \{u, v\}, \quad \sum_{e=(t,t') \in E} f(e) = \sum_{e=(t',t) \in E} f(e)$$

The size (or cardinality) of a flow f, represented as $|f|$, is defined as:

$$|f| = \sum_{e=(u,t) \in E} f(e) - \sum_{e=(t,u) \in E} f(e)$$

A flow f is said to be maximum if, for every flow f' between the same pair of nodes, $|f| \leq |f'|$.

Let $u, v \in V$ be nodes of the graph G. A *cut* between u and v is a set of edges C so that removing all edges in C from the graph G, u and v are not connected. The size (or cardinality) of a cut C, represented as $|C|$, is defined as the cardinality of the set C. A cut C is said to be minimum if, for every cut C' between the same pair of nodes, $|C| \leq |C'|$. For every pair of nodes of the network, the maximum flow and the minimum cut have the same cardinality, and are computed with the same algorithms [4]. So, this work will use both terms interchangeably.

Figure 2 shows the algorithm that is run when node n has to route a packet to a given destination. $\Gamma(G, e)$ is an evaluation function, specified below.

The evaluation of the edges to be used in the routing process is computed on a subgraph of the digraph that corresponds to the local representation of the network topology. This subgraph is obtained with the removal of the nodes already visited by the packet, and of the edges that are adjacent to these nodes. This strategy guarantees there will not be loops.

There is a specific case in which edges that lead to loops are used. Considering that topology information is not necessarily up-to-date in all nodes, a node can choose an edge based on a path that is not available anymore, or is faulty. When a packet reaches a node that already has up-to-date information, it is possible that the only available paths to the destination pass through nodes already visited. In this case, the packet needs to be delivered back to the node from which it came. However, the node that receives this packet probably has out-of-date information about the topology, since its selection led to a node without available route options. So, in order to make it possible for this node to have up-to-date information, the update message programmed to be sent to this node is anticipated, and is sent before the packet is sent back to the node. This way, the new node can take the decision for a new path based on more recently updated information about the topology, and so avoiding paths with no routing options.

In order to make the information about the availability of the routes reach all nodes in the network, a topology update process is run on each node. This process is run every α seconds, where α is a parameter of the algorithm. Each node sends

1. Add node n to the list of visited nodes of the message.
2. If there is an edge from node n to the destination, send the message through this edge and finish.
3. Create an auxiliary graph G', corresponding to the known topology, removing the visited nodes of the message.
4. Evaluate each adjacent edge of node n, using function $\Gamma(G,e)$ in graph G'. Edges reaching visited nodes are not evaluated, as well as edges without available paths to the destination.
5. If at least one edge was evaluated, send the message through edge e with the largest $\Gamma(G,e)$.
6. If no edge could be evaluated:
   (a) Remove n from the list of visited nodes.
   (b) If n is the source of the message, return an error.
   (c) If n is an intermediate node, send an update message, followed by the routed message, to the last node on the list of visited nodes.

Fig. 2. The algorithm for choosing the next edge

for all its neighbors recently learnt information about topology changes. When a node receives a packet through an edge that was considered faulty, the node adds the edge to its local representation of the topology. If an update message is expected and is not received through an edge after a timeout, the edge is considered faulty and is removed from the local representation of the network topology. This timeout is called β ($\beta > \alpha$), and is also a parameter of the algorithm.

After receiving an update message, each node replies with an acknowledgement. After this acknowledgement is received, all information is marked so that the sender does not need to resend the information again in the next update message.

2.2   Edge Evaluation: Path Redundancy and Distance

The computation of the edge evaluation function $\Gamma(G,e)$ is based on a set of quantitative criteria related to the redundancy and to the size of the paths that pass through the evaluated edge. For each of these criteria, a weight is associated, so that the computation can be adapted to the priority given to each criterion. Each weight is a parameter of the algorithm.

The following formula corresponds to the computation of the edge evaluation:

$$\Gamma(G,e) = \sum_{c_n \in C} \omega_n \times c_n(e) \tag{1}$$

In this equation, $\Gamma(G, e)$ is the evaluation function, e is the edge being evaluated, C is the set of criteria (described below) and ω_n is the weight associated to criterion c_n.

The criteria used for edge evaluation are functions that receive a graph representing the topology as input and an edge, and return a numeric value. This work uses two criteria: the cardinality of the maximum flow (or the minimum cut) from the node adjacent to the evaluated edge to the destination node (c_1) and the length of the shortest path between these nodes (c_2).

The main criterion used in this work for the evaluation of the edges for routing is the maximum flow (or minimum cut) from the node adjacent to the evaluated edge to the destination. This criterion is called c_1. A classic algorithm for the computation of the maximum flow is the Ford and Fulkerson algorithm [4,5]. This algorithm uses an edge-valued graph structure, in which, for a graph $G = (V, E)$ there is a function $c : E \rightarrow \Re$, that associates a value for each edge, corresponding to the capacity of the edge. Our algorithm assumes that $c(e) = 1$ for all edges. The complexity of this algorithm, when the capacity is an integer, is $O(NM)$, where N is the number of nodes and M is the number of edges of the graph [5]. For the weight associated with this criterion (ω_1) a positive value is used, since the evaluation of an edge is intended to be proportional to the result of this function.

In order to select routes that are not only robust but also short, one of the criterion used for the evaluation of an edge is the minimum distance from the node adjacent to the evaluated edge to the destination. This criterion is called c_2. As this work considers that all edge capacities or costs are equal to one, a breadth-first search on the graph, in which the number of rounds, or levels, passed through to find the destination node, starting at the evaluated node, is used as the result of the criterion. The breadth-first search is run in $O(M)$ steps, where M is the number of edges in the network [6,5]. For the weight associated to this criterion (ω_2) a negative value is used, since a shorter distance is better for evaluation of the edge.

2.3   Example Executions

Figure 3 shows an example execution of the algorithm. In this figure, suppose node s has to send a packet to node t, The routing algorithm is run on s, evaluating all adjacent edges, i.e., (s, a), (s, b) and (s, c), and choosing the one that has the best evaluation and that will be used for the routing. Suppose the chosen edge is (s, b), the packet is then sent from s to b through this edge.

When node b receives the packet sent by s to t, it evaluates edges (b, d) and (b, e). Edge (b, s) is not evaluated, since node s has already been visited and, so, is removed from the graph used for the evaluation. Suppose the chosen edge is (b, e). The packet is then sent to node e. Similarly e evaluates its neighbor edges, discarding (e, b) and choosing (e, h). Finally, node h evaluates its adjacent edges. As it has an edge that goes directly to the final destination t, this edge is used. So, the packet is sent to node t through edge (h, t), achieving the final destination.

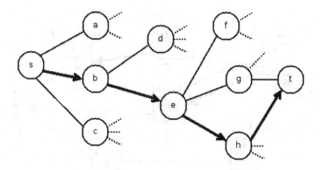

Fig. 3. An example execution

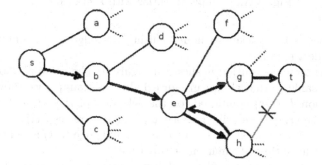

Fig. 4. Rerouting after an edge becomes faulty

Consider another example. Suppose that, in the same network described above, a fault occurs on edge (h, t), that is used on the path between s and t. Figure 4 shows the resulting network after this fault. Suppose, again, that s has a packet to send to t, immediately after the fault occurs. Suppose that, when the packet is sent, only nodes h and t (adjacent to the faulty edge) have information about the occurrence of the fault. The algorithm is run by node s, which sends the packet to b, that sends the packet to node e, that sends the packet to node h. This procedure is executed in the same way it was in the previous example, since these nodes have not had their topology information changed.

When node h receives the packet to be sent to node t, it finds out that the only possible paths leading to t pass through nodes already visited by the packet, such as node e. Since there is no alternative route for sending the packet, node h sends a topology update message to node e. As node e receives this message, it will be able to take a decision based on more recent topology information. Finally, after sending the update message, node h sends the original packet back to e. When node e receives the original packet, it will take a new decision about the edge that should be used, now considering that the edge (h, t) is not employable. So, another edge is chosen, for example, edge (e, g), sending the packet to node g.

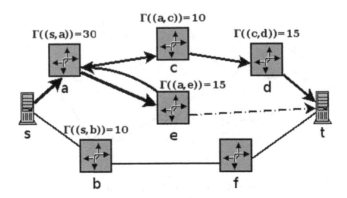

Fig. 5. An example execution with Γ evaluation

This node sends the packet to node t, using the edge (g, t), and the packet achieves its destination.

Another example execution is shown in figure 5. The network shown in this figure is the same as that shown in figure 1. In this example we show the evaluation function $\Gamma(G, e)$ computed for the selection of the edges. Suppose the weights for the criteria described above, ω_1 and ω_2, are respectively 20 and -5. Suppose node s has a packet to send to node t, and edge (e, t) is faulty, but only edges e and t have this information at this time.

Initially, node s evaluates all its adjacent edges, i.e. edges (s, a) and (s, b). Both evaluations are made in a subgraph G', that is equivalent to the original topology representation in node s, except for node s itself. Note that edge (e, t), even faulty, is still in graph G', since node s does not have the information that it is faulty. In graph G', the maximum flow from node a to node t is equal to two, and from node b to node t is equal to one, so $c_1((s, a)) = 2$ and $c_1((s, b)) = 1$. The minimum path from node a to node t is $a - e - t$, with distance 2. The minimum path from node b to node t is $b - f - t$, also with distance 2. So, $c_2((s, a)) = c_2((s, b)) = 2$. Applying these values to the $\Gamma(e)$ equation, we have: $\Gamma((s, a)) = 30$ and $\Gamma((s, b)) = 10$, and thus edge (s, a) is selected.

When the packet arrives at node a, it evaluates edges (a, c) and (a, e). Edge (a, s) is ignored, since node s was already visited. Now the evaluation is made on a subgraph G'', similar to the original topology representation in node a, but removing nodes s and a, already visited. Note that edge $e - t$, even faulty, is still in subgraph G'', since node a does not have the information it is faulty. In subgraph G'', the maximum flow from both nodes c and e to the destination t is equal to 1, so $c_1((a, c)) = c_1((a, e)) = 1$. The minimum path from node c to node t is $c - d - t$, with distance 2. The minimum path from node e to node t is $e - t$, with distance 1. So, $c_2((a, c)) = 2$ and $c_2((a, e)) = 1$. Applying these values to the $\Gamma(e)$ equation, we have: $\Gamma((a, c)) = 10$ and $\Gamma((a, e)) = 15$, and thus edge (a, e) is selected.

Node e, receiving the packet, has no alternatives for routing, as its only non-faulty adjacent edge leads to node a, already visited. So, a topology update message is sent to node a, containing the information about edge (e, t), followed by the packet itself. When node a receives both the message and the packet, it re-evaluates all its adjacent edges. Edge (a, e) is now ignored, as it does not have any available path to the destination. Edge (a, s) is ignored, and $\Gamma((a, c)) = 10$, as described above, and (a, c) is select.

Now node c receives the packet, and it evaluates the only possible edge (c, d), with $c_1((c, d)) = 1$, $c_2((c, d)) = 2$ and $\Gamma((c, d)) = 15$. The packet is delivered to node d, that has a direct available link to node t, and sends the packet to the destination through this link.

3   Proofs

In this section we present proofs of correctness of the algorithm, as well as proofs for the number and size of the update messages, the edge selection complexity and the latency of the algorithm.

3.1   Correctness

The first proof corresponds to the correctness of the algorithm, i.e., if there is a route between two nodes, the algorithm will route a packet successfully between these two nodes. This proof assumes the following hypotheses. The first hypothesis states that nodes that are adjacent to an edge (or to another node) have correct information about the state of this edge (or node). The second hypothesis states that the source node has at least one non-faulty path to the destination in its local representation, i.e., in the local representation of the topology in the source node at least one available path between source and destination must be fully working; please note that this is not necessarily the selected route. Another hypothesis states there is no topology change from the time the packet leaves the source and the time it arrives at the final destination, or until the source learns that there is no available path to the destination.

Initially a lemma is proved stating that if a packet is sent through all edges with paths in the source's local representation of the network and returns to the source in every path, the source will learn there is no route to the destination and the routing will correctly fail. After that, another lemma proves that, if there is a non-faulty path to the destination through the selected edge, this edge is used in the route. The next lemma proves that if there is one or more paths in the local representation of the network in the source that are not faulty, then an edge that is part of one of these paths is chosen to the route. Finally, using the proved lemmas, the theorem stating the correctness of the algorithm is proven.

Lemma 1. *Consider graph $G = (V, E)$, and two non-faulty nodes $s, t \in V$ of this graph. Consider all nodes have the correct state information of their adjacent edges in their local representations of the topology. If s sends a packet with destination t using the proposed algorithm, and no edge adjacent to s is* *selected, or if after the message is sent in several tries through all adjacent edges and all return an update message to the source, then s learns there is no available route to the destination.*

Proof. Assume the set of adjacent non-faulty edges of s is the set $\{e_1, e_2, \ldots e_n\}$. Edges that do not have available paths leading to the destination are ignored by the algorithm, and so are not included in this set. Proving by induction, assume initially that this set is empty, i.e., s does not have any fault-free adjacent edge. The proof in this case is trivial, since s learns that there is no available route to the destination.

Assume now the lemma is true for set $\{e_1, e_2, \ldots e_{n-1}\}$. Assume that the set is $\{e_1, e_2, \ldots e_{n-1}, e_n\}$. Assume, without loss of generality, that the chosen edge for routing is edge e_n. So, the packet is sent through edge e_n to the next node, say node u. As there is no path to the destination, the packet has to return to the node from where it came from. One of the hypotheses assumes the packet is sent back through the same edge, e_n, but this happens only after u sends s a message with all topology updates learned by u, considering u has no available route to the destination t. After s receives this update message, it updates its local representation of the topology. When the original packet arrives, a new evaluation will start, and this time edge e_n is ignored, since the received topology information points to the nonexistence of paths to the destination t through edge e_n. So the set of available edges is changed to $\{e_1, e_2, \ldots e_{n-1}\}$, for which the lemma is true. So, by induction, the lemma is true, and s learns there is no available route to the destination.

Lemma 2. *Consider $G = (V, E)$ is a graph, and $s, t \in V$ are two non-faulty nodes of this graph. Consider all nodes have the correct state information of their adjacent edges in their local representations of the topology. Consider there is a path from s to t, and that (s, u) is the first edge of this path (u and t may be the same node). If s sends a packet with destination t through the edge (s, u) using the proposed algorithm, the packet will either reach its destination or return to the source s.*

Proof. We prove by induction. First assume graph G has only two nodes. These nodes have to be s and t and, by definition, they are not the same node. The only edge that can be evaluated by node s is edge (s, t), since there is no other possible edge in the graph. So, $t = u$. If this edge is faulty, s has the information about this fault (hypothesis) and so (s, u) cannot be evaluated. However, if the edge is not faulty, then the packet is sent by node s directly to node t through the edge (s, u), arriving node t. When $t = u$ a similar proof can be given.

Assume now that the lemma is true for a graph with $(n - 1)$ nodes. Suppose that G has n nodes. When s sends a packet through the edge (s, u), the hypotheses assert s has the information that this edge is not faulty. Node u, on receiving the packet and after evaluating its adjacent edges, removes node s from the graph used for the evaluation, and so continues the execution on a subgraph containing $(n - 1)$ nodes, for which the lemma is true. So, by induction, the lemma is proven true for every number of nodes.

Lemma 3. *Consider graph $G = (V, E)$, and two non-faulty nodes $s, t \in V$. Consider all nodes have the correct state information of their adjacent edges in their local representations of the topology. Consider s has a available path leading to t in its local representation. If s has to send a packet to t, using the proposed algorithm, an edge that belongs to a fully available route is chosen.*

Proof. Proving by induction, consider s has only one neighbor, called u. As there is an available path leading to t, this path has to pass through u (which can be t itself). When the edges are evaluated, edge (s, u) is chosen because s has a non-faulty route passing through this edge in its local representation, and it is the only available edge. So, the lemma is true for one neighbor.

Now consider the lemma is true for $(n - 1)$ neighbors. Suppose s has n neighbors, called $u_1, u_2, \ldots u_{n-1}, u_n$. Using the proposed algorithm, some edges are going to be discarded, as they do not belong to available paths to the destination, as proven by the previous lemma. Suppose, without loss of generality, (s, u_n) is discarded. So, the algorithm continues with $(n-1)$ neighbors, for which case the lemma is true.

Consider now that no edge is discarded. Without loss of generality, consider the edge evaluated as the best is (s, u_n). The algorithm sends a packet through this edge. If the edge belongs to a available path leading to t, the lemma is proven. If, however, there is no available path leading to t through (s, u_n), the packet returns to node u_n, as proven by lemma 2, and a routing message is sent back to node s with more recent information about the network topology. So, edge (s, u_n) is discarded, as it does not belong to an available to node t. The algorithm continues with $(n - 1)$ neighbors, for which it is true. Thus the lemma is proven for any number of neighbors.

Theorem 1. *Consider graph $G = (V, E)$, and two non-faulty nodes $s, t \in V$. Consider all nodes have the correct state information of their adjacent edges in their local representations of the topology. Consider s has at least one available non-faulty path leading to t in its local representation. If s sends a packet to t using the proposed algorithm, the packet is delivered to t.*

Proof. Initially consider there is a non-faulty edge linking s to t. In this case, as s is adjacent to the edge and, so, has the information about its state, the packet is sent from s to t through the edge (s, t), arriving at t, as proposed.

Consider now there is no direct link between s and t, or it exists, but is faulty. According to lemma 3, as s has a non-faulty path leading to destination t in its local representation of the topology, an edge that belongs to a non-faulty route is chosen. According to lemma 2, as the chosen edge leads to a available path, the packet arrives its destination. So, the packet arrives the destination t.

3.2 Number and Size of Update Messages

Theorem 2. *Consider a network that employs the proposed algorithm for routing. The number of topology update messages sent by all nodes is $O(M)$ every α seconds, and each message has $O(M)$ entries.*

Proof. The proposed algorithm employs periodic topology update messages. According to the algorithm specification, each node sends a message every α seconds for each of its neighbors. If g_v is the degree of node v, i.e. the number of adjacent edges of node v, each node sends g_v messages every α seconds. Thus $\sum_{v \in V} g_v = 2M$ $2M$ messages are sent by all nodes every α seconds, and the number of messages sent is $O(M)$ every α seconds.

The worst case of the message size is when it has information about all links in the network. As each edge is counted twice (once for each adjacent node), the largest possible message has $2M$ entries, so the message size, in the worst case, is $O(M)$ entries.

3.3   Edge Selection Complexity

Theorem 3. *Consider a network that employs the proposed algorithm for routing. The complexity for evaluating and selecting an edge for routing is $O(M^2)$.*

Proof. For the selection of an edge, the proposed algorithm computes $\Gamma(G, e)$ for each of its neighbor edges, i.e. for g_v edges. The $\Gamma(G, e)$ computation includes the computation of two criteria: the criterion c_1, corresponding to the maximum flow, that has a complexity of $O(NM)$ [5]; and the criterion c_2, corresponding to the breadth-first search, with complexity of $O(M)$ [5]. Thus, the complexity for the computation of $\Gamma(e)$ is $O(NM + M) = O(NM)$. As this function is computed for each neighbor edge, the selection of an edge is done in $O(NM\overline{g_v})$ steps. As $N\overline{g_v} = 2M$, the selection is done in $O(M^2)$ steps.

3.4   Latency

In this subsection, we evaluate the time required after a topology change for a message to be properly routed.

Theorem 4. *Consider a network that employs the proposed algorithm for routing. Consider that the source node has an available route to the destination in its local representation of the topology. Consider that the state of an edge toggles. The time elapsed from the occurrence of this event until a packet can be successfully delivered to the destination is β seconds.*

Proof. Assume that there is a route to the destination in the source's local representation of the topology, and that this route does not pass through the edge that toggled state. This can be assumed as the route was assumed to be available. In this case, only the nodes adjacent to the edge have information about the state change. If the edge becomes faulty, each neighbor will learn the state after β seconds without receiving any message through the faulty edge. If the state change is the recovery of a faulty edge, or a new edge that is added to the network, then the neighbors will learn the state change after at most α seconds, when the next topology update message is sent. As $\beta > \alpha$, in this case the latency is β seconds.

Theorem 5. *Consider a network that employs the proposed algorithm for routing. Consider, now, there is no available route to the destination in the source's local representation of the network. Consider that the state of an edge toggles. The time elapsed after the occurrence of this event until a packet can be successfully delivered to the destination is $O(D(G)\alpha)$ seconds, where $D(G)$ is the diameter of the graph representing the network topology.*

Proof. In this case the source node does not have any available path to the destination in its local representation of the network. However, there is a path leading to the destination passing through a faulty link that becomes available. The neighbors of this link learn the state change in at most α seconds. This information has to be sent to the neighbor's neighbors, and so on until the information arrives at the node that has a packet to send. In each step the information takes at most α seconds to arrive at the next node. As each node sends the message to all its neighbors, the message will arrive at the node that needs the information in a number of steps equivalent to the minimum distance between this node and the edge that has its state changed. As the maximum shortest distance of two nodes in a graph is the diameter of the graph, or $D(G)$, the latency of the proposed algorithm for this case is $O(D(G)\alpha)$.

4 Implementation and Experimental Results

A simulator for the proposed routing algorithm was implemented in Java [3], version J2SE (*Java 2 Standard Edition*) 1.4.2. A running applet is available at http://www.inf.ufpr.br/jonatan/mfrp.

The implementation was divided in three modules. The first module is the main module, which contains internal procedures, such as those employed for the communication between nodes and edges, the edge evaluation for routing, and the procedures for sending and receiving the topology update messages. The second module is the graphical interface module, used for setting parameters and visualizing the execution of the algorithm; the user can draw the topology, observe the flow of routing information, determine the state of links and nodes, and check selected routes. The third module is the simulation module, employed to obtain experimental results on random graphs with random events.

The random graphs were generated using the *Power Law* distribution model [7]. This model is proven to generate topologies that are very similar to those of real networks, such as the Internet [8,9,10]. The simulation module, mentioned before, implements the algorithm by Bu and Towsley [11] for creating random Power Law graphs.

The experimental results presented in this paper take into account the number of messages that successfully arrive at the destination. For each simulation, several graphs of 100 nodes each were generated. We could not employ larger graphs due to lack of resources for the simulation. For each graph, a set of events was generated. An event corresponds to either the change of the state of an edge, the change of the state of a node state or the creation of a packet for routing. Each event has an associated timestamp.

The graph generator employed the Bu and Towsley algorithm with the following parameters: m_0 (initial backbone size) corresponding to 5 nodes, p (related to the number of edges) equal to 0.6, and β (related to the graph sparsity) equal to 0.2. In each graph random events were scheduled for about 10 minutes. About every 120 seconds a randomly chosen node toggled its state; a random edge state change was scheduled for about every 60 seconds; a packet was generated about every two seconds. In all tests, the simulation was run several times for each graph, using a representative result as the final result for each simulation.

Since for all simulations the same set of events was used, packets were ignored in case they did not arrive at the destination because (1) the source or destination failed or (2) there is no available route between source and destination. Each simulation generated a total of 286 messages for each graph in average, and about 25 messages were discarded for one of the reasons presented above.

In the first simulation experiment a varying time interval between topology update messages, known as α, was employed. The following values were used for α: 10 milliseconds, 0.5 seconds, 1 second, 2 seconds, 5 seconds, 10 seconds and 20 seconds. In all simulations, β was defined as 2α, the *delay* for a message transmission through an edge was 200 milliseconds and the values 20 and -5 were used respectively for the weights of the criteria c_1 and c_2 (ω_1 and ω_2). The results are presented in figure 6, in (A). In this figure, the average number of messages arriving at the destination in all graphs is used as result.

We can observe through the results of experiment 1 that the algorithm performance is worse for higher values of α. The same occurs for very low values, as 10 milliseconds. In the latter case, only five messages were successfully routed to their destinations. This happens because, for a very low α, the number of messages in the network is higher, causing congestion at some points and the topology update messages get delayed. With a higher value of α, there is a reduction in the number of messages and most topology update messages can be received in time. However, as α increases, the time for a node to receive topology update messages also increases, and the local representation of the topology at the nodes get out-of-date for longer periods. Thus, for this experiment we can conclude that the best range for α is between 500 milliseconds and two seconds.

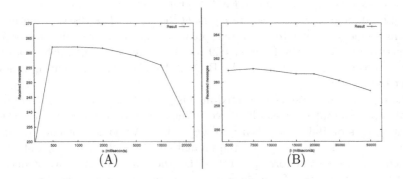

Fig. 6. Simulation results for a varying α and β

Another experiment varied the *timeout* interval for receiving information from a given neighbor, called β. The simulation was run having α equal to 5 seconds, and using the following values for β: 5, 7.5, 10, 15, 20, 30 and 50 seconds. In all simulations, the *delay* for a message to pass through an edge is 200 milliseconds, and the values 20 and -5 were used respectively for the criterion weights ω_1 and ω_2. The result is shown in figure 6, in (B). In this figure, as above, results correspond to the average of the number of packets arriving at the destination when routed with the proposed algorithm.

The results obtained show that there is a very low variation for the value of β (note that the scales are different than the ones of the previous figure), however the result is better for shorter values of β, closer to α. For higher values, the algorithm's latency is increased, and the time for a node to acknowledge the failure of an edge is also increased, and so rising the probability of sending a message through a faulty edge.

5 Related Work

The dependability requirements for modern networks is increasingly high. The convergence latency of current Internet routing protocols, especially BGP is a problem [2,12]. During this interval packets are lost and connections are broken. This situation can persist even when the physical network is redundant, offering alternative physical routes for communication.

Several approaches have been proposed in order to decrease BGP's convergence latency and/or to avoid its consequences. Recently, Sahoo et al. [13] presented a strategy for adjusting BGP parameters, specially MRAI (*Minimum Route Advertisement Interval*) and for reducing the processing overhead of routers, allowing the reduction of the convergence latency after large-scale failures. A set of tools for monitoring BGP routers, as well as determining relevant events that may result in routing anomalies are presented in [14]. In [15] an alternative BGP version is proposed, with messages for reporting faults that allow new information to be distinguished from old information. The authors show that their strategy avoids part of BGP instability problems.

Another strategy is FRTR (*Fast Routing Table Recovery*), introduced in [16], which was proposed to detect and correct inconsistencies in neighbor routers tables; the paper shows that the original BGP neither detects nor solves several types of inconsistencies. An evaluation of the packet loss rate during the convergence latency is presented in [17]. The authors conclude that increasing the network connectivity causes a decrease of the packet loss rate, and that the ability of the protocol of quickly propagating network state information is also important to reduce the packet loss rate. Two papers [18,19] propose strategies for path dependence analysis, in order to reduce the number of paths considered during the convergence, and so reducing the convergence latency. None of these papers proposes a solution that solves completely the problem.

An approach for finding robust paths, proposed in [20], is based on the identification of nodes that belong to highly connected components on the network, in order to find paths that pass through these nodes. Two connectivity criteria are defined, named #C(v) and MCC(v), or the connectivity number and the maximum connectivity component of a vertex, respectively. Polynomial algorithms based on Gomory and Hu's cut tree [21] are proposed for computing these criteria. However, this approach is intended to be used for internal routing only, as nodes are required to to maintain a complete and up-to-date topology representation of the network.

Another related work refers to QoS routing, in which besides distance other criteria are taken into account such as bandwidth, jitter and delay. In this case, even if there are no link or node failures, and communication is not totally interrupted, the previously agreed quality of service (QoS) level has to be maintained. When a QoS violation is predicted or detected, *rerouting* is required [22]. The MPLS (*Multi Protocol Label Switching*) protocol [23] is usually employed in this setting. Using MPLS, it is possible to establish virtual circuits that carry flows with specific QoS requirements. When a MPLS router has to change the virtual circuit used for transmitting a flow, rerouting occurs for *QoS restoration* [24].

Several strategies for MPLS rerouting have been proposed. In [25], an architecture is presented based on mobile agents for monitoring virtual circuits and rerouting after a QoS failure tendency is detected. This kind of approach is said to be proactive, as opposed to reactive approaches which cause rerouting only after detecting that the agreed parameters have been broken. In the proactive approach periods when the network does not offer the required QoS levels are avoided; on the other hand, rerouting is some times executed without being necessary, as a QoS fault tendency is not always confirmed. Most proactive QoS restoration techniques are based on back-up routes that are reserved for the flow from the time it is established to the time it is released [26], even when they are not necessary. A comparison between proactive and reactive strategies based on traffic engineering is presented in [27]. Tanaka et al. [28] take into account the physical network technology to evaluate rerouting strategies, considering IP routers and optical devices, such as PXC's (*Photonic Cross Connects*) and DWDM (*Dense Wavelength Division Multiplexing*).

6   Conclusion

This work introduced a new fault-tolerant dynamic routing algorithm. Routes are dynamically selected with maximum flow evaluation and distance. The proposed algorithm does not require that routers be initialized with the complete network topology. Intermediate routers are able to switch the path employed, and this path itself is selected based on robustness, i.e. the number of edge-disjoint routes it offers. The proposed routing approach was formally specified. The correctness of the algorithm was proven in as well as the complexity, latency, and the number and sizes of messages. Experimental results obtained through simulation in Internet-like topologies were presented, allowing an evaluation of choices for the algorithm parameters.

Future work includes extending the proposed algorithm to deal with QoS (Quality of Service) routing, allowing the selection of paths based on delay, cost and bandwidth. The development of a path cache, for which the first message for a source-destination pair establishes a path for others to follow, and so reducing overflow, is under study. Employing additional criteria for evaluating edges, such as the number of paths leading to the destination and the average distance of such paths, is also under consideration, as well as simulation tests comparing the algorithm with other well-known routing algorithms, such as Dijkstra and Bellman-Ford. Implementations on larger networks and on real networks are also planned for the future. Finally, a protocol using the proposed algorithm is being developed. In order to be practical when deployed in large networks, this protocol must employ techniques for enhancing the performance of the algorithm, such as off-line route evaluation, and routing flows instead of single packets.

References

1. Huitema, C.: Routing in the Internet, 2nd edn. Prentice Hall, Upper Saddle River (1999)
2. Labovitz, C., Ahuja, A., Bose, A., Jahanian, F.: Delayed internet routing convergence. In: SIGCOMM, pp. 175–187 (2000)
3. Java Technology: http://java.sun.com
4. Ford Jr., L.R., Fulkerson, D.R.: Flows in networks. Princeton University Press (1962)
5. Cormen, T.H., Leiserson, C.E., Rivest, R.L.: Introduction to Algorithms, 2nd edn. McGraw-Hill, New York (1990)
6. Dijkstra, E.W.: A note on two problems in connexion with graphs. Numerische Mathematik 1, 269–271 (1959)
7. Faloutsos, M., Faloutsos, P., Faloutsos, C.: On Power-Law Relationships of the Internet Topology. In: Proceedings of the ACM Conference on Applications, Technologies, Architectures, and Protocols for Computer Communication (SIGCOMM'99), Cambridge, Massachusetts, USA, pp. 251–262. ACM Press, New York (1999)
8. Medina, A., Matta, I., Byers, J.: On the Origin of Power Laws in Internet Topologies. SIGCOMM Computer Communication Review 30(2), 18–28 (2000)
9. Chen, Q., Chang, H., Govindan, R., Jamin, S., Shenker, S., Willinger, W.: The Origin of Power-Laws in Internet Topologies Revisited. In: Proceedings of the 21st Annual Joint Conference of the IEEE Computer and Communications Societies (INFOCOM'2002). IEEE Computer Society Press, Los Alamitos (2002)
10. Tangmunarunkit, H., Govindan, R., Jamin, S., Shenker, S., Willinger, W.: Network Topology Generators: Degree-Based vs. Structural. In: Proceedings of the ACM Conference on Applications, Technologies, Architectures, and Protocols for Computer Communication (SIGCOMM'2002), pp. 147–159. ACM Press, New York (2002)
11. Bu, T., Towsley, D.F.: On Distinguishing between Internet Power Law Topology Generators. In: Proceedings of the 21st Annual Joint Conference of the IEEE Computer and Communications Societies (INFOCOM'2002). IEEE Computer Society Press, Los Alamitos (2002)

12. Pei, D., Zhang, B., Massey, D., Zhang, L.: An analysis of convergence delay in path vector routing protocols. Computer Networks 50(3) (2006)
13. Sahoo, A., Kant, K., Mohapatra, P.: Improving bgp convergence delay for large-scale failures. In: The 7th IEEE/IPIP International Conference on Dependable Systems and Networks (DSN'06), Philadelphia, U.S.A (2006)
14. Wong, T., Jacobson, V., Alaettinoglu, C.: Internet Routing Anomaly Detection and Visualization. In: The 6th IEEE/IPIP International Conference on Dependable Systems and Networks (DSN'05), Yokohama, Japan (2005)
15. Zhang, H., Arora, A., Liu, Z.: A Stability-Oriented Approach to Improving BGP Convergence. In: The 23rd IEEE International Symposium on Reliable Distributed Systems (SRDS'04), Florianópolis, Brazil (2004)
16. Wang, L., Massey, D., Patel, K., Zhang, L.: FRTR: A scalable mechanism for global routing table consistency. In: Proceedings of the IEEE/IFIP International Conference on Dependable Systems and Networks (DSN'2004), Florence, Italy, pp. 465–474 (2004)
17. Pei, D., Wang, L., Massey, D., Wu, S.F., Zhang, L.: A Study of Packet Delivery Performance During Routing Convergence. In: The 4th IEEE/IPIP International Conference on Dependable Systems and Networks (DSN'03), San Francisco, U.S.A (2003)
18. Chandrashekar, J., Duan, Z., Zhang, Z.L., Krasky, J.: Limiting Path Exploration in BGP. In: The 24th IEEE INFOCOM (INFOCOM'04), Miami, U.S.A. IEEE Computer Society Press, Los Alamitos (2005)
19. Pei, D., Zhao, X., Wang, L., Massey, D., Mankin, A., Wu, S., Zhang, L.: Improving BGP Convergence through Consistency Assertions. In: The 21st IEEE INFOCOM (INFOCOM'02), New York, U.S.A. IEEE Computer Society Press, Los Alamitos (2002)
20. Duarte Jr. E.P., Santini, R., Cohen, J.: Delivering packets during the routing convergence latency interval through highly connected detours. In: Proceedings of the IEEE/IFIP International Conference on Dependable Systems and Networks (DSN'2004), Florence, Italy, pp. 495–504 (2004)
21. Gomory, R.E., Hu, T.C.: Multi-terminal network flows. SIAM Journal on Applied Mathematics 9, 551–556 (1961)
22. Funagalli, A., Valcarenghi, L.: Restauration vs. WDM Protection: Is There an Optimal Choice? IEEE Network (2000)
23. Rosen, E., Viswanathan, A., Callon, R.: RFC 3031: Multi-Protocol Label Switchin (2001)
24. Hellstrand, F., Sharma, V.: RFC 3469: Framework for MPLS-based Recovery (2004)
25. Correia, R.B., Pirmez, L., et al.: Rerroteamento Parcial Pró-Ativo em Redes Baseadas em Circuito Virtual no Suporte ao Gerenciamento de Desempenho Pró-Ativo. In: XXIII Simpósio Brasileiro de Redes de Computadores (SBRC'2005), Fortaleza, Brazil (2005)
26. Medhi, D.: A Perspective on Network Restoration. Handbook of Optimization in Telecommunications (2005)
27. Puype, B., Yan, Q., Colle, D., et al.: Multi-Layer Traffic Engineering in Data Centric Optical Networks. In: COST266-IST OPTIMIST Workshop on Optical Networks, Budapest, Hungary (2003)
28. Tanaka, S., et al.: Field Test of GMPLS All Optical Path Rerouting. IEEE Photonics Technology Letters 17(3) (2005)

On the Implementation of
Communication-Optimal Failure Detectors*

Mikel Larrea[1], Alberto Lafuente[1], Iratxe Soraluze[1], Roberto Cortiñas[1],
and Joachim Wieland[2]

[1] The University of the Basque Country
20018 San Sebastián, Spain
{mikel.larrea,alberto.lafuente,iratxe.soraluze,roberto.cortinas}@ehu.es
[2] RWTH Aachen University
52056 Aachen, Germany
joachim.wieland@rwth-aachen.de

Abstract. Several algorithms implementing failure detectors have been
proposed in the literature. In particular, we have proposed a family of
communication-efficient $\Diamond \mathcal{P}$ algorithms, i.e., algorithms using n links to
carry messages forever, being n the number of processes in the system.
Moreover, we have recently proposed a $\Diamond \mathcal{P}$ algorithm that uses only $\mathcal{C}$
links, being $\mathcal{C}$ the number of correct processes. In this paper, we show
that $\mathcal{C}$ is the minimum number of links required to implement $\Diamond \mathcal{P}$. We
also show that, assuming that there is at least one incorrect process,
$\mathcal{C}$ is optimal not only for $\Diamond \mathcal{P}$ but also for $\Diamond \mathcal{S}$ and Ω. We revisit our
Reliable Broadcast based communication-optimal $\Diamond \mathcal{P}$ algorithm, and
we show that, regarding QoS measures, it performs better than the
communication-efficient algorithms.

Keywords: Distributed algorithms, fault tolerance, Consensus, unreliable failure detectors.

1 Introduction

Unreliable failure detectors, proposed by Chandra and Toueg [5], have been used
to address the Consensus problem [16] and several related problems in asynchronous crash-prone distributed systems. In this paper, we mainly focus on the
Eventually Perfect failure detector class, denoted $\Diamond \mathcal{P}$, which satisfies (1) strong
completeness: eventually every process that crashes is permanently suspected
by every correct process, and (2) eventual strong accuracy: there is a time after
which correct processes are not suspected by any correct process. Nevertheless,
Consensus can be solved with a weaker failure detector class called *Eventually
Strong*, denoted $\Diamond \mathcal{S}$, which satisfies strong completeness and eventual *weak* accuracy: there is a time after which *some* correct process is not suspected by any

---

* Research partially supported by the Spanish Research Council, under grants
TIN2004-07474-C02-02 and TIN2006-15617-C03-01, the Basque Government, under
grant S-PE06IK01, and the Comunidad de Madrid, under grant S-0505/TIC/0285.

A. Bondavalli, F. Brasileiro, and S. Rajsbaum (Eds.): LADC 2007, LNCS 4746, pp. 25–37, 2007.
© Springer-Verlag Berlin Heidelberg 2007

correct process. Specifically, a particular failure detector called Ω, equivalent to $\Diamond S$, has been proved to be the weakest failure detector to solve Consensus [4]. The Ω failure detector provides eventual agreement on a common *leader* among all non-faulty processes in a system. Specific algorithms for implementing Ω and/or $\Diamond S$ have been proposed in the literature, e.g., [1,2,3,11]. Note that since $\Diamond P$ is strictly stronger than $\Diamond S$, any implementation of $\Diamond P$ trivially implements $\Diamond S$. Observe also that $\Diamond P$ can be easily transformed into Ω, e.g., by choosing as leader the non-suspected process with lowest identifier.

In [13,15] we have proposed a family of heartbeat-based algorithms which implement $\Diamond P$ using a logical ring arrangement of processes. In these algorithms, every process p tries to determine which is its correct successor in the ring, i.e., the process to which p should send heartbeats forever, and also which is its correct predecessor in the ring, i.e., the process from which p should receive heartbeats forever. Attached to heartbeats, processes propagate around the ring a list of suspected processes, which provides the properties of $\Diamond P$. This list is updated whenever p receives a new heartbeat from its predecessor, and then used to set p's current successor in the ring. The algorithms are *communication-efficient* following Aguilera et al. [1], i.e., eventually only n unidirectional links carry messages forever. With regard to this performance measure, heartbeat-based ring algorithms outperform other ring algorithms based on polling [10] or algorithms using a centralized communication pattern [1,12]. By all means, algorithms using an all-to-all communication pattern, as Chandra-Toueg's algorithm, are far away from being communication-efficient. Our communication-efficient algorithms sporadically broadcast failure suspicions and —when required— suspicion refutations. Since the heartbeat flow keeps on following the ring arrangement, and eventually no new broadcasts occur, communication efficiency is preserved.

In the Brief Announcement of [14] we show that even *communication-optimal* algorithms for $\Diamond P$ can be implemented, in which eventually only $\mathcal{C}$ unidirectional links carry messages forever, being $\mathcal{C}$ the number of correct processes. The algorithm proposed in [14] does no longer propagate a list of suspected processes. Instead, it uses a Reliable Broadcast primitive [5] to communicate the sporadic suspicions and refutations. Doing like that, no information about suspected processes has to circulate around the ring. Now, the list of suspected processes satisfying the properties of $\Diamond P$ is inferred directly by a process p from its balance of suspicions and refutations received about every process q.

Our Contribution. In this paper, we show that $\mathcal{C}$ is the minimum number of unidirectional links carrying messages forever needed for an algorithm to provide the properties of $\Diamond P$ in a crash-prone system. Furthermore, when $\mathcal{C} < n$, we show that $\mathcal{C}$ is also minimal for Ω. We then revisit the communication-optimal $\Diamond P$ algorithm of [14], providing a correctness proof. We also evaluate its performance in terms of QoS measures, comparing it to the communication-efficient $\Diamond P$ algorithm of [15].

Despite Ω has been extensively used to solve Consensus, we focus our work on implementing communication-optimal failure detectors of the class $\Diamond P$, instead of providing specific implementations for Ω. This is mainly justified by the fact that, as we will show, communication optimality is nearly the same for both $\Diamond \mathcal{P}$ and Ω, and every $\Diamond \mathcal{P}$ failure detector trivially implements Ω. Moreover, for certain problems [8] and Consensus protocols [17] failure detector $\Diamond \mathcal{P}$ is required. Finally, $\Diamond \mathcal{P}$ is more *natural*, in the sense that all correct processes can produce a list containing just the faulty processes, providing a higher degree of accuracy. This may be a relevant QoS parameter for some applications.

The rest of the paper is organized as follows. In Section 2, we describe the system model considered in this work. In Section 3, we show the communication optimality results for $\Diamond \mathcal{P}$ and Ω. In Section 4, we revisit the algorithm of [14], and provide a proof of correctness. In Section 5, we evaluate its performance. Finally, Section 6 concludes the paper.

2   System Model

We consider a distributed system composed of a finite set Π of $n > 1$ processes, $\Pi = \{p_1, p_2, \ldots, p_n\}$, that communicate only by sending and receiving messages. Every pair of processes (p_i, p_j) is connected by two unidirectional and reliable[1] communication links $p_i \rightarrow p_j$ and $p_j \rightarrow p_i$.

Processes can only fail by crashing, that is, by prematurely halting. Moreover, crashes are permanent, i.e., crashed processes do not recover. In every run of the system we identify two complementary subsets of Π: the subset of processes that do not fail, denoted *correct*, and the subset of processes that do fail, denoted *crashed*. We use $\mathcal{C}$ to denote the number of correct processes in the system in the run of interest, which we assume is at least one, i.e., $\mathcal{C} = |correct| \geq 1$.

We consider that processes are arranged in a logical ring. Without loss of generality, process p_i is preceded by process p_{i-1}, and followed by process p_{i+1}. As usual, p_1 follows p_n in the ring. In general, we will use the functions $pred(p)$ and $succ(p)$ respectively to denote the predecessor and the successor of a process p in the ring.

Concerning timing assumptions, we consider a partially synchronous model [5,7] which stipulates that, in every run of the system, there are bounds on relative process speeds and on message transmission times, but these bounds are not known and they hold only after some unknown but finite time (called *GST* for *Global Stabilization Time*). Actually, the bounds must exist and hold only for the $\mathcal{C}$ links that eventually form the ring of correct processes, i.e., the links from every correct process to its correct successor in the ring. Hence, the bounds must only hold for a linear number of links.

Finally, in the algorithms presented in this paper we assume that a local clock that can measure real-time intervals is available to each process. Clocks are not synchronized.

---

[1] The definition of reliable link that we consider is the following: if both the sender and the receiver do not crash, then all messages that are sent are eventually delivered. Reliable communication is usually implemented using retransmission techniques and acknowledgment messages.

Every process p executes the following:

To execute r-broadcast(m):
    send m to all (including p)

r-deliver(m) occurs as follows:
    when receive m for the first time
        if $sender(m) \neq p$ **then**
            send m to all[a]
        end if
        r-deliver(m)

---

[a] An optimization consists in not relaying m to p, $sender(m)$, and the process q from which m has been received for the first time (if $q \neq sender(m)$).

Fig. 1. Reliable Broadcast by message diffusion

2.1   Reliable Broadcast

Reliable Broadcast is a communication primitive for asynchronous systems guaranteeing that all correct processes deliver the same set of messages. This set includes at least all messages broadcast by correct processes. Formally, Reliable Broadcast is defined in terms of two primitives, r-broadcast(m) and r-deliver(m), and satisfies the following properties [9]:

- Validity. If a correct process r-broadcasts a message m, then it eventually r-delivers m.
- Agreement. If a correct process r-delivers a message m, then all correct processes eventually r-deliver m.
- Uniform integrity. For any message m, every process r-delivers m at most once, and only if m was previously r-broadcast by $sender(m)$.[2]

Figure 1 presents a simple Reliable Broadcast algorithm for asynchronous systems with up to $n - 1$ crash failures [5]. Informally, when a process receives a message for the first time, it relays the message to all processes and then r-delivers it.

3   On Communication Optimality

In this section, we show that $\mathcal{C}$, i.e., the number of correct processes in the system, is the minimum number of unidirectional links carrying messages forever needed for an algorithm to provide the properties of $\Diamond \mathcal{P}$. Then, we show that, assuming

---

[2] We assume that messages include the identity of the sender and a sequence number, which make every message unique.

that at least one process crashes, i.e., $\mathcal{C} < n$, $\mathcal{C}$ is also minimal for implementing Ω.[3] Both results hold when there are at least two correct processes in the system, i.e., $\mathcal{C} \geq 2$.

Theorem 1. *$\mathcal{C}$ is the minimum number of unidirectional links carrying messages forever needed for an algorithm to provide the properties of $\Diamond\mathcal{P}$ in a crash-prone system.*

Proof. Given a run R, observe that every process must periodically inform that it is still alive by sending a message, which after every incorrect process has crashed gives us the minimum number of $\mathcal{C}$ unidirectional links. Otherwise, if less than $\mathcal{C}$ unidirectional links carry messages forever, there is some correct process p that eventually stops sending messages. Let t be the time instant in which p stops sending messages. Consider now another run R', identical to R until time t, and assume that p crashes at time t in R'. For any correct process q, if q does not eventually and permanently suspect p, then the strong completeness property of $\Diamond\mathcal{P}$ is violated. Hence, q will eventually and permanently suspect p in R'. Observe that both executions R and R' are indistinguishable. Hence, in run R q will also eventually and permanently suspect p, violating the eventual strong accuracy property of $\Diamond\mathcal{P}$.

Theorem 2. *If at least one process crashes, then $\mathcal{C}$ is the minimum number of unidirectional links carrying messages forever needed for an algorithm to provide the property of Ω in a crash-prone system.*

Proof. The proof is by contradiction. Assume that we have an implementation of Ω in which only $\mathcal{C} - 1$ unidirectional links carry messages forever. Observe that such an implementation would be possible only if correct processes are arranged in a tree topology, being the leader the root of the tree and propagating heartbeat messages —directly or indirectly— to the rest of correct processes.[4] Consider a run R of the algorithm in which $\mathcal{C}$ processes are correct and let t be the time instant after which only $\mathcal{C} - 1$ unidirectional links carry messages forever. Consider now another run R', identical to R until time t, and assume that a process q different from the leader, which is correct in R, crashes at time t in R'. Observe that both executions R and R' are indistinguishable, and there is no way for the leader to know that q has crashed, and hence it will not stop sending messages to q. Since the number of correct processes in run R' is $\mathcal{C} - 1$, the algorithm should use only $\mathcal{C} - 2$ unidirectional links to carry messages forever, which contradicts the fact that the leader will not stop sending messages to q.

In [3], Aguilera et al. propose an algorithm implementing Ω such that eventually only f links carry messages forever, being f the maximum number of processes that can crash. They also show that in the crash-failure model no algorithm using fewer than f links exists. Hence, if $f = n - 1$ (as in our system model), Ω can be implemented with $n - 1$ links carrying messages forever, even if no

---

[3] By equivalence, the reasoning regarding Ω applies to $\Diamond\mathcal{S}$ too.

[4] Observe that a star is a particular case of a tree topology.

process crashes, i.e., $\mathcal{C} = n$. However, the algorithm of [3] uses always $n - 1$ links, independently of the actual number of correct processes $\mathcal{C}$. As we will see, the algorithm we propose in this work, besides implementing $\Diamond\mathcal{P}$, dynamically adapts the number of links used to the actual number of correct processes.

4   Communication-Optimal Implementation of $\Diamond\mathcal{P}$

In this section, we revisit our communication-optimal implementation of $\Diamond\mathcal{P}$ of [14] that uses Reliable Broadcast, providing a correctness proof and showing its optimality. In the algorithm, each process sends heartbeats to its successor in the ring, and monitors its predecessor by hearing heartbeats from it. Figure 2 presents the algorithm in detail, which uses a $Balance_p$ variable for every process p, accounting suspicions and refutations for every process. If $Balance_p(q) > 0$ with $q \neq p$, then p suspects q; else, q is trusted by p. As we will see, $Balance_p$ provides the properties of $\Diamond\mathcal{P}$. Every process p starts sending periodically an $(ALIVE, p)$ message to its successor in the ring, denoted by the variable $succ_p$ (Task 1). Also, every process p waits for periodical $(ALIVE, pred_p)$ messages from its predecessor in the ring, denoted by the variable $pred_p$. If p does not receive such a message on a specific time-out interval of $\Delta_p(pred_p)$, then p suspects that $pred_p$ has crashed, and r-broadcasts a $(SUSPICION, p, pred_p)$ message (Task 2). In Task 3, when p r-delivers a $(SUSPICION, q, r)$ message, p increments $Balance_p(r)$ and calls the *update_pred_and_succ* procedure. Besides this, if $r = p$, i.e., p has been erroneously suspected by q, p r-broadcasts a $(REFUTATION, p)$ message. In Task 4, when p r-delivers a $(REFUTATION, q)$ message, p decrements $Balance_p(q)$, increments $\Delta_p(q)$, and calls the *update_pred_and_succ* procedure. Variables $pred_p$ and $succ_p$ are updated from $Balance_p$ to the nearest predecessor and the nearest successor in the ring having a non-positive balance respectively.[5] If all the components of the $Balance_p$ vector are positive, then p sets both $pred_p$ and $succ_p$ to p.

4.1   Correctness Proof

We show now that the algorithm of Figure 2 implements a failure detector of class $\Diamond\mathcal{P}$ and that it is communication optimal. In the proof, we consider that all the time instants are after all the incorrect processes have already crashed, and all the messages they have sent before crashing have already been delivered. We start making the following observations.

Observation 1. $\forall p \in correct$, *eventually and permanently* $Balance_p(p) = 0$. *This derives from the following: (1) initially* $Balance_p(p) = 0$, *(2) for every* $(SUSPICION, -, p)$ *message that p r-delivers in Task 3, eventually p r-delivers*

---

[5] Here we informally use the terms *nearest predecessor* (or *nearest successor*) of a process p to denote the first process preceding (or succeeding) p following the ring arrangement and fitting a particular condition.

Every process p executes the following:

procedure *update_pred_and_succ()*
(1)   **if** $\forall r : Balance_p(r) > 0$ **then**
(2) $pred_p \leftarrow p$
(3) $succ_p \leftarrow p$
(4)   **else**
(5) $pred_p \leftarrow$ *p's nearest predecessor r such that* $Balance_p(r) \leq 0$
(6) $succ_p \leftarrow$ *p's nearest successor r such that* $Balance_p(r) \leq 0$
(7)   **end if**
end procedure

(8) $pred_p \leftarrow pred(p)$ {*p's estimation of its nearest correct predecessor*}
(9) $succ_p \leftarrow succ(p)$ {*p's estimation of its nearest correct successor*}
(10)   **for all** $q \in \Pi$:
             $\Delta_p(q) \leftarrow$ default time-out interval
(11)   **for all** $q \in \Pi$:
             $Balance_p(q) \leftarrow 0$

(12)   **cobegin**

(13) $\|$ *Task 1:* **repeat periodically**
(14)   **if** $succ_p \neq p$ **then**
(15)   send $(ALIVE, p)$ to $succ_p$
(16)   **end if**

(17) $\|$ *Task 2:* **repeat periodically**
(18)   **if** $pred_p \neq p$ **and** *p did not receive* $(ALIVE, pred_p)$
                             during the last $\Delta_p(pred_p)$ *ticks of p's clock* **then**
(19)   r-broadcast $(SUSPICION, p, pred_p)$
(20)   **end if**

(21) $\|$ *Task 3:* **when** r-deliver $(SUSPICION, q, r)$
(22) $Balance_p(r) \leftarrow Balance_p(r) + 1$
(23)   *update_pred_and_succ()*
(24)   **if** $r = p$ **then**
(25)   r-broadcast $(REFUTATION, p)$
(26)   **end if**

(27) $\|$ *Task 4:* **when** r-deliver $(REFUTATION, q)$
(28) $Balance_p(q) \leftarrow Balance_p(q) - 1$
(29) $\Delta_p(q) \leftarrow \Delta_p(q) + 1$ {*not needed if q = p*}
(30)   *update_pred_and_succ()*

(31)   **coend**

Fig. 2. Communication-optimal $\Diamond\mathcal{P}$ using Reliable Broadcast

in Task 4 a (REFUTATION, p) message that compensates the previous incre-ment of $Balance_p(p)$, and (3) eventually every correct process stabilizes with its correct predecessor in the ring, after which it stops r-broadcasting suspicions.

Observation 2. $\forall p$, *if* $pred_p = q$ *with* $q \neq p$ *then* $Balance_p(q) \leq 0$. *Also, if* $succ_p = r$ *with* $r \neq p$ *then* $Balance_p(r) \leq 0$. *This derives directly from the fact that both* $pred_p$ *and* $succ_p$ *are only updated by* p *inside the procedure* update_pred_and_succ().

Observation 3. *For every pair of correct processes* p, q, *when no more failure suspicions occur,* $Balance_p(r) = Balance_q(r)$ *for every process* r. *By the proper-ties of Reliable Broadcast, both* p *and* q *r-deliver the same set of (SUSPICION, $-$, r) and (REFUTATION, r) messages. Consequently, both* p *and* q *apply the same modifications to* $Balance_p(r)$ *and* $Balance_q(r)$ *respectively.*

Lemma 1. *For every pair of consecutive correct processes* q, p *in the ring, even-tually* p *stops r-broadcasting (SUSPICION, p, q) messages.*

Proof. The proof is by contradiction. Assume that p r-broadcasts $(SUSPICION, p, q)$ messages infinitely often. Since both p and q are correct, for each message $(SUSPICION, p, q)$ q will r-broadcast a $(REFUTATION, q)$ message that will be delivered by p. Upon delivery, p will increment $\Delta_p(q)$. Since the commu-nication link between q and p is eventually timely, eventually $\Delta_p(q)$ will reach the unknown bound on message transmission times, after which p will receive a $(ALIVE, q)$ always before $\Delta_p(q)$ expires, and p will no more suspect q in Task 2. This contradicts the fact that p suspects q infinitely often.

Lemma 2. *For every pair of non-consecutive correct processes* q, p *in the ring, eventually* p *stops r-broadcasting (SUSPICION, p, q) messages.*

Proof. By Lemma 1, eventually p will permanently monitor another correct pro-cess r, being r its correct predecessor in the ring. After that, p will never r-broadcast any $(SUSPICION, p, q)$ message any more.

Lemma 3. *For every pair of correct processes* p, q, *eventually and permanently* $Balance_p(q) = 0$.

Proof. Follows from Lemma 1 and Lemma 2, and the fact that, being initially $Balance_p(q) = 0$, by the algorithm p delivers the same number of $(SUSPICION, -, q)$ and $(REFUTATION, q)$ messages, compensating the increment and decrement operations over $Balance_p(q) = 0$.

Lemma 4. *For every incorrect process* q, *eventually and permanently* $Balance_p(q) > 0$ *for every correct process* p.

Proof. Note that after q crashes it will not be able to r-broadcast any message $(REFUTATION, q)$. Also, at least process r, being r the correct successor of q in the ring, will eventually r-broadcast a $(SUSPICION, r, q)$ message that q will not refute, and consequently $Balance_r(q) > 0$ permanently. Then, by Observation 3, $Balance_p(q) > 0$ for every correct process p.

Lemma 5. *Eventually, for every correct process p, $pred_p$ will be permanently set to p's correct predecessor in the ring, and $succ_p$ will be permanently set to p's correct successor in the ring.*

Proof. Follows directly from Lemma 3, Lemma 4, and Observation 2.

Theorem 3. *The algorithm of Figure 2 implements a failure detector of class $\Diamond \mathcal{P}$.*

Proof. From Lemma 3 and Lemma 4, for every correct process p, eventually and permanently $Balance_p(q) = 0$ for every $q \in correct$, and $Balance_p(r) > 0$ for every $r \in crashed$. The rule "if $Balance_p(q) > 0$, then p suspects q; else, p does not suspect q" provides the properties of strong completeness and eventual strong accuracy of $\Diamond \mathcal{P}$.

Theorem 4. *The algorithm of Figure 2 is communication-optimal, i.e., eventually only $\mathcal{C}$ links carry messages forever.*

Proof. From Lemma 5, for every correct process p, eventually and permanently $succ_p$ will be set to p's correct successor in the ring and, by Task 1, p will send $(ALIVE, p)$ messages to it forever. No other periodical messages will be sent. Furthermore, since no more suspicions will occur, no new $SUSPICION$ (and hence $REFUTATION$) messages will be broadcast. Thus, if there are $\mathcal{C}$ correct processes in the system, just a number of $\mathcal{C}$ unidirectional links will be permanently used.

Observe that if there is just one correct process in the system, i.e., $\mathcal{C} = 1$, the algorithm of Figure 2 eventually uses no links, by an optimization introduced in Task 1. Hence, when $\mathcal{C} = 1$ both $\Diamond \mathcal{P}$ and Ω can be implemented using 0 links carrying messages forever.

5   Performance Evaluation

Figure 3 summarizes the costs of the communication-efficient algorithm of [15] and the communication-optimal algorithm presented in this paper, in terms of the number of links used forever and the number of messages needed to manage a suspicion. Chandra-Toueg's all-to-all algorithm is also included as a reference.

Besides communication efficiency, there are QoS measures that are of interest when evaluating the performance of failure detector algorithms, as those related

Algorithm	Periodic cost (#links used forever)	Sporadic cost (#msgs to manage a suspicion)
Chandra-Toueg [5]	$\mathcal{C}(n-1)$	0
Comm.-efficient [15]	n	$O(n)$
Comm.-optimal (Figure 2)	$\mathcal{C}$	$O(n^2)$

Fig. 3. Costs of different algorithms implementing $\Diamond \mathcal{P}$

to the accuracy of the information provided to querying processes. In particular, we focus on the *query accuracy probability*, defined as the probability that a failure detection module which is queried by its associated process gives the right answer. This measure is based on [6], but has been extended in this work to scenarios with more than two processes.

We have used the ns-2 simulator (http://www.isi.edu/nsnam/ns/) to test the comparative performance of the algorithms. In Figure 4 we show the simulation settings for a typical local area network scenario. The simulation generates message delays at random with a uniform distribution. However, we have set minimum and maximum message bounds. Apparently, this contradicts our partially synchronous system model. Nevertheless, the algorithms do not exploit the knowledge of the maximal message delay when initializing the timeouts. This allows us to generate erroneous suspicions under the same conditions for both algorithms. Moreover, from a practical point of view the setting of a maximum message delay allows to determine the duration of the simulations.

Parameter	Value
Minimum message delay	0.001
Maximum message delay	0.005
Periodicity of $ALIVE$ messages	0.5
Initial timeouts	0.5
Timeout increment	0.001

Fig. 4. Simulation settings (in seconds)

The tests have been carried out for a number of nodes going from 3 to 24, with a duration of 2000 seconds, that has been empirically proved to be sufficient for comparative purposes. In fact, using the settings of Figure 4, after this duration the simulations have either stabilized or are near stabilization. Every simulation has been executed a sufficiently large number of times.[6] We assume that no process crashes during the simulation. This assumption does not really lose any generality. On the one hand, in our algorithms erroneous suspicions are actually more complex to handle than real crashes.[7] On the other hand, although a crash during the execution of the Reliable Broadcast may delay the delivery of the message, the probability of such a failure in practice is very low. Also, this delay is really small in a LAN, thus our assumption has not any impact in the QoS measures.

Figure 5 shows the average results obtained. For clarity, values express the complement of the right answer probability, i.e., the probability that a failure detection module gives a wrong answer. In the communication-efficient algorithm of [15], the circulation of the list of suspected processes around the ring, while

---

[6] We have repeated every simulation 20 times. In fact, the averages become stable after few executions.

[7] Observe that crashed processes do not send any refutation message.

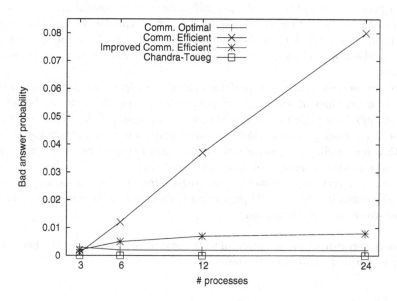

Fig. 5. Comparative query accuracy, expressed as bad answer probability (percentage)

required for a correctness point of view, had a negative impact over the newest information about suspicions-refutations sent by processes. For example, a list of suspected processes received from the predecessor in the ring may cancel a recent suspicion directly received from another process. That is why, as shown in Figure 5, we have also tested an improved implementation of the communication-efficient algorithm that mitigates this effect by delaying updates.

In Figure 5, it can be observed that both the communication-optimal and Chandra-Toueg's algorithms provide constant bad answer probabilities (negligible in the latter). This is due to the use of an all-to-all communication pattern. However, while Chandra-Toueg's algorithm uses this pattern periodically and forever, the communication-optimal algorithm uses it sporadically, and eventually stops using it. Regarding the communication-efficient algorithms, the aforementioned effect caused by the circulating lists produces worse results, partially mitigated in the improved version.

6 Conclusion

In this paper, we have explored communication efficiency, a performance parameter that refers to the number of unidirectional links that carry messages forever. We have shown that failure detector class $\Diamond \mathcal{P}$ requires at least $\mathcal{C}$ unidirectional links to carry messages forever, being $\mathcal{C}$ the number of correct processes. Moreover, when at least one process crashes, $\mathcal{C}$ links are also required for $\Diamond \mathcal{S}$ and Ω. We have revisited our communication-optimal $\Diamond \mathcal{P}$ algorithm of [14] and given a proof of correctness and optimality. Since this algorithm uses exactly $\mathcal{C}$ unidirectional links to carry messages forever, it can be derived that communication optimality for $\Diamond\mathcal{P}$ is achieved. Since $\Diamond\mathcal{P}$ trivially implements Ω, communication optimality can be considered achieved also for $\Diamond\mathcal{S}$ and Ω failure detectors.

Also, we have evaluated the performance of our algorithm compared to the communication-efficient algorithm of [15], showing that it performs better in terms of QoS. The price to pay is a higher cost in terms of the number of messages sent for managing suspicions. In this regard, our communication-optimal algorithm uses Reliable Broadcast to communicate suspicions and refutations, involving a quadratic number of messages. Since this can be a drawback in some scenarios, e.g., very large networks, our current research is focused on variants of the algorithm in which, while preserving QoS, Reliable Broadcast is replaced by point-to-point communication.

Acknowledgments. We are grateful to the anonymous reviewers for their comments, which helped to improve this paper.

References

1. Aguilera, M., Delporte-Gallet, C., Fauconnier, H., Toueg, S.: Stable leader election. In: Welch, J.L. (ed.) DISC 2001. LNCS, vol. 2180, pp. 108–122. Springer, Heidelberg (2001)
2. Aguilera, M., Delporte-Gallet, C., Fauconnier, H., Toueg, S.: On implementing Ω with weak reliability and synchrony assumptions. In: Proceedings of the 22nd ACM Symposium on Principles of Distributed Computing (PODC'2003), Boston, Massachusetts, pp. 306–314 (July 2003)
3. Aguilera, M., Delporte-Gallet, C., Fauconnier, H., Toueg, S.: Communication-efficient leader election and consensus with limited link synchrony. In: Proceedings of the 23rd ACM Symposium on Principles of Distributed Computing (PODC'2004), St. John's, Newfoundland, Canada, pp. 328–337 (July 2004)
4. Chandra, T.D., Hadzilacos, V., Toueg, S.: The weakest failure detector for solving consensus. Journal of the ACM 43(4), 685–722 (1996)
5. Chandra, T.D., Toueg, S.: Unreliable failure detectors for reliable distributed systems. Journal of the ACM 43(2), 225–267 (1996)
6. Chen, W., Toueg, S., Aguilera, M.K.: On the quality of service of failure detectors. IEEE Transactions on Computers 51(5), 561–580 (2002)
7. Dwork, C., Lynch, N., Stockmeyer, L.: Consensus in the presence of partial synchrony. Journal of the ACM 35(2), 288–323 (1988)
8. Guerraoui, R., Kapalka, M., Kouznetsov, P.: The weakest failure detector to boost obstruction-freedom. In: Dolev, S. (ed.) DISC 2006. LNCS, vol. 4167, pp. 399–412. Springer, Heidelberg (2006)
9. Hadzilacos, V., Toueg, S.: Fault-tolerant broadcasts and related problems. In: Mullender, S.J. (ed.) Distributed Systems, 2nd edn., ch. 5, pp. 97–146. Addison-Wesley, Reading (1993)
10. Larrea, M., Arévalo, S., Fernández, A.: Efficient algorithms to implement unreliable failure detectors in partially synchronous systems. In: Jayanti, P. (ed.) DISC 1999. LNCS, vol. 1693, pp. 34–48. Springer, Heidelberg (1999)

11. Larrea, M., Fernández, A., Arévalo, S.: Optimal implementation of the weakest failure detector for solving consensus. In: Proceedings of the 19th IEEE Symposium on Reliable Distributed Systems (SRDS'2000), Nurenberg, Germany, pp. 52–59 (October 2000)
12. Larrea, M., Fernández, A., Arévalo, S.: Eventually consistent failure detectors. Journal of Parallel and Distributed Computing 65(3), 361–373 (2005)
13. Larrea, M., Lafuente, A.: Brief announcement: Communication-efficient implementation of failure detector classes $\Diamond Q$ and $\Diamond P$. In: Fraigniaud, P. (ed.) DISC 2005. LNCS, vol. 3724, pp. 495–496. Springer, Heidelberg (2005)
14. Larrea, M., Lafuente, A., Wieland, J.: Brief announcement: Communication-optimal implementation of failure detector class $\Diamond P$. In: Dolev, S. (ed.) DISC 2006. LNCS, vol. 4167, pp. 569–571. Springer, Heidelberg (2006)
15. Larrea, M., Lafuente, A., Wieland, J.: Communication-efficient implementation of $\Diamond P$ with reduced detection latency. Technical Report EHU-KAT-IK-02-06, The University of the Basque Country (February 2006), Available at http://www.sc.ehu.es/acwlaalm/
16. Pease, M., Shostak, R., Lamport, L.: Reaching agreement in the presence of faults. Journal of the ACM 27(2), 228–234 (1980)
17. Wu, W., Cao, J., Yang, J., Raynal, M.: A hierarchical consensus protocol for mobile ad hoc networks. In: Proceedings of the 14th Euromicro International Conference on Parallel, Distributed, and Network-Based Processing (PDP'2006), Montbeliard-Sochaux, France, pp. 64–72. IEEE Computer Society Press, Los Alamitos (2006)

Connectivity in Eventually Quiescent Dynamic Distributed Systems*

Sara Tucci Piergiovanni and Roberto Baldoni

Dipartimento di Informatica e Sistemistica
Università di Roma "La Sapienza"

Abstract. A distributed dynamic system is a fully distributed system subject to a continual arrival/departure of the entities defining the system. Another characterizing dimension of these systems is their, possibly, arbitrary large size (number of entities) and the possible arbitrary small part of the system a single entity directly interacts with. This interaction occurs through data exchange over logical links, and the constantly changing graph, formed by all links connecting entities, represents the *overlay* network of the dynamic distributed system. The *connectivity* of such overlay is of fundamental importance to make the whole system working. This paper gives a precise definition of the connectivity problem in dynamic distributed systems while formally defining assumptions on arrival/departure of entities and on the evolution of the system size along the time. The paper shows the impossibility of achieving connectivity when an arbitrary large number of entities may arrive/depart concurrently at any time, doing so for an arbitrarily long time. A solution is presented achieving overlay connectivity during *quiescent periods* of the system: periods in which no more arrivals and departures take place. The paper conveys the fact that the finite but not known duration of the perturbed period before quiescence makes the solution of the problem far from being trivial. The paper also provides a simulation study showing that the solution not only achieves connectivity in quiescent periods but it rearranges entities in an overlay that shows good scalability properties.

1 Introduction

Recently researchers have been paying more and more attention to so-called dynamic systems. Basically named in the peer-to-peer literature, dynamic systems do not have an agreed and precise definition yet, but it is possible to recognize some features characterizing them [4,6], listed below:

1. **Full decentralization.** A dynamic system is a fully decentralized system in which each entity plays the same role;
2. **Dynamicity.** Dynamicity concerns a possible continually changing membership of the very entities defining the system;

---

* This work has been done in the context of the European Network of Excellence ReSIST (Resilience for Survivability in IST).

A. Bondavalli, F. Brasileiro, and S. Rajsbaum (Eds.): LADC 2007, LNCS 4746, pp. 38–56, 2007.

3. **Locality.** Locality concerns how entities interact in the system. Generally speaking, the system may show a possible arbitrary size while each entity has a possible arbitrary small knowledge about the system it is member of. It is also said that this knowledge defines the entity's neighborhood, *i.e.*, the other entities an entity will directly interact and communicate with.

These characteristics may be abstracted in a unique unifying concept: the concept of a *dynamic graph* (also called *overlay network*) that includes as vertices all system entities and that depicts through its arcs the neighbors each entity knows of, along the time.

The concept of overlay is well-known in the peer-to-peer literature, but in this paper we want to attribute to this concept an abstract flavor by simply considering this overlay as the communication graph of the system. In static distributed systems this graph is defined at the very beginning and may change only by losing vertices (if entities fail) or arcs (if links shutdown). In a sense the communication network in static systems abstracts the physical network and the communication network topology is tightly coupled to the physical network topology. Contrarily, in dynamic systems the communication network is defined on top of – and generally independently of – the underlying physical computer network by a specific *overlay protocol* always running at each entity. This protocol is in charge to set and maintain the entity's neighborhood, and its output defines a new communication graph for each change it makes.

In this paper we want to formally tackle the problem of keeping the dynamic overlay connected over the time. It is obvious that the connectivity of the overlay is of fundamental importance as it enables communication among entities. If the overlay is connected any pair of entities is able to communicate through at least one path. On the other hand, losing connectivity leads to a partitioned overlay. In a partitioned overlay, entities group in components and communication between entities in different components stops. The logical nature of the network gives here the opportunity of designing an overlay protocol that could try to avoid logical partitions or detect and recover from them [1].

Unfortunately, there is no formal definition of the overlay connectivity problem, and the precise definition of an appropriate computing model where to study the problem is still an open research issue [4]. In particular, [4] proposes a computing model embedding the concept of dynamic communication graph. This graph varies along the time by adding and removing (possibly concurrently) an arbitrary large number of entities. In this computing model, however, the communication graph is assumed *always connected*, *i.e.*, the existence of an overlay protocol able to maintain the dynamic graph connected all the time is *assumed*. The study about the implementability of this assumption is exactly the scope of this paper.

This study led to the following contributions: (i) the adoption of a distributed computing model where the connectivity problem may be solved; (ii) a formal

---

[1] In the reminder of this paper the term partition will be always referred to logical partitions, physical partitions are not handled.

specification of the connectivity problem and (iii) a protocol which satisfies the specification under the model proposed.

More specifically, the system model assumes *an arbitrarily large* number of processes that along the time join and leave the system when considering the *access to the overlay of simultaneous joins is not serialized*. Specifically, we assume a finite arrival model [10] where the (finite) number of processes simultaneously joining/leaving the overlay is arbitrary and unknown. Assuming a finite arrival model has the following implications:

- Each system run can be divided in two intervals of time: a first *finite* interval in which joins and leaves take place (*perturbed period*) and then an infinite period of time in which no more join and leave occurs (*quiescent period*). The perturbed period lasts for an unknown time.
- The overlay has an unknown (but finite) size where process failures accumulate over time as processes join. Thus, the number of failures tend to an arbitrary large number as time passes and the proportion among the total number of processes and faulty ones, at any time, is arbitrary[2].

As any run of these systems can be characterized by a perturbed period followed by a quiescent period, we call these systems *eventually quiescent dynamic systems*.

Then, the paper presents the connectivity problem specified through a property called *eventual strong connectivity*, which expresses the ability for overlay entities to communicate from an arbitrary time onwards. Complementary properties are specified to guarantee overlay progress, *i.e.*, to avoid trivial solutions that systematically prevent joins to the overlay.

At this point, it may seem trivial solving eventual strong connectivity in an eventually quiescent dynamic system. However, this is far from being true for the following reasons:

- The paper shows that there exists no protocol which can assure connectivity during the perturbed period, *i.e.*, a partition may occur during this period. This comes from the effect of the admitted level of concurrency. In fact, many overlay protocols proposed in the literature are proved to maintain connectivity in face of a limited and a priori-known level of dynamicity[6], while in this paper we assume that an arbitrary number of joins and leaves may happen concurrently.
- No protocol can detect when quiescence begins.

From the first point it follows that any protocol can achieve connectivity only in quiescent periods. Moreover, from the second point, it follows that it has to do its best during the perturbed period to face partition occurrences. In particular, *any protocol must detect any partition and subsequently recover it.*

---

[2] It is worth to note that this computational model departs from classical static distributed system models in which: (i) the number of processes is fixed and a-priori known and (ii) solutions are designed to behave correctly under fixed and known threshold of failures.

In this paper we present a protocol able to eventually detect and restore connectivity each time a partition occurs and able to output an overlay in the quiescent period which is an undirected tree. The tree topology eases the task of detecting partitions. More specifically, each failure triggers a restoring and in order to reduce the number of restorings, voluntary leaves are managed in a different way than failures. In particular, voluntary leaves are handled in an active way, i.e., a piece of code is executed before the actual deletion of the vertex from the overlay [3].

Through an experimental analysis, we also investigate the nature of the trees the protocol is able to output during quiescence, dependently on the level of dynamicity experienced during the perturbed period. In particular we found that the higher the level of dynamicity was, the more unbalanced the resulting tree becomes, showing a few number of vertices with a huge number of children. Then we discuss and evaluate a mechanism to converge to a $k - ary$ balanced tree when the system becomes quiescent.

The paper is organized as follows. Section 2 presents our distributed computing model while Section 3 defines the connectivity problem and presents the impossibility of ensuring connectivity all the time. Section 4 presents a tree-based protocol solving the problem. In Section 5 the overlay maintained by the protocol is evaluated. Section 6 presents related work, and Section 7 concludes the paper. Due to lack of space the proof of the protocol correctness is not included but it can be found in [12].

2   System Model and Basic Definitions

We consider an infinite set of processes Π, uniquely identified. We denote processes by i, j, k. Processes communicate by exchanging messages through point-to-point *reliable channels*. We assume no bound on process relative speeds and message transmission delays. A process may be correct or faulty. A correct process never fails. A faulty process fails by crashing. To simplify the description without losing generality, we assume the existence of a fictional global clock, whose output is the set of positive integers denoted by $\mathcal{T}$.

Process State. Each process $i \in \Pi$ has a finite set $i.X$ of variables $x \in \Pi \cup \{nil\}$, where nil is a special process that does not belong to Π. There is no communication channel from/to nil. $i.x$ denotes a *neighbor* variable x of process i. By definition the nil process does not have any neighbor variable. The state of a process i is represented by $i.X$. Each neighbor variable $i.x$ initially assumes a nil value.

Overlay Definition. At any time, the global state constituted by the set of processes and their neighbor variables define the *overlay*. Formally,

Definition 1 (Overlay O(t)). *The overlay $O(t)$ is the set constituted by each pair $\langle i, i.X \rangle : \exists i.x \in i.X \neq nil$ at time t.*

---

[3] In [11] is shown that, without failures, connectivity can be assured all the time.

Any process $i : \langle i, i.X \rangle \in O(t)$ is called a *vertex* of the overlay $O(t)$.

Process Actions. Each process i is characterized by the following actions: $init_i$, $join_i$, $leave_i$, $stop_i$.

The $init_i$ action is an output action coming from the outside world (by an application). The effect of the $init_i$ action is the initialization of the neighbor variables.

The $join_i$ action is an internal action. The effect of the $join_i$ action is the assignment of a non-nil value to some neighbor variable of i, from a state in which all neighbor variables have a nil value, i.e., the $join_i$ action determines the addition of the process i to the overlay.

The $leave_i$ action is an internal action. The effect of the $leave_i$ action is the assignment of nil values to each neighbor variable of i, from a state in which at least one neighbor variable has a non-nil value, i.e. the $leave_i$ action determines the deletion of the process i from the overlay.

The $stop_i$ action is an input action that *models* a crash of the process (it is not actually executed). The effect of this action is the same for the $leave_i$ action, i.e., the $stop_i$ action determines the deletion of the process i from the overlay.

The need of using two different actions for leaves and failures ($stop_i$ and $leave_i$ respectively) gives the opportunity of treating these two events in a different manner, as done in the protocol of Section 4.

Eventually Quiescent Dynamicity. We assume a *finite arrival model* [2,7,9], i.e., the number of processes in the system is infinite but only finitely many might be added to the overlay for any system execution. The admitted level of simultaneous concurrency allows the number of processes concurrently added/deleted to/from the overlay at any time to be finite, arbitrary and unknown. This implies that at any time t the number of pairs $\langle i, i.X \rangle \in O(t)$ is finite but can grow until an unknown bound. Once a vertex i is deleted from the overlay (by $leave_i$ or $stop_i$), it is deleted forever. This assumption is not restrictive as a process can become a vertex with a different identifier an unbounded number of times (remember that Π, the set of processes, is infinite).

A vertex may be *stable* or *transient*. A stable vertex, once added to the overlay, belongs to the overlay forever. A transient process belongs to the overlay only a finite interval of time.

The contact() function. Any process, to be added to the overlay, must set one (or more) of its own neighbor variables to a non-nil value. The need for getting at least one vertex identifier arises as no a-priori knowledge is assumed. To join the overlay, a process invokes a *contact()* function. The *contact()* function returns a set of processes called *contacts*.

3   The Overlay Connectivity Problem

The goal of an overlay protocol is to dynamically manage the overlay in order to add and delete vertices while keeping the overlay connected. In the following, we precisely define the properties that such a protocol should ensure. Namely, we give (i) a property which captures a fundamental requirement on the state of the overlay and (ii) a set of properties that guarantee the progress of the overlay.

3.1   Eventual Strong Connectivity

The overlay $O(t)$ is said to be connected if for any pair of vertices there is at least a path of neighbor variables connecting them. At any time the overlay may be viewed as a directed graph (digraph) with an arc (i, j) iff $j \in i.X$. With some abuse of terminology we will refer to the overlay either as a global state or as the graph defined by its neighbor variables.

A *directed path* from i to j at time t is denoted by $i \rightarrow_t j$ and is defined as follows:

Definition 2 (Directed Path). *For any* $i, j : \langle i, i.X \rangle, \langle j, j.X \rangle \in O(t)$, *then* $i \rightarrow_t j$ *iff at time t one of the following conditions holds:*

$$\exists i.x \in i.X : i.x = j \text{ or } \exists k \in \Pi : (i \rightarrow_t k) \wedge (k \rightarrow_t j)$$

Two vertices are *weakly* connected if there exists a directed path in between; more precisely:

Definition 3 (Weak Connection between Two Vertices). *For any* i, j : $\langle i, i.X \rangle, \langle j, j.X \rangle \in O(t)$ *(i may be equal to j) are* weakly *connected, iff* $i \rightarrow_t j \vee j \rightarrow_t i$.

Two vertices are *strongly* connected if there exist two directed paths (one in each direction) in between; more precisely:

Definition 4 (Strong Connection between Two Vertices). *For any* i, j : $\langle i, i.X \rangle, \langle j, j.X \rangle \in O(t)$ *(i may be equal to j) are* strongly *connected, iff* $i \rightarrow_t j \wedge j \rightarrow_t i$.

The following property, called *Eventual Strong Connectivity (ES)*, guarantees that every pair of vertices in the overlay are strongly connected from an arbitrary point of time onwards. A protocol ensuring eventual strong connectivity is not necessarily able to maintain strong connectivity at any time, *e.g.*, some overlay disconnection is allowed. In this case the protocol should be able to restore the overlay. The meaning of having an eventual connectivity instead of a connectivity at any time comes from the impossibility of maintaining connectivity at any time in the model assumed (see Section 3.3).

Property 1 (Eventual Strong Connectivity (ES)). $\exists t : \forall t' \geq t$,

$$\forall i, j : \langle i, i.X \rangle, \langle j, j.X \rangle \in O(t') \Rightarrow (i \rightarrow_{t'} j) \wedge (j \rightarrow_{t'} i)$$

3.2 Overlay Progress

The *ES* property characterizes the connectivity of an overlay that may change arbitrarily often due to finite arrival model assumed. However, a trivial (and bogus) connectivity maintenance protocol may systematically avoid the addition of any element in the overlay.

Thus, to prevent trivial implementations, properties on the progress of the overlay are needed. We define two different progress properties: *Global Progress* and *No-Lockout*.

Property 2 (Global Progress). If there exists a correct $i \in \Pi$ that executes the $join_i$ action at time t, then $\exists t', j : t' > t \wedge \langle j, j.X \rangle \in O(t') \wedge \langle j, j.X \rangle \notin O(t)$.

This property does not guarantee that the access to the overlay is granted to all processes executing the connectivity protocol, *i.e.*, it allows a process j to be repeatedly granted the access to the overlay, while another process i trying to obtain the access is forever prevented from doing so. The following stronger progress property precludes this scenario.

Property 3 (No-Lockout). For each correct process $i \in \Pi$ that executes the $join_i$ action, $\exists t : \langle i, i.X \rangle \in O(t)$.

3.3 Impossibility of Avoiding Overlay Partitions

Each graph has its level of connectivity that defines the resilience the graph has to vertex removal. More formally, the connectivity level of a graph is the minimum number of vertices that must be removed, to disconnect it. A graph is said to be k-connected if it disconnects by removing at least k vertices.

Let us remark at this point that the only way to tolerate any number of concurrent failures is to maintain a clique along the time, while maintaining a topology with some a priori-defined level of connectivity t means tolerating an arbitrarily small number of simultaneous failures with respect an arbitrary system size N, since it could be $t << N$ at some point of time.

Thus, the aim of this section is proving that even starting from an overlay with a clique topology, the way in which vertices can arrive and depart may lead the overlay to show a monotonically decreasing level of connectivity, until disconnection. Let us consider ideally that there is a clique of k vertices, in a system, thus, starting with k vertices. The decrease of the overlay connectivity is due to the following facts:

- Impossibility of maintaining a clique (see below) along the time when considering non-serialized access of an arbitrarily large number of concurrent joins. The number of vertices of the overlay in this case may increase to some $N > k$ while the level of connectivity remains k (this happens, for instance, when each new vertex connects with k arcs to the k vertices of the original clique).

– Now, the departure of one of the k vertices which belonged to the original clique makes the connectivity of the overlay decreasing to some $h < k$.

Note that this pattern may provoke a disconnection if all k vertices in the original clique simultaneously depart.

The Impossibility of a Clique. We give a formal proof of the impossibility of maintaining a clique at any time. The proof is based on the following abstract solution of the problem. Let us consider two atomic operations, namely *contact()* and *update()*. *contact()* is a a very powerful contact function that allows processes to get the complete snapshot of the overlay at the time they invoke the function. *contact()* returns in *contacts* the finite number of vertices in the overlay. Then, on the basis of the information got from the contact function, the process enters the overlay invoking an *update()* function. Once the update function returns the process has been added in the overlay [4]. The update consists in adding i as new neighbor of each vertex in *contacts* and adding each vertex in *contacts* as neighbor of i.

Let us note that at the heart of the impossibility lies the non-atomic execution of *contact()* and the subsequent *update()*. In fact, this modelling let us consider a non-serialized access to the overlay and the effect of an arbitrary number of concurrent leaves/failures. Formally:

Let us denote as $|O(t)|$ the number of vertices of the overlay O at time t.

Theorem 1. *If there exists a time t: $\forall\langle i, i.X\rangle \in O(t)$, $i.X$ variables define a clique, then there exists a time $t' > t$ in which the graph defined by each $\langle i, i.X\rangle \in O(t')$ it is not a clique and has connectivity $k < (|O(t')| - 1)$.*

Proof. Let us suppose by contradiction that for all $t' > t$, the graph defined by $\langle i, i.X\rangle \in O(t')$ is a (undirected) clique. This implies that for each $t' > t$, $\forall\langle i, i.X\rangle, \langle j, j.X\rangle \in O(t')$, $\Rightarrow j \in i.X \land i \in j.X$.

Let us consider any run R in which only two processes $i, j \in \Pi$ are added to the overlay after time t. In particular, they invokes the *contact()* function at the point of time, respectively, $t_i^r, t_j^r > t$ and the *update()* function at the point of time, respectively, $t_i^w, t_j^w > max(t_i^r, t_j^r)$. The *contact()* function returns all processes in $O(t)$ (not comprising i and j). Then at time $t' = max(t_i^w, t_j^w)$ the overlay $O(t')$ contains $\langle i, i.X\rangle$ and $\langle j, j.X\rangle$ but $i \notin j.X$ and $j \notin i.X$ with a connectivity $k = |O(t)| - 1 = |O(t')| - 3$ contradicting the initial hypothesis.

4   The Protocol

This section presents the protocol. Section 4.1 contains a detailed description of the protocol, while Section 4.2 presents the assumptions underlying the correctness of the protocol. In particular, assumptions about the *contact()* function and the type of used failure detection are discussed, giving an intuition of their necessity.

---

[4] To avoid to solve our problem with the contact function, we also suppose that the invocation of the contact function is only intended to solve the bootstrap, *i.e.*, it can be invoked at most once and before the invocation of the *update()* function.

4.1   Protocol Description

Our protocol arranges the vertices of the overlay in a routed tree topology. A process i that wishes to join the overlay establishes a connection with an arbitrary node of the tree j, becoming a child of j. Note that any number of nodes (less than the number of current nodes in the overlay) may simultaneously be added to the overlay.

The tree may disconnect because of any leave or failure, however, leaves and failure are managed in a different manner. In particular, leaves are handled in an active way: before leaving any node repairs the tree without causing a partition. More specifically, a node i that wishes to leave the overlay ensures, before leaving, that its sub-tree (rooted by i) is being connected to i's parent. Adjacent and concurrent leaves on the same branch are properly managed establishing a departure order.

Any non-leaf failure, on the other hand, causes a partition. The recovery from the partition is enabled by a dynamic restoring mechanism. This mechanism provides that any i's failure in the tree triggers a re-connection of the sub-tree routed by i to another live node in the tree. In this case, the re-connection must be carefully handled to avoid scenarios in which i reconnects to a node belonging to its sub-tree. To this end, upon joining, nodes set a particular variable called *rank* and re-connection is driven by the node ranking defined at the join time. This mechanism allows to properly select a new parent not belonging to the disconnected sub-tree.

Process state. In the following the overlay will be denoted as $T(t)$. Each element of $T(t)$ is composed of a pair $\langle i, (i.parent, i.children) \rangle$ where $i.parent$ and each $x \in i.children$ are neighbor variables. With respect to the process state described in Section 2, the state is enriched by the variable s and the variable $rank$; the variable s can contain values $\{in, out, joining, leaving, restoring\}$, while $rank$ is a natural number.

Process actions. Each process i performs a *Tree()* task to maintain the overlay. We detail the effects of actions $init_i$, $join_i$, $leave_i$ described in Section 2. The $init_i$ action: (i) it initializes the neighbor variables to nil values [5]; (ii) it initializes the s variable to *out* and (iii) invokes the *Tree()*. The $join_i$ action sets the s variable to *joining*. The $leave_i$ action sets the s variable to *leaving*.

$T(t)$ *initialization.* The overlay is initialized by an initiator r, *i.e.*, $T(t_0) = \langle r, (r.parent = r, \forall x \in r.children, x := nil) \rangle \wedge r.state = in$. It means that r is a special process with an $init_r$ action occurring at time t_0, which is slightly different from the *init* of all other processes. Upon the $init_r$ action, r (i) sets $s := in$, (ii) $r.parent := r$ and $\forall x \in r.children, x := nil$, and (iii) $r.rank = 0$. Then, r invokes task $Tree()$.

---

[5] The set of neighbor variables is unbounded, *i.e.*, the number of neighbor variables is a-priori-unknown, thus this static initialization models a dynamic initialization of neighbors variables.

The Tree() task. The $Tree()$ task handles the addition/deletion [6] of the pair $\langle i, (i.parent, i.children) \rangle$ to/from $T(t)$, *i.e.*, it sets and updates neighbor variables.

As soon as a process i wishes to join the overlay, it sets its variable s to *joining*. Any vertex in the tree wishing to leave the overlay sets variable s to *leaving*. Any vertex in the tree wishing to restore after disconnection has its s variable equal to *restoring*. $Tree()$ handles the s state transitions: [*joining/in*], [*leaving/out*] and [*restoring/in*]. The completion of the transition [*joining/in*] at time t denotes the addition of the pair $\langle i, (i.parent, i.children) \rangle$ to $T(t)$. The completion of the transition [*leaving/out*] at time t', denotes the deletion of the pair $\langle i, (i.parent, i.children) \rangle$ from $T(t)$. With this mechanism, all *in* processes are vertices of the tree, while all *out* processes are not vertices of the tree, *i.e.*, each *out* process i has $i.parent = nil \wedge \forall x \in i.children, x = nil$.

A faulty vertex disconnects all its sub-tree (if any). To cope with faults $Tree()$ has access to a failure detector module FD_i reporting a list of faulty processes. In this case all children enter a restoring state when their FD module reports their parent. $Tree()$ recovers the overlay reconnecting restoring nodes to a new live parent.

In Figure 3 the $Tree()$ pseudo-code is shown. In the following we detail the mechanism to join, leave, and restore.

The join mechanism. When the variable $i.s$ assumes the *joining* value (line 4), i obtains a vertex a of the tree through the $contact()$ function. Then i sends a "JOIN" message to a (line 5). Upon receiving the "JOIN" message, a adds i to its *children* if its $a.s = in$ (the role of the *rank* variable is detailed for the restore mechanism), by setting $a.children$ to i and sending an "ACK_JOIN" message back to i (lines 16,19). Upon receiving the "ACK_JOIN" message, i sets $i.parent$ to a (line 8) and sets the variable $i.s = in$ (lines 31-32). At this point the [*joining/in*] transition completes. With this mechanism, if the joining process establishes its connection at time t with a vertex j, *i.e.*, $i \rightarrow_t j$, then there exists a time $t' < t$ in which $j \rightarrow_{t'} i$ (see Fig.1). This mechanism allows to couple i to a possible transient *parent*. As we see in the following, this parent before leaving will give a notice to all its children, i comprised. At line 9, the process i sets also its own variable $i.rank$ to the rank of its parent plus one (not shown in Fig.1).

Due to concurrency, asynchrony, and failures the a vertex given by the $contact()$ function could be out or failed before receiving the "JOIN" message from i [7]. In this case we assume that FD_i will report a in its list, at this point i restarts by getting another contact a.

The leave mechanism. When the variable $i.s$ assumes the *leaving* value, the protocol allows to update the i's neighbors before deleting i from the overlay. In practice, it ensures that the parent of i becomes the parent of each child of i. In case of two (or more) concurrent leaving processes i, j which are adjacent

---

[6] Deletions of only voluntary leaves.

[7] We assume that a process which has left the overlay (an *out* process) is not obligated to respond to messages associated with the maintenance of the overlay connectivity.

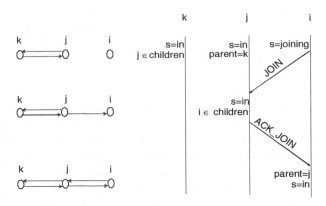

Fig. 1. Change of topology and message pattern for joining

on a same path, the deletion of the pairs $\langle i, i.X \rangle$ and $\langle j, j.X \rangle$ during the concurrent diffusion of the corresponding updates may lead to a partition. To avoid partition, the two updates are serialized: before deleting j, the i's update takes effect (or vice versa). After that, j updates its neighbor variables and sends a new update to new neighbors. In the presented protocol the deletion order is given by the distance from the root. The process closest to the root leaves first.

In particular, the pseudo-code includes a sequence of asynchronous basic steps, where a basic step is the sending and the receiving of a "LEAVE" and its "ACK_LEAVE" message, respectively (lines 12-15). The [*leaving/out*] transition completes when a basic step succeeds (line 15), $s = out$. More in details, during each step, a "LEAVE" message containing the children of i is sent to update the neighbor variables of the current i's parent (line 12).

In the simple case where the i's parent k is *in* when the "LEAVE"(*i.children*) message is received (line 21), k updates its children variable, it sends a "NEW_PARENT"(k) message to all new children and it sends an "ACK_LEAVE" message to i (line 23). In Fig. 2 the message pattern and the consequent changing of connectivity relations is described.

After line 23 (executed at time t), we have: (i)$\forall j \in i.children, j \in k.children$, then $k \to_t j$ and (ii) $k \not\to_t i$ by eliminating i from $k.children$. When at time t' the "ACK_LEAVE" is received by i (line 13), i sets its neighbor variables to nil, then only the relation $k \to_{t'} j$ holds. When at time t'' "NEW_PARENT"(k) is received by each j (lines 24-25), then the following relations hold: $k \to_{t''} j \wedge j \to_{t''} k$.

In a more difficult case, the i's parent k is *leaving* when the "LEAVE" message is received. In that case an order on the departures of i and its parent k is needed, to break the tie. The rule is the following: if i and its parent k have concurrent leaves, k leaves the system before j. In this case, while a step is running for i, a basic step succeeds for k. Then a new (strong) connectivity relation involves i and the k's parent j, i.e., $i \to_{t''} j \wedge j \to_{t''} i$. A this point i will have to start a new step since the variable *parent_change* has been set to true (line 19).

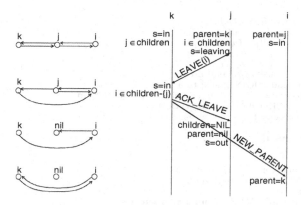

Fig. 2. Change of topology and message pattern for leaving

In the worst case scenario all ancestors of i are leaving processes. In this case the tree root is also involved in a leave, and thus a new root has to be found. Mechanisms to elect a new root are out of the scope of the paper. Thus, we consider only the case where *the root is a stable process* (see 4.2 for a discussion about protocol assumptions) avoiding to consider election mechanisms. In this case the number of steps, before i ends successfully a basic step (at line 13), is bounded by its depth in the tree.

The dynamic restoring mechanism. Initially, the transition [*joining/in*] brings the process i to select one *parent*, namely j, which includes i as one of its children. When i belongs to the overlay (line 8), thanks to lines 27-28, the previous selected *parent* j is monitored. If the failure detector reports the *parent* j as faulty, then the variable degree turns to 0 and the process i switches in a *restoring* state (lines 29-30). Subsequently, i is in charge of restoring the overlay by connecting its sub-tree to a new live parent. To avoid cycles, each process uses the variable *rank* that gives an indication of the position of the vertex in the overlay. The value of *rank*, defined during the [*joining/in*] transition, is never modified. The root r has $r.rank = 0$. If a process i joins through a process j, $i.rank$ is set to $j.rank+1$. When a process i turns into a restoring state, it avoids to select as parent any parent k with $k.rank \geq i.rank$.

We depict in Fig. 4 a possible overlay evolution and the use of ranks. After a growing phase in which only joins occur (Fig.4(a)), a leaving phase in which only leaves occur is depicted (Fig. 4(b)). Then a failure and the corresponding restoring is described in Fig. 4(c) and Fig. 4(d).

4.2   Protocol Assumptions and Correctness

Due to lack of space, formal proofs of the protocol correctness are included in [12] where we prove that the protocol is able to maintain strong connectivity in quiescent periods of the overlay. When the overlay is affected by failures the

```
Tree()_i
1   var : parent_change := ⊤  Boolean;
2         degree := null    {0, 1, null};
3         rank := ∞         {null} ∪ Integer;


4   when (s = joining ∨ s = restoring) do
5     a := contact(); send ["JOIN", rank] to a;
6     wait until (degree = 1 ∨ a ∈ FD_i ∨ receive ["RETRY"] from a)
7   when (receive ["ACK_JOIN", r] from a) do
8     parent := a; degree := 1;
9     if (rank = ∞)
10      then rank = r + 1;


11  when ((s = leaving) and (parent_change)) do
12    send ["LEAVE"(children)] to parent;
13    parent_change := ⊥;
14  when (receive ["ACK_LEAVE"] from a = parent) do
15    parent := nil; ∀k ∈ children := nil; s := out;


16  when ((receive ["JOIN,r"] from j)) do
17    if ((s = in) ∧ (rank < r))
18      then children := children ∪ {j};
19           send ["ACK_JOIN",rank] to j
20      else send ["RETRY"] to j
21  when ((receive ["LEAVE"(j.children)] from j ∈ children) ∧ (s = in)) do
22    children := children ∪ j.children − {j};
23    send ["NEW_PARENT"(i)] to each j.children; send ["ACK_LEAVE"] to j;
24  when (receive ["NEW_PARENT"(j)] from a) do
25    parent := j;
26    parent_change := ⊤; degree := degree + 1;
27  while parent ≠ nil do
28    degree := |parent| − |parent ∩ FD_i|;
29  when (degree = 0) do
30    s := restoring;
31  when (degree = 1) do
32    s := in;
```

Fig. 3. The Tree-based Protocol at i

protocol does not avoid partitioning but is able to eventually restore the overlay. We discuss here the assumptions underlying the correctness of our protocol, giving an intuition of their necessity.

By the protocol, anytime i switches in a restoring state, if i never completes lines $4 − 8$, then ES will be violated. This is precisely why we assume the following:

Assumption 1. *contact() eventually returns a stable vertex with $s = in$ and $rank = 0$.*

This assumption implies that the overlay has to be initialized by a stable root in absence of an election protocol. In fact, if a root with rank 0 fails, its children go to a restoring phase. As already said, in order to complete the restoring phase, they have to connect to a process with rank 0 and *already part of the overlay* (s=in). By the protocol this process could be only the root. This implies that the root cannot be transient. Practically, Assumption 1, states the *contact()*

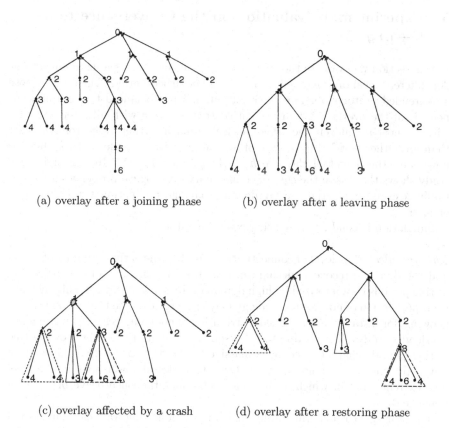

(a) overlay after a joining phase   (b) overlay after a leaving phase

(c) overlay affected by a crash   (d) overlay after a restoring phase

Fig. 4. An example of overlay evolution

function should eventually return, to a restoring process i, a process which does not belong to the sub-tree of i and which remains in the overlay enough time to be selected and used as entry point.

The protocol uses a perfect failure detection mechanism[5] satisfying the following properties:

Assumption 2 (completeness). *There exists a time t after which a faulty vertex is permanently suspected by every correct process.*

Assumption 3 (accuracy). *No process is suspected before it crashes.*

It is worth to note that completeness is necessary as it ensures that a broken overlay will be eventually restored by first detecting failures. On the other hand accuracy is not necessary but simplifies the problem. The effects of a non perfect failure detection are extensively studied in [11].

5   Experimental Evaluation on the Convergence to a $k - ary$ Tree

In this section we evaluate the tree topologies our protocol is able to output under different level of dynamicity during the perturbed period. Then we propose an extended protocol version which outputs a k-ary balanced tree in quiescent periods of the overlay. A k-ary balanced tree is a tree with all internal nodes with at most k children and where no leaf is much farther away from the root than any other leaf [8]. In the case of an overlay with N nodes with k children per-nodes, the height of the tree $h = \lceil \log_k N(k - 1) + 1 \rceil$. Interestingly, this study shows that, as in the case of connectivity, topological properties are eventually restored when the overlay does not change population for a time long enough.

Simulation is conducted by using Ns-2 simulator [1].

The star effect. The level of connectivity assured by the active handling of leaves and the dynamic recovery mechanism is at the cost of a loss of tree balancing during periods characterized by high dynamics. In particular, with a highly transient population of nodes, the topology may converge to some tree configurations showing, for instance, a very tailed distribution of node-degrees resulting in a few overloaded nodes. This is due to a brusque reduction of the height of the tree during periods characterized by a massively departure of internal nodes since any departing node hangs up its children to nodes at lower level in the tree. The extreme case in which all internal nodes simultaneously leave brings to a star-like overlay.

The star effect is experimentally shown in the following way: each simulation starts with a topology in an ideal state. In particular, at initial time t_0^{sim}, $T(t_0^{sim})$ is a k-ary balanced tree with $k = 7$ and 1000 nodes. The simulation time is divided in time intervals called *rounds*. We fixed the round duration to $20sec$. Let μ be the churn rate, at each round of the protocol, μ nodes join and μ nodes leave. Then, at the end of each round the number of vertices is still 1000. The state of the overlay is checked every second. We report what is the velocity (in term of seconds) of reaching a star-like topology varying the churn rate [9]. To point out the relation between the churn rate and the time taken to reach a star-like topology, the y-axis reports round numbers instead of seconds. In this simulation we have considered that the overlay reaches a star topology when at least one node has a number of children greater than 100[10]. The plot in Fig. 5(a) shows that an increasing churn rate reduces the time the overlay converges to a star-like topology. Note that we chose very high churn rates to show the extreme behavior of the protocol.

---

[8] There may exist a difference between two leaves of at most 1 level.

[9] Each point in the plots has been computed as an average of 40 simulation distinct runs. For each point all the results of these runs were within 4% each other, thus variance is not reported in the plots.

[10] One order of magnitude greater than $\log_7 1000$.

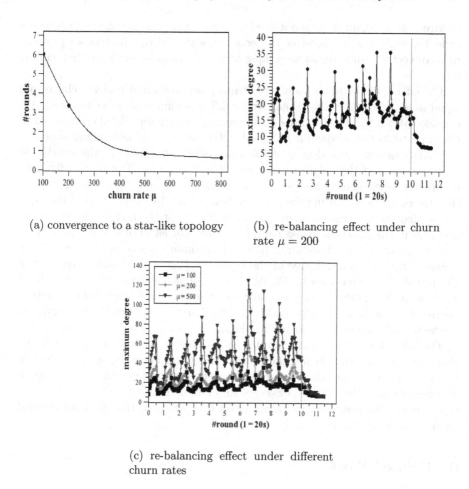

(a) convergence to a star-like topology

(b) re-balancing effect under churn rate $\mu = 200$

(c) re-balancing effect under different churn rates

Fig. 5. Protocol effects on topology without and with the re-balancing mechanism

The re-balancing mechanism. To contend with the star effect, we propose a simple mechanism to re-balance the tree and we evaluate its effectiveness under dynamics.

Assuming that the topology in the ideal state is a k-ary balanced tree, the mechanism is the following: any node i periodically selects a number of exceeding children equal to $|i.children| - k$. These children may be chosen at random or by following more sophisticated rules, *e.g.*, choosing the youngest children). We consider a random choice. The node i sends a message to these exceeding children, inviting them to find another parent between their (not exceeding) siblings. Then each exceeding child j that is a *leaf* immediately tries to connect to one of its siblings k. If the connection successes, (i) j results connected to k with a rank $j.rank = k.rank+1$ (ii) i deletes j from its children. In a pure star overlay this mechanism is very effective, because all the children of the overloaded node are leaves. Unfortunately, if an overloaded node has any children with just one children the mechanism does not work anymore. For this reason, each exceeding child i dismisses all its sub-tree to become a leaf, and the mechanism provides to reconnect the sub-tree as an unique flat level around a not exceeding sibling of i.

The effects of the re-balancing mechanism are evaluated under a churn rate equal to $\mu = 200$ (see fig. 5(b)) and under different churn rates (see fig. 5(c)). We consider also a fixed percentage of failures equal to 1 for all experiments. The churn perturbs the overlay for 10 rounds (200 seconds) and after churn subsides. We have evaluated the degree of the most overloaded node in the overlay at every second and the height of tree after the it subsides. The plot in fig. 5(b) points out a periodic counter-effect due to the re-balancing mechanism striving the star convergence during the perturbation period. In the first round the most overloaded node reaches a degree equal to 25 but at the end of the round the re-balancing mechanism shrinks the degree to 8. The effect of a continuous churn leads to increase the minimum degree and maximum degree per round, *e.g.*, in round 8, the maximum degree of the most overloaded is 36 and at the end of the round the degree goes to 15. At the end of perturbation the re-balancing mechanism brings the overlay to converge again to a well-balanced tree with a degree of the most overloaded node equal to 7 and a height of the tree equal to 8 (the height does not appear in the plots).

The impact of different churn rates in Fig. 5(c) reveals that the higher the churn rate is, the faster the degradation towards a star becomes, and less effective is the re-balancing mechanism during the perturbation interval. In any case in absence of churn the overlay converges to a balanced tree (the height is always equal to 8). The time for converging again to a balanced tree does not depend on the churn suffered previously.

6 Related Work

To the best of our knowledge, [8] is the only work which presents a precise definition of the connectivity problem for ring-shaped overlays in a finite arrival model. More specifically, an invariant for a ring overlay protocol was defined stipulating that the ring topology is eventually restored after overlay changes subside. A protocol that satisfies the invariant in the *absence of failures* was then presented. A ring-based redundant structure was also proposed, however, the model they assume considers a *known number of failures*, which can be arbitrary small with respect the number of entities part of the system. Our problem specification is more general in the sense that we consider any topology. In addition, our protocol tolerates any number of failures.

The more general problem of defining a computing model for dynamic systems is an active research area, *e.g.*, [3,10,4]. In [10] system dynamicity is modelled through a finite arrival model with an arbitrary large number of failures. However, there is no concept of dynamic communication graph: the communication graph is "hidden" by two communication primitives, namely a query-response and a broadcast. The behaviour of these two primitives implies the assumption of connectivity among process entities.

In [4] the communication graph is part of the very definition of a dynamic system. Moreover, differently from what assumed in our paper, [4] adopts an infinite arrival model to abstract the continual arrival and departure of nodes to/from the graph. This implies that no quiescence is assumed since arrivals and departures never subside. As regards the dynamic communication graph, in [4] different levels of graph dynamicity are proposed, by ruling the way the graph diameter and the number of vertices may vary along the time. Nevertheless, the graph is here assumed connected at any time, then it can vary growing and shrinking arbitrarily, but it never disconnects by assumption.

7   Concluding Remarks

The paper has provided a formal definition of the connectivity problem in eventually quiescent dynamic systems. In particular it has been presented the property of eventual strong connectivity which states that from an arbitrary point of time any pair of nodes must be able to communicate–the overlay is strongly connected. We believe that this form of connectivity has the double advantage to be (i) loose enough to encompass a wide range of protocols and (ii) strong enough to be useful in practice.

The paper has presented a protocol that maintains a tree as overlay topology. This is actually the first provably correct protocol guaranteeing eventual connectivity of the communication graph in a model including an arbitrary large number of simultaneous arrival and departures.

Finally, the paper presented a simple extension of the protocol with the aim of converging to a k-ary tree during system quiescence. A simulation study confirmed this result.

References

1. Ns-2 simulator: http://www.isi.edu/nsnam/ns
2. Aguilera, M.K.: A Pleasant Stroll through the Land of Infinitely Many Processes. ACM SIGACT News, Distributed Computing Column 35(2), 36–59 (2004)
3. Anceaume, E., Defago, X., Gradinaru, M., Roy, M.: Towards a Theory of Self-organization. In: Anderson, J.H., Prencipe, G., Wattenhofer, R. (eds.) OPODIS 2005. LNCS, vol. 3974. Springer, Heidelberg (2006)
4. Baldoni, R., Bertier, M., Raynal, M., Piergiovanni, S.T.: Towards a Definition of Dynamic Distributed Systems. In: Malyshkin, V. (ed.) PaCT 2007. LNCS, vol. 4671, Springer, Heidelberg (2007)
5. Chandra, T., Toueg, S.: Unreliable Failure Detectors for Reliable Distributed Systems. Journal of the ACM 43(2), 225–267 (1996)
6. Karger, D., Liben-Nowell, D., Balakrishnan, H.: Analysis of the Evolution of Peer-to-Peer Systems. In: Proceedings of the 21st ACM Annual Symposium on Principles of Distributed Computing (PODC02), pp. 233–242 (2002)

7. Gafni, E., Merritt, M., Taubenfeld, G.: The Concurrency Hierarchy, and Algorithms for Unbounded Concurrency. In: Proceedings of the 20th annual ACM symposium on Principles of Distributed Computing (PODC01), pp. 161–169 (2001)
8. Li, X., Misra, J., Plaxton, G.: Active and Concurrent Topology Maintenance. In: Guerraoui, R. (ed.) DISC 2004. LNCS, vol. 3274, pp. 320–334. Springer, Heidelberg (2004)
9. Merritt, M., Taubenfeld, G.: Computing with Infinitely Many Processes. In: Proceedings of the 14th International Conference on Distributed Computing, pp. 164–178 (2000)
10. Mostefaoui, A., Raynal, M., Travers, C., Patterson, S., Agrawal, D., El Abbadi, A.: From Static Distributed Systems to Dynamic Systems. In: Proceedings of the 24th IEEE Symposium on Reliable Distributed Systems (SRDS05). IEEE Computer Society Press, Los Alamitos (2005)
11. Tucci-Piergiovanni, S.: Concurrent Connectivity Maintenance with Infinitely Many Processes. Ph.D. Thesis, http://www.dis.uniroma1.it/~midlab/publications
12. Tucci-Piergiovanni, S., Baldoni, R.: Connectivity in Eventually Quiescent Dynamic Systems, Technical Report,
http://www.dis.uniroma1.it/~midlab/publications

Implementing Fault Tolerance Using Aspect Oriented Programming

Ruben Alexandersson and Peter Öhman

Dept. of Computer Science & Engineering, Chalmers University of Technology,
SE-41296, Gothenburg, Sweden
{ruben,peter.ohman}@chalmers.se

Abstract. Aspect oriented programming (AOP) is a promising technique for implementing fault tolerance. Still there exist few actual implementations. One reason is that most present day AOP languages do not offer the level of control needed. This paper addresses the problem by defining a representative set of fault tolerance mechanisms. The set can be used for evaluating the feasibility of languages and for finding needs for improvements. It has been used to evaluate the AspectC++ language, and a number of limitations have been revealed. AspectC++ was then extended in order to address this. It is also demonstrated how reusable fault tolerance mechanisms can be built using aspect oriented C++, and the advantages compared to using standard C++ are discussed.

Keywords: Aspect Oriented Programming, Fault Tolerance.

1 Introduction

Software implemented fault tolerance is a well known technique for dealing with failures caused by both hardware and software faults. Compared to hardware implemented fault tolerance it has the advantage of being more flexible and cost efficient. Today a number of techniques are available when implementing fault tolerance (e.g. libraries, program transformation or meta programming). A new approach to software implementation is aspect oriented programming (AOP) [1]. It has seen a rapid development in the past few years and is presently reaching a state at which it can be considered a useful and functioning technique. AOP allows the programmer to implement fault tolerance functionality separately from the functional code and to combine these implementations to form the final system. As discussed below, and demonstrated by the implementations presented in this paper, this gives a number of benefits when implementing fault tolerant software.

Still, very few actual implementations that use AOP to achieve fault tolerance exist. One reason is, as demonstrated in this paper, that present day AOP languages do not provide the level of control needed for fault tolerance frameworks. Although a great deal of effort is currently being made in the development of different general purpose AOP languages, the needs of fault tolerance implementations have not been addressed in these languages. Hence there is a need for stating the language level requirements given by fault tolerance implementations. To elicit these requirements a

A. Bondavalli, F. Brasileiro, and S. Rajsbaum (Eds.): LADC 2007, LNCS 4746, pp. 57–74, 2007.

representative set of fault tolerance mechanisms has been defined. The mechanisms have then been used to evaluate the AspectC++ language [2]. This revealed the limitations of the language and the necessary requirements for improvements. To certify that the requirements were sufficient and could be met, AspectC++ was extended and again evaluated against the set of mechanisms.

2 Aspect Oriented Programming

Any normal industrial size software system is a combined implementation of multiple functionalities such as diagnostics, fault tolerance, data persistence, logging, authentication, security, multithread safety and so on. These are known as concerns.

The system design and modularization are chiefly conducted to reflect the primary function of the application. The effect of this is that all other concerns can not be modularized in a good way and their implementation is then scattered throughout the program modules. These secondary concerns are therefore called crosscutting concerns since they crosscut all (or many) of the program modules. As an example, control flow checking (see section 3.5) affects every function of every module of the application program and is therefore scattered throughout the implementation. Although the mechanism can syntactically be defined with just a few lines of code, object oriented techniques require that a very large amount of code be added throughout the entire software. Code scattering is one effect of this lack of modularization. Code tangling is another effect, meaning that each module includes code related to many concerns. Hence the code related to different concerns becomes tangled within a module or function. A number of problems with the software and its development arise as a result of code tangling and scattering. One is the problem of less code reuse. Code tangling makes it difficult to reuse the primary function of the module in another set-up since the code is tangled with secondary functionalities. Reusing secondary functionalities, such as fault tolerance, is even harder since the code is both scattered around the application and tangled together with other concerns. AOP is an approach that can be used to overcome this and other problems by separating the implementation of a concern from the rest of the program. AOP allows the programmer to implement any (or all) concerns in a loosely coupled fashion and to combine these implementations with the rest of the program to form the final system.

The use of AOP is supported by AOP languages. An AOP language compiler is normally implemented as a source-to-source compiler that weaves the different concern specific sources together. One view of an AOP language is therefore that it is a highly programmable source-to-source compiler. This is why the technique is so well suited for implementing systematic fault tolerance mechanisms that can be introduced automatically. However, in contrast to a pure code transformation tool, AOP allows the utilization of application knowledge to cover only the parts of the implementation that are critical and can thereby reduce the overhead. Another view of an AOP language is that it is a well integrated extension to a programming language that lets the programmer produce implementation specific code. Hence both systematic and implementation specific mechanisms can be implemented in a uniform way, allowing them to smoothly cooperate in a single fault tolerance framework. This gives the developer the freedom to choose the most efficient mechanism to achieve fault tolerance for each part of the implementation. However, this is only possible if most or at least a wide range of fault tolerance mechanisms can be implemented efficiently using the chosen AOP language. This is unfortunately not the case in most present day AOP languages.

3 Defining the Representative Set

When developing fault tolerance frameworks, or researching new mechanisms for fault tolerance, target programs are used to measure and assess the effectiveness of the mechanisms or frameworks. To be able to compare the results for different mechanisms and frameworks originating from different studies, the same target programs and fault loads should be used. Further, in order to be able to draw general conclusions, a set of diverse and representative programs and fault loads is needed. When developing implementation techniques, there is a similar need for a set of fault tolerance mechanisms that can be used for evaluating the feasibility of different techniques for implementing fault tolerance. No such set exists today that can be used to evaluate the feasibility of different AOP languages or of AOP in general.

To be able to conduct this study, a small set of fault tolerance mechanisms was thus defined. If all mechanisms included can be implemented in a satisfactory way using a certain language, that language can be considered generally feasible for fault tolerance purposes. The mechanisms are intentionally chosen so that they place as high and diverse demands as possible. Hence one can not draw the conclusion that a language is unfeasible in all situations because it fails on a single or a couple of mechanisms; rather, this points out the limitations of the language and sets the boundaries for its applicability. This information can serve as an input to language designers about the needs of fault tolerance implementations and be useful when considering different implementation techniques or languages for a specific fault tolerance implementation. It should be noted that the mechanisms were chosen for the purpose of evaluating implementation techniques and languages from a programming or software engineering point of view. This gives a set that is probably different from one that would be chosen for a representative performance benchmark. Hence this set should not be used for performance evaluations without proper adaptation.

Software implemented fault tolerance is built on run time checks that can detect errors originating from activated faults. This is done by monitoring different aspects of the program. The first criterion for language feasibility is therefore that monitoring all parts of both the functional and data domain of the program must be supported. Hence this should be covered by the set.

Both detection and recovery mechanisms make use of redundancy as the underlying concept. Detection mechanisms compare the program state with redundant information in order to detect differences, and recovery mechanisms use redundancy to create a correct or acceptable program state. Redundancy can either be in the form of replication or diversity. As with checks, it can be applied to either the functional or the data domain of the program yielding (on the implementation level) four different forms of redundancy: function duplication, function diversity, data duplication and data diversity. Since these different forms of redundancy have different requirements on the implementation language, the set must cover all of them.

As high and diverse demands on the implementation language as possible were the main criteria for selecting the set of representative mechanisms, the end result was a set of mechanisms that includes both error detection and error recovery mechanisms. They range from systematic to implementation specific and include mechanisms designed for both hardware and software fault tolerance. Although this set was defined with the purpose of assessing the feasibility of AOP languages, it is still applicable for assessing other languages or techniques as well. This is true since the mechanisms were not chosen directly on the basis of language features used but on underlying properties such as accessibility of data and functional code. The chosen set is presented in Table 1 and explained in detail in the sections below.

Table 1. Set of representative mechanisms

Name	Check	Redundancy
Incremental recovery cache	-	Data replication
Time redundant execution	Function output	Function replication
Runtime checks	Data	Data diversity
Recovery blocks	Function input / output	Function diversity
Control flow checking	Function flow	-

3.1 Incremental Recovery Cache

A large number of fault tolerance implementations rely on the concept of backward error recovery to return to a previously saved state. A checkpointing mechanism builds on the principle of data replication and provides support for backward error recovery by allowing the program to return to the state it held when a checkpoint was established. There are basically two different approaches when implementing support for checkpointing. Either a backup of the complete state is made and stored at the checkpoint or the mechanism starts to monitor state changes and stores only the part of the state that is changed. The latter is called incremental checkpointing. There are also two distinct types of incremental mechanisms. The first makes a complete backup at the first checkpoint and then starts monitoring changes to the program state. When a new checkpoint is reached, only the part of the state that has been changed since the last one is updated. The second type is called an incremental recovery cache [3]. The recovery cache does not make a total snapshot of the state when it sets up a checkpoint but starts monitoring changes to state variables. When a variable is changed for the first time after the checkpoint, a copy of the old value is immediately stored in the cache. Considering these three basic types of mechanisms, they place a rising demand on access to and control over the program state. All three require access to all state variables in order to be able to store or restore them. The two that are incremental in addition to this also need to detect changes to these variables. The first type of incremental mechanism must only detect a change afterwards, while the recovery cache needs to detect the change prior to its being made in order to be able to fetch the old value before it is overwritten. This means that, if a language is powerful enough so that a recovery cache can be implemented in a satisfactory way, the other types of checkpointing mechanisms can be built as well. Compared to some other mechanisms for data replication, the recovery cache lacks the need to detect read accesses on data. However, this is covered by the set through the runtime check mechanism described below. Hence the recovery cache was chosen to represent data replication mechanisms in the set.

3.2 Time Redundant Execution

A technique for detecting and masking transient faults through function replication is time redundant execution [4]. An error originating from a transient fault can be detected by executing a function two times and comparing the results. If the function is executed a third time, the fault can be masked by voting between the three runs. Since the error masking version follows the same structure as the non masking, with the exception that it executes the function a third time and calls a voting algorithm instead of signaling an error, it does not place any additional demands on the language. Hence the mechanism chosen is the basic version that detects an error and signals that a fault has occurred. A common extension to this mechanism is to duplicate the actual program code in memory having each execution run on its own copy. Static duplication of code, although very useful in the fault tolerance domain, is out of the scope of any general purpose programming language. Hence it was not included in this study. However, should the set be applied to implementation techniques where this can be supported, e.g. code transformation tools, it should be included.

3.3 Recovery Blocks

Recovery blocks [5] are a structured way of adding software fault tolerance to a program based on the concept of function diversity. This technique consists of an acceptance test that verifies the output of an algorithm and one or more alternative implementations that are executed should the test fail. The recovery block implementation included in the set has one alternative algorithm, but implementations with more alternatives follow the same basic structure.

3.4 Runtime Checks

Runtime checks (also known as executable assertions) are used to monitor the properties of data stored in variables or passed to and from functions. Monitoring function input and output is covered by the set through the time redundant execution and recovery block mechanisms. Hence only monitoring of variable data needs to be further included. The check included in the set should monitor a counter variable. When the variable is written to it asserts that it is only reset or raised by one. When read from it asserts that the variable is in the range of zero to ten.

3.5 Control Flow Checking

Function checks either assert the correctness of function code or that the correct code is executed. The first case is done at runtime by monitoring the results the code produces, i.e. by data checks. Hence this is already covered by the chosen mechanisms. To cover the second case, control flow checking [6] was included. This mechanism is used to detect an erroneous program flow caused by illegal branches. Such a branch could e.g. be caused by transient faults that affect the program counter. The mechanism is built on the principle that, if a program enters a block of code, it must be the same block that it exits the next time it exits a code block. An identifier that is unique to each block is placed at the beginning and at the end of the block. When a block is entered, the identifier is pushed on a stack and, when the block is exited, it is pulled and compared with the identifier placed at the end. If they do not match, a control flow error has been detected. A code block can be defined with different granularity. The highest granularity used in practice in software is achieved by defining a block as a branch free sequence of the code. Another common approach is to use function bodies as blocks.

4   AOP Language Evaluation

In a preparatory study [7] we evaluated the feasibility of present day AOP languages for building fault tolerance. The only language that showed satisfactory results was AspectJ, which is an AOP extension to Java. However, since our research targets embedded safety critical systems, the usability of Java is very limited. Therefore, AspectC++ [2], which is an AOP extension to C++, is the most promising candidate as an AOP platform for implementing fault tolerance in this domain. Hence, this was the language chosen for further evaluation and extension.

4.1   AOP Language Concepts

An aspect oriented implementation of a crosscutting concern consists of two parts, the actual implementation of the functionality associated with the concern and the information on how that code should be integrated into the rest of the program. Any traditional language, such as C or C++, is well suited for the first part. However, the traditional languages lack primitives for specifying how the concern specific code should be composed, or weaved, together to form the final system. An AOP language therefore defines a way to specify rules for composing different implementation pieces together. The AOP language is then built as an extension to a traditional language to give that language aspect oriented capabilities in the same way that C++ was built as an extension to C to provide object oriented capabilities to the C language.

The main characteristics of an AOP language are what base language it extends and what joinpoints it supports. A joinpoint is an accessible point in the application execution where concern specific code can be inserted when conducting system weaving. An AOP language lets the programmer declare a pointcut that accesses a set of joinpoints. The pointcut can then be linked to a concern specific code segment called advice.

4.2   Evaluating AspectC++

When trying to implement the mechanisms using AspectC++ it was found that only two of the five could be implemented while still retaining the separation of concerns (see Table 2). An analysis showed that the reason was the same for the recovery cache and the runtime check, namely the lack of joinpoints for targeting the data domain. In the case of the control flow check, AspectC++ could not generate a unique function

Table 2. Evaluation results

	AspectC++ v.1.0pre3	Extended AspectC++
Recovery cache		✓
Time redundant execution	✓	✓
Recovery blocks	✓	✓
Runtime checks		✓
Control flow checking		✓

identifier that can be used by the check. In order to know whether these problems could be solved, we decided to extend the official release of AspectC++ with the needed functionality by modifying the publicly available source code. After adding the two extensions described in section 4.3, all the mechanisms could be implemented in a satisfactory way.

In addition, a few more language improvements that could further improve the implementations in terms of runtime performance, applicability and reusability were revealed while implementing the set of mechanisms. The ability to pointcut implicitly declared operators would improve the performance of the recovery cache implementation. The ability to use multiple proceed() statements without restriction would make the time redundancy mechanism applicable to all target functions and the ability to pass joinpoint information as function argument would enable reuse of the recovery block structure. These improvements, and the ability to pointcut the data domain implemented in the extension, would be generally useful for a larger number of fault tolerance mechanisms, e.g. most data redundancy mechanisms and N-version programming. This proves the usability of the chosen set in finding limitations shared by a larger number of fault tolerance mechanisms.

4.3 AspectC++ Extensions

Two extensions were added to the official release of AspectC++ addressing the limitations found. The first deals with the need for detecting and controlling data accesses. In other AOP languages, joinpoints for targeting the data domain are known as get and set joinpoints. These are used for monitoring read and write accesses on variables. One reason for why AspectC++ does not yet support these joinpoints is that C++ allows overloading of assignment operators. This makes it difficult to define the set joinpoint. The possibility to overload the operator can be used instead of a set joinpoint in order to monitor variable change for non primitive data types (i.e. Class types). Class types can hence be monitored by automatic introduction of assignment operators or by execution joinpoints on already declared operators. This reduces the need for set joinpoints to primitive data types and pointers that lack operator overloading capabilities. Hence AspectC++ was extended with set joinpoints only for these types. By combing these techniques a fault tolerance implementation can monitor variables of all data types. A second problem in set and get joinpoints is commonly known as the alias problem. In a language that supports pointers, a data field might be accessible through several pointers or variables. This problem is generally difficult to solve since the use of pointer arithmetics makes it impossible to know at compile time which variables might be accessed by address. For now, the alias problem is not considered in the implementation of the get and set joinpoints, which can therefore be considered to monitor a specific access path to a data field rather than the field itself. Implications of this approach for the mechanisms that use the joinpoints are discussed below.

The other limitation found was that AspectC++ could not generate a unique identifier for each function that can be used by the control flow check. However, the language has a very similar feature that gives a unique identifier for each joinpoint called JoinPoint::JPID. Hence this structure was extended with an identifier, FID (Function ID), which works in a similar way and identifies the function containing the joinpoint.

5   AspectC++ Implementations

This section describes the implementations of the mechanisms. Advantages and limitations of the AspectC++ implementations and AOP in general are discussed. The implemented and suggested extensions to the language are also put into context and explained.

5.1 Incremental Recovery Cache

The complete implementation of the recovery cache is far too tedious to fit in the size restriction of this paper. Therefore only the general principles together with advantages and limitations are discussed. A more extensive description of the implementation can be found in [8].

The functionality of the actual cache is provided by the class shown in Figure 1. This class is not specific to AOP and hence the internal implementation is not needed to understand the AOP approach. The core functionality of the class is provided by three functions, establish, restore and discard, which are used to set up, restore to and discard checkpoints. The cache accepts an object for storing through the *store* function. By encapsulating any such object in a generic object type by instantiating a template class, the cache can remain oblivious to the type of the stored object and hence support all types of objects. The cache must also keep track of when objects are created so that only objects created before the checkpoint are cached. This is assured by calling the functions objectCreated and objectDeleted upon object construction and destruction. The cache also prevents memory allocated prior to the checkpoint from being freed before the checkpoint is discarded and assures that memory allocated after the checkpoint is freed when the checkpoint is restored. This is handled by calling memoryAllocated when an object is created on the heap and by allowing the cache to control the release of memory by calling free.

```
class RecoveryCache {
public:
  static void establish();
  static void discard() ;
  static void restore();

  static void store(Recoverable* r);

  static void objectCreated(void* p);
  static void objectDeleted(void* p);

  static void memoryAllocated(void* p);
  static bool free(void* p);
};
```

Fig. 1. The RecoveryCache class

The first three functions are publicly available for any part of the fault tolerance framework that needs the functionality of the cache and can be used when desired. The other functions must be called whenever an object that may potentially be cached is created, deleted or modified. Much of this can be achieved by having all affected classes inherit from a common base class. In this way, the base class constructor and destructor can signal the creation and deletion of objects to the cache. New and delete operators can also be placed in the base class in order to refer memory allocation and deallocation to the cache. Furthermore, some object modifications can be detected by having the base class define its own assignment operator. This assignment operator is only called if there is no operator already defined in the inheriting class. This is a limitation in the base class approach, which in a standard C++ implementation would require that an explicit call to the base class operator is manually added to all assignment operators. In addition, if standard C++ is used, the base class must be manually added to the inheritance tree of all affected classes. When AspectC++ is used, both these things can automatically be assured by the aspect. Still, there is the case when primitive or pointer fields are modified. Standard C++ has no means to detect this. This most significantly limits the usefulness of standard C++ implementations of the recovery cache. This limitation is also shared with the current release of AspectC++. As described in section 4.3, AspectC++ was therefore extended with a set joinpoint that targets changes to these fields.

```
aspect RecoveryCacheAspect {
public:
  pointcut virtual cachedClasses() = 0;


  pointcut filteredClasses() = cachedClasses()
    && !"RecoveryCache" && !"Recoverable"
    && !derived("RecoveryCacheAspect")
    && !"CachedObject";


  advice filteredClasses(): baseclass(Recoverable);



    ...



  pointcut assignmentOp() =
    execution("% %::operator=(...)"
    &&  within(filteredClasses());


  pointcut primitiveChange() = set("%::%")
    &&  target(filteredClasses());


  pointcut change() = assignmentOp()
    || primitiveChange();


  advice change() : before() {
    RecoveryCache::store((Recoverable*)tjp->that());
  }
};


aspect CompleteCache : public RecoveryCacheAspect {
  pointcut cachedClasses() = "%";
};
```

Fig. 2. The RecoveryCache aspect

The RecoveryCache aspect shown in Figure 2 is the aspect oriented part of the implementation and what glues the cache implementation and the target program together. The cachedClasses pointcut defines what objects should be stored in the cache. This pointcut is declared as true virtual in order to make the implementation generic. The filteredClasses pointcut assures that all classes that are part of the cache implementation itself are removed from the set of classes that should be stored. The advice then adds the common base class described above to the classes. The added set joinpoint is used in the primitiveChange pointcut. The change pointcut is the union of user defined assignment operators and of changes to primitive and pointer fields. This pointcut is then used for an advice that updates the cache.

A further language improvement that may lower the runtime cost of the mechanisms would be the ability to pointcut implicitly declared operators. This would remove the need for having an assignment operator in the base class. Because of multiple inheritances in C++, the base class operator might be called multiple times when an object is changed. If it would be possible always to intercept calls to the assignment operator in the top level class, multiple calls to the cache could be avoided.

The cache is applied to a target program by writing a subaspect that defines the cachedClasses pointcut. In the CompleteCache aspect in Figure 2, it is set to pointcut all of the target program classes. This will monitor the complete program so that all changes to the system state are reverted when a restore to the checkpoint is made. Alternatively, knowledge of the target program can be used to minimize overhead by only caching a wanted subset of objects. The AOP implementation also places almost no restriction on the target classes and can hence easily be applied to legacy code. The restriction that is placed is that a primitive member field should not be directly aliased. This is a small restriction, since primitive member fields should always be accessed through the object. What we have is thus a fully transparent recovery cache that can be applied to an application without knowledge of that application's inner working, and at the same time a recovery cache that can be targeted to only cache wanted parts of the program state by simply modifying a single line pointcut definition.

5.2   Time Redundant Execution

The TimeRedundancy aspect in Figure 3 implements a generic time redundancy mechanism. Time redundancy illustrates well how simple it is to apply an AOP implementation to a target program. It is only a matter of declaring which function(s) should be executed in a time redundant manner by subclassing the aspect and defining the timeRedundantFunctions pointcut. This is exemplified by the TRFunctions aspect in Figure 3 that will execute all functions in the "Critical" class in a time redundant manner. The timeRedundantCall pointcut makes use of the "!cflow" expression. This guarantees that a function called by a function (itself or another) that is already executed in a time redundant manner will not also execute multiple times within each execution of the calling function. This is a very good example of the power of the pointcut syntax. This program wide property can be difficult and error prone to ensure when using standard C++ but is guaranteed with just a single expression using AOP. As presented here, the mechanism assumes that the targeted functions are fully deterministic and does not depend on external actions. However, if the result is dependent on varying external values (e.g. sensor values), the mechanism can be extended to capture calls to these and provides the function with a consistent value for both runs. The exact implementation depends on the nature of the interface used for accessing external values and is thus dependent on the architecture of the target program.

The time redundancy mechanism shown here makes use of the recovery cache to set up a checkpoint and return to the previous state before each run. Normally, some other checkpointing mechanism should be used, since the recovery cache is designed only for software fault tolerance. However, since the recovery cache is included in the chosen set of mechanisms, it is used here to demonstrate the structure of the time redundancy mechanism.

```
aspect TimeRedundancy {

  pointcut virtual timeRedundantFunctions() = 0;

  pointcut timeRedundantCall() =
    call (timeRedundantFunctions()) &&
    !cflow(execution (timeRedundantFunctions()));

  advice timeRedundantCall() : around() {
    RecoveryCache::establish();
    tjp->proceed();
    JoinPoint::Result r1 = *tjp->result();
    RecoveryCache::restore();
    tjp->proceed();
    JoinPoint::Result r2 = *tjp->result();
    if(r1 != r2) throw "TransientFaultException";
    RecoveryCache::discard();
  }
};


aspect TRFunctions : public TimeRedundancy {

  pointcut timeRedundantFunctions() =
    "% Critical::%(…)";
};
```

Fig. 3. Time redundant execution implementation

There is one limitation to the applicability of this mechanism that has to do with the implementation of the AspectC++ compiler. If the result of the targeted function is a class instance that is returned by value, there can be unintended effects when calling proceed() multiple times within an advice. The reason is that the result of the first run is simply overwritten without executing the class assignment operator. This can be handled by certifying that the assignment operator does not do anything critical, or by using return by reference instead. Although it can be handled, this is a limitation in AspectC++ that should be addressed in order to remove the restrictions on the target program.

The main advantage of this implementation is that it is implemented in a generic way and allows the programmer to simply apply it to a function. This is not possible in an OO only language, which requires that wrapper functions be written to individual functions. Thus, the properties described above and the fact that the fault tolerance code is completely separate from the primary function modules, make AOP a very compelling approach to implementing this type of mechanism.

5.3 Runtime Checks

Runtime checks do not benefit from one common general AOP implementation as the structure of the AOP joinpoints and advice in itself give an ideal environment for implementing each check. Checks that are implementation specific can be implemented directly as a custom built aspect, and ones that are common can be implemented as a reusable aspect. An appealing property of runtime checks implemented with the use of aspects is that they can easily be made to continuously monitor for instance a state variable at all accesses. The source code needed is equally simple as the code needed for monitoring a single crucial location in a program. Monitoring all accesses gives a higher runtime overhead but is still an effective way of assuring that only legal state transitions occur in a critical system. There is one limitation to this, caused by the alias problem. This means that a runtime check set up to monitor accesses to an object or field will only detect accesses through the variable it is set to monitor. If an access is made through an unmonitored aliasing variable, it will not be detected. Aliasing critical variables is not recommended and, if done, the effects must be well understood and handled. AspectC++ does not at present free the programmer of this responsibility.

```
aspect CounterAssertion {

  pointcut writeCounter() =set("int Aclass::_counter");

  pointcut readCounter() =get("int Aclass::_counter");

  advice writeCounter() : before() {
    if ( !(0 == *tjp->source() ||
      1 == *tjp->source() - *tjp->dest()) )
      throw "CheckFailedException";}

  advice readCounter() : before() {
    if ( !(0 <= *tjp->dest() && 10 >= *tjp->dest()) )
      throw "CheckFailedException";}
};
```

Fig. 4. Counter property assertion

This runtime check requires the set and get joinpoints added in the extended version of AspectC++. The code in Figure 4 asserts the counter property of a variable, as well as that it is within the range of zero to ten.

The advantages of using AOP for runtime checks are, apart from the separation of function and assertion code, that program properties can be continuously monitored in a simple way and that common checks can be reused.

5.4 Recovery Blocks

The RecoveryBlock aspect in Figure 5 is applied to an algorithm (encapsulated in a function) by both declaring the pointcut and implementing the acceptance test and an alternative algorithm. Since it is not possible to pass the tjp data structure as a function argument, the aspect can not be built generically and the functions implemented in a subclass. This is a limitation of AspectC++ that should be addressed in the future.

```
aspect RecoveryBlock {

  pointcut function() =
    execution ("int aClass::afunction(int)");


  bool acceptanceTest(int arg, int result){
    // implementation of acceptanceTest
  }
  int alternativeImp(int arg){
    // alternative implementation of function.
  }


  advice function() : around() {
    RecoveryCache::establish();
    tjp->proceed();
    if (!acceptanceTest(*tjp->arg<0>(),
    *tjp->result())){
      RecoveryCache::restore();
      *tjp->result() =
        alternativeImp(*tjp- >arg<0>());
      if (!acceptanceTest(*tjp->arg<0>(),
      *tjp->result())){
        RecoveryCache::discard();
        throw "SoftwareFaultException";
      }
    }
    RecoveryCache::discard();
  }

};
```

Fig. 5. Recovery block implementation

```
aspect ControlFlowChecking{

  pointcut monitoredFunctions() = "% ...::%(...)";
  pointcut ControlFlowExe() =
    execution(monitoredFunctions())
    && !execution("% ...::main(...)")
    && !within("ControlFlowChecking");
  pointcut ControlFlowCall() =
    call(monitoredFunctions())
    && !call("% ...::main(...)")
    && !within("ControlFlowChecking");


  stack<int> s;

  advice ControlFlowCall() : around() {
    s.push((int)JoinPoint::FID);
    try {
      tjp->proceed();
    } catch (...) {
      if ((int)JoinPoint::FID != s.top())
        throw "ControlFlowFaultException";
      s.pop();
      throw;
    }
    if ((int)JoinPoint::FID != s.top())
      throw "ControlFlowFaultException";
    s.pop();
  }


  advice ControlFlowExe() : before() {
    if ((int)JoinPoint::FID != s.top())
      throw "ControlFlowFaultException";
  }


  advice ControlFlowExe() : after(){
    if ((int)JoinPoint::FID != s.top())
      throw "ControlFlowFaultException";
  }
};
```

Fig. 6. Control flow checking implementation

A recovery block is an example of a mechanism that is not a crosscutting concern. It is built to monitor a single function and is applied at a single location in the program. This is normally true for all software fault tolerance mechanisms built on design diversity, unless the functionality monitored is in itself crosscutting. This weakens the case for using AOP for this type of mechanism. However, the advantages of using AOP for recovery blocks are still twofold. The syntactical separation of the fault tolerance code and the target program is in itself a good thing that improves reusability. The other reason for using AOP is that, although the single mechanism is not crosscutting, the complete fault tolerance framework that it is part of is. For example, the recovery block uses the crosscutting implementation of the recovery cache for doing backward error recovery.

5.5 Control Flow Checking

The implementation of the control flow check mechanism is a good example of both the advantages and limitations of present day AOP languages. Since AOP languages lack statement level joinpoints, code can not be added to specific points within a function body. However, there are discussions on integrating statement level annotations into the AspectC++ language in the future, which would remove this limitation. As of today, a block granularity finer than function bodies can not be implemented.

The implementation shown in Figure 6 verifies that the function entered is the one that was called. When the end of a function body is reached, it verifies that it is the same function that was entered and, finally, after returning, it verifies that it was the same function that was returned from.

The control flow mechanism is strictly systematic and as such has been implemented as a reusable aspect that can be applied to any target program without modification.

6 Related Work

AOP has been discussed for some time in the area of distributed fault tolerance. Fabry [9] defined custom built AOP languages and used them for a transparent reusable distributed replication framework. Herrero et al. [10] define an AOP language specifically designed for writing object replication policies. In [11] AOP is used to move some functionality from the FT-CORBA middleware to the application while still retaining transparency to the application programmer. This is shown to give performance benefits.

AOP has many characteristics in common with reflection or meta programming. Meta programming has been successfully used for introducing fault tolerance in software, and a number of publications exist on the topic. In [12] Juan Carlos Ruiz et al. summarize their experience of using meta programming for building fault tolerant distributed applications. The current work [13] by this group tries to extend the techniques beyond the application layer in order to create a unified meta protocol that can affect all abstraction layers from kernel OS and up. Jie Xu et al. [14] address the area of software fault tolerance and show how meta programming can be used in this context. Other work on fault tolerance and meta programming is reported in [15] and [16], which define meta level design patterns for fault tolerance.

7 Conclusion

This paper defines a representative set of mechanisms that can be used for feasibility evaluations of implementation languages and techniques for fault tolerance purposes. It consists of five fault tolerance mechanisms including recovery cache [3], time redundant execution [4], recovery blocks [5], runtime checks and control flow checking [6].

Such evaluations can be used both for selecting implementation techniques and to serve as a valuable tool in communicating the need of fault tolerance implementations to language designers.

The representativeness of the chosen set of mechanisms has been argued theoretically from a structural viewpoint. The usefulness is also verified in a study evaluating the AspectC++ language [2].

The study showed that only two out of five mechanisms can be implemented using the current version of AspectC++.

In order to address this, AspectC++ has been extended to fulfill two vital requirements elicited from the evaluation. With this extension it is verified that the complete set can be implemented, thus showing that AspectC++ when extended is generally feasible for fault tolerance implementations. Hence the advantages introduced by the aspect oriented programming paradigm can be utilized when implementing fault tolerant software in C++.

In addition, a few more language improvements that could further improve the implementations in terms of runtime performance, applicability and reusability were revealed by implementing the mechanisms. These improvements, as well as the language extensions implemented, are required or useful for a larger number of fault tolerance mechanisms, thus proving the usability of the defined set.

Furthermore, the implementations included in this paper demonstrate how reusable fault tolerance mechanisms can be built using aspect oriented C++, and the advantages compared to using standard C++ are discussed.

Acknowledgements

This research was conducted within the CEDES (Cost Efficient Dependable Electronic Systems) project, which is funded by IVSS – Intelligent Vehicle Safety Systems - a Swedish industry and government joint research program. The authors would like to thank Johan Magnusson for his part in extending AspectC++.

References

1. Elrad, T., Filman, R.E., Bader, A.: Aspect-oriented programming: introduction. Communications of the ACM 44(10), 29–32 (2001)
2. Spinczyk, O., Gal, A., Schröder-Preikschat, W.: AspectC++: An Aspect-Oriented Extension to C++. In: Proceedings of the 40th International Conference on Technology of Object-Oriented Languages and Systems (TOOLS Pacific 2002), Sydney, Australia, pp. 18–21 (2002)

3. Rodgers, P., Wellings, A.J.: An incremental recovery cache supporting software fault tolerance. In: González Harbour, M., la de Puente, J.A. (eds.) Ada-Europe 1999. LNCS, vol. 1622, pp. 385–396. Springer, Heidelberg (1999)

4. Damm, A.: The effectiveness of software error-detection mechanisms in real-time operating systems. FTCS Digest of Papers. In: 16th Annual International Symposium on Fault-Tolerant Computing Systems, Washington DC, USA (1986)

5. Randell, B.: System structure for software fault tolerance. IEEE Transactions on Software Engineering SE 1(2), 220–232 (1975)

6. Oh, N., Shirvani, P., McCluskey, E.J.: Control-Flow Checking by Software Signatures. Center for Reliable Computing, Stanford Univ., CA, CRC-TR-00-4 (CSL TR num 00-800) (2000)

7. Alexandersson, R., Öhman, P., Ivarsson, M.: Aspect oriented software implemented node level fault tolerance. In: Ninth IASTED International Conference on Software Engineering and Applications (SEA 2005), Phoenix AZ, USA (2005)

8. Alexandersson, R.: Techniques for software implemented fault tolerance. Technical report 22L, ISSN 1652-876X, Department of Computer Science and Engineering, Chalmers University of Technology, Sweden (2006)

9. Fabry, J.: A Framework for Replication of Objects using Aspect-Oriented Programming. Phd Thesis, University of Brussel (1998)

10. Herrero, J.L., Sanchez, F., Toro, M.: Fault tolerance as an aspect using JReplica. In: Proceedings of the Eighth IEEE Workshop on Future trends of Distributed Computing Systems, October 31- November 2, pp. 201–207. IEEE Computer Society Press, Los Alamitos (2001)

11. Szentivanyi, D., Nadjm-Tehrani, S.: Aspects for improvement of performance in fault-tolerant software. In: Proceedings of the 10th IEEE Pacific Rim International Symposium on Dependable Computing, 3-5 March, pp. 283–291 (2004)

12. Ruiz, J.C., Killijian, M.O., Fabre, J.C., Thévenod-Fosse, P.: Reflective Fault-Tolerant Systems: From Experience to Challenges. IEEE Transactions On Computers 52(2), 237–254 (2003)

13. Taiani, F., Fabre, J.C., Killijian, M.O.: A multi-level meta-object protocol for fault-tolerance in complex architectures. In: Proceedings of the International Conference on Dependable Systems and Networks, 2005 (DSN 2005), 28 June-July 1, pp. 270–279 (2005)

14. Xu, J., Randell, B., Zorzo, A.F.: Implementing Software-Fault Tolerance in C++ and Open C++. In: Min, Y., Tang, D. (eds.) Proceedings of the 1996 International Workshop on Computer-Aided Design, Test, and Evaluation for Dependability (CADTED '96), Beijing China, pp. 224–229 (1996)

15. Cheynet, P., Nicolescu, B., Velazco, R., Rebaudengo, M., Sonza Reorda, M., Violante, M.: Experimentally evaluating an automatic approach for generating safety-critical software with respect to transient errors. IEEE Transaction on Nuclear Science 47(6), 2231–2236 (2000)

16. Lisboa, M.L.B.: A new trend on the development of fault-tolerant applications: software meta-level architectures. In: Proceedings of the International Workshop on Dependable Computing and its Applications (IFIP'98) (1998)

Architecture-Centric Fault Tolerance with Exception Handling

Patrick H. S. Brito[1], Rogério de Lemos[2],
Eliane Martins[1], and Cecília M. F. Rubira[1]

[1] Institute of Computing – State University of Campinas (Unicamp)
P.O. Box 6176, 13084-971, Campinas, SP, Brazil
{pbrito,eliane,cmrubira}@ic.unicamp.br
[2] Computing Laboratory – University of Kent
Canterbury, U.K.
r.delemos@kent.ac.uk

Abstract. When building dependable systems by integrating untrusted software components that were not originally designed to interact with each other, it is inevitable the occurrence of architectural mismatches related to assumptions in the failure behaviours. These mismatches if not prevented during system design have to be tolerated during run-time. This paper presents an architectural abstraction based on exception handling for structuring fault-tolerant software systems. This abstraction comprises several components and connectors that transform an existing untrusted software element into an idealised fault-tolerant architectural element. The proposed rigorous approach relies on a formal representation for analysing exception propagation, and verifying important dependability properties. Beyond this, the formal models are also used for generating unit and integration test cases that would be used for validating the final software product. The feasibility of the proposed approach was evaluated on an embedded critical case study.

1 Introduction

The adoption of software components, which used to be restricted to the construction of enterprise systems, has expanded to other application areas where the cost of failure might be unacceptable. Software systems that can cause risks for human lives or great financial losses can be made fault-tolerant, so that they are capable of providing their intended service, even if only partially, despite the presence of faults. Amongst the several existing techniques for building fault-tolerant systems, exception handling is a well-known mechanism for structuring error recovery in software systems [13]. Exception handling complements other techniques for error recovery, such as atomic transactions [19], and aims to support the construction of programs that are more reliable, concise, and easy to evolve [25]. The use of exception handling to develop large-scale software systems [9,27], together with the fact that it is implemented by several modern object-oriented languages, such as, Java, Ada, C#, and C++, and component

A. Bondavalli, F. Brasileiro, and S. Rajsbaum (Eds.): LADC 2007, LNCS 4746, pp. 75–94, 2007.

models, such as, CCM, EJB, Ice, and .NET, confirms its importance to the current practice of software development. Furthermore, in applications where a rollback is not possible, such as those that interact with physical environments, exception handling may be the only choice available. On the other hand, it is also accepted that exception handling mechanism might have its disadvantages, if we consider the fact that a large part of a system's code is devoted to error detection and handling [13,27,31]. As a consequence, abnormal (exceptional) behaviour has to be carefully structured, in order to reduce its impact on the overall complexity of the software.

In this paper, we present an architectural approach for structuring fault-tolerant software systems so that mechanisms for detecting and handling errors have minimal impact on the overall system complexity. The motivation for this work is twofold. First, it is widely accepted that the architecture of a software system has a strong impact on its capacity to meet its intended quality requirements [4]. And second, it is also accepted that dependability of a software system is inherently associated with its structure [26]. The contribution of this paper is on the provision of an architectural solution, which is integrated with a development approach for improving the dependability of component-based software systems. The paper will focus into three major issues: (i) the specification and verification of the architectural abstraction using a combination of the B-Method and CSP, what includes the refinement of the exceptional behaviour with more details about exception types and the way the architectural element reacts with each exception type; (ii) the definition of architectural properties for analysing exception propagation and fault tolerance aspects of architectural elements; and (iii) the generation of unit and integration test cases from the architectural specification.

The architectural abstraction adopted in this work, namely the idealised fault tolerant architectural element (iFTE), was initially proposed as an abstraction for structuring complex fault-tolerant systems [17]. The formal definition and verification of the iFTE, as an architectural abstraction, was subsequently performed in terms of the B-Method and CSP [7]. This formal modelling has enabled the representation of architectural configurations based on the iFTE, thus allowing the formal verification of error handling properties, including exception propagation, and the automatic generation of test cases for integration of iFTEs. In this paper, that previous work is expanded by defining the internal structure of an iFTE, in terms of further components and connectors that enable the integration of existing components into architectural configurations based on iFTEs. Besides that, we have formally specified the iFTE abstraction in such a way the formal model of an iFTE element can be used as part of a complementary model for dependable software architectures, where are verified properties regarding exception propagation among iFTEs and non-iFTE elements disposed together according to an architectural configuration. The detailed modelling of the iFTE also enforces the separation between normal and exceptional behaviours and allows us to verify and validate how the iFTE internal elements are able to implement the behaviour of the architectural elements.

The rest of this paper is organised as follows. The following two sections present, respectively, some related work and a brief background about the area of architectural fault tolerance based on exception handling. Section 4 describes an architectural solution for structuring dependable architectural elements. The formal verification of this structuring solution, as well as its formal representation, are presented in Section 5. Section 6 presents the method for generating test cases for the architectural elements. In Section 7 the feasibility of the overall approach is evaluated in the context of an embedded critical case study. Finally, the last section provides some concluding remarks and future directions of research.

2 Related Work

A contribution of a structuring technique for error confinement is the idealised C2 component (iC2C) [16], based on the idealised fault-tolerant component [3]. It has been proposed for structuring software systems compliant with the C2 architectural style [30]. The internal protocol followed by the internal elements of an iC2C enforces error confinement and makes it possible to define multiple exception handling contexts at the architectural level. Later work by Castor et al. [11] defined and implemented an architectural level exception handling mechanism based on the concept of iC2C. The work presented in this paper can be seen as an extension of the iC2C for a broader class of software architectures that adhere to the peer-to-peer architectural style [12].

In a previous work, Brito et al. [15] have proposed a systematic approach for the specification and validation of exceptional behaviour for component-based software systems in which the validation was provided through the generation of unit test cases. The work reported in this paper is different from that work on several fronts, although the validation process is similar. The main focus in this paper is on the formal specification of iFTE-based software architectures from which both unit and integration test cases are automatically generated.

In another related work, the Aereal framework leverages existing languages and tools to support the description and analysis of exception flow in software architectures adhering to multiple architectural styles [10]. In terms of verification, both works have similar goals, however Aereal did not model the interplay between an architectural element and the error recovery mechanisms that make it fault-tolerant. Another important difference is that in the proposed approach the architectural behaviour related to error handling is specified in terms of scenarios, which increases its scalability because it reduces the number of states generated during the architectural verification.

Seminal work by Issarny and Banâtre [20] describes an extension to architectural description languages that allows for the specification of architectural invariants. Violations of these invariants, called configuration exceptions, trigger architectural reconfigurations. This work differs from ours because it emphasises fault handling at the architectural level. Our work, on the other hand, emphasises error recovery.

3   Background

3.1   iFTE: Idealised Fault-Tolerant Architectural Element

The idealised fault-tolerant architectural element (iFTE) [17] is an architectural abstraction for structuring fault-tolerant systems, which enforces the principles associated with the concept of the idealised fault-tolerant component [23], and includes responsibilities for detecting errors in the architectural elements, as well as handling and propagating exceptions in a structured way.

The general model of an iFTE defines four types of external interfaces, and these are clearly partitioned into normal and abnormal (exceptional) behaviour: (i) I_iFTE_PS defines an access point for the (fault-tolerant) services provided by the iFTE; (ii) I_iFTE_RS specifies services required by the iFTE for implementing its normal behaviour or handling exceptions; (iii) I_iFTE_PE defines an access point where iFTE signals its external exceptions; and (iv) I_iFTE_RE specifies the external exceptions that the iFTE is able to handle. These interfaces can be detailed according to specific provided and required services of an iFTE, as well as its exception types. As it could be seen, while the two first interfaces (I_iFTE_PS and I_iFTE_RS) are responsible for the normal behaviour, the two last ones are responsible for the abnormal behaviour.

Looking for the iFTE as an architectural abstraction, there are seven different scenarios that describe the relationship that can be established between the external interfaces of an iFTE. After a request is made through I_iFTE_PS, the iFTE may respond in two different ways: returns normal services through I_iFTE_PS (1st scenario); signals an interface exception through I_iFTE_PE (2nd scenario); or signals a failure exception through I_iFTE_PE (3rd scenario). Besides that it is possible to request external services through I_iFTE_RS. After requesting external services, four scenarios are possible. If the external architectural element returns normal services through I_iFTE_RS, the iFTE either returns normal services through I_iFTE_PS (4th scenario), or signals an exception through I_iFTE_PE (5th scenario). If the external architectural element signals an exception, the iFTE either propagates the error through I_iFTE_PE (6th scenario), or recover its state, returning normally through I_iFTE_PS (7th scenario).

3.2   Formal Anotation and Verification

The B-Method [1] is a formal method based on set theory, where sets and relations among sets are used for data modelling, and operations describe state modifications. A limitation of the B-Method is its inability to easily restrict the correct order of operations. Communicating Sequential Process (CSP) [8] is a process algebra that allows an easy representation of execution sequences. In this way, when used for guiding the execution of B-Method operations, CSP compensates the mentioned limitation of B-Method [28,24].

Because of their complementary characteristics, there are many approaches that combine set-based notations with algebra processes. ProB [24] is a model checker that combines B-Method and CSP into a complementary way. As a joining point between the two notations, the B-Method operations in ProB are represented as single events in the CSP specification. Thus, when it is used a CSP model to guide a B-Method machine, ProB uses the order of the CSP events for restricting the B-Method operations that can be executed.

4   Detailing the iFTE

4.1   Structure of the iFTE

The detailed design of an iFTE is shown in Figure 1, and it contains five architectural elements: (i) the Normal component implements the normal behaviour of the iFTE; (ii) the Abnormal component handles the exceptions raised (or created) by the Normal component, and those propagated (or signalled) from the environment of the iFTE; (iii) the Provided component acts like a bridge between the services provided by the iFTE and its environment, including the signal of exceptions; (iv) the Required component also acts like a bridge, but between the required services of the iFTE and its environment; and (v) the Coordinator connector coordinates the interaction between the four internal components of an iFTE.

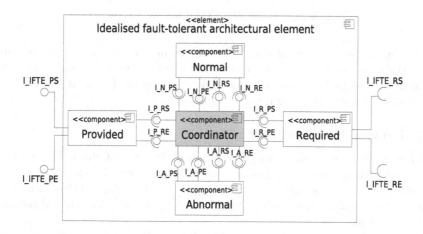

Fig. 1. Internal structure of the idealised fault-tolerant architectural element (iFTE)

To maintain the separation of concerns, between the normal and exceptional behaviours, the Abnormal component is the only one that handles exceptions. The Provided and Required only propagate exceptions to the Abnormal, mediating the access between the iFTE and the external environment. About the Normal component, besides propagating exceptions to the Abnormal, it can identify exceptional conditions and raise exceptions. The internal architectural elements of the iFTE interact through internal interfaces, and these interfaces also enforce the separation between normal and exceptional behaviours.

Since the Normal component is responsible for providing functionalities of the iFTE, it might be an existing component that needs to be incorporated into the architecture. Before using a COTS component as the Normal element of an iFTE, it is necessary to adapt it, in order to make it compatible with the four internal interfaces of the Normal. As presented in Figure 2, the structure of the Normal after reusing a COTS component is composed of three elements: the COTS component, which has to be reused; a NormalProvided adapter, which is responsible to convert all the provided interfaces of the COTS into the I_N_PS and I_N_PE interfaces; and a NormalRequired adapter, which is responsible to convert all the required interfaces of the COTS into the I_N_RS and I_N_RE interfaces.

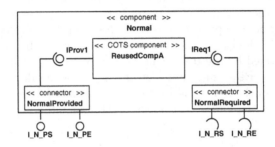

Fig. 2. Adaptation of a COTS Normal component

Besides the adaptation of a COTS Normal component, the iFTE also supports the adaptation of inconsistencies among architectural elements. This complementary and high-level adaptation is provided by the Provided and Required components presented in Figure 1.

4.2   Detailed Execution Scenarios

Analysing the interaction among the internal elements of the iFTE, we have identified 12 basic scenarios. These scenarios do not consider the requests that the Abnormal component can do for providing the handling services, which includes its internal requests to the Normal component, and its external requests to the Required.

After a request is made through I_iFTE_PS, the Provided component may respond in two different ways: (i) signals an interface exception through I_iFTE_PE (1st basic scenario); or (ii) requests the respective service of the Normal component from I_P_RS to I_N_PS, mediated by the Coordinator connector. When the Normal component receives a service request, it can behave in three different ways: (i) returns normally to the Provided from I_N_PS to I_P_RS (2nd basic scenario); (ii) signals an internal exception through I_N_PE; or (iii) requests an external service. When the Normal component signals an exception through I_N_PE, the Coordinator connector propagates it to the Abnormal through I_A_RE. After executing the handler, whose behaviour is omitted here, the Abnormal either signals a failure exception through I_A_PE (3rd basic scenario), or return normally through I_A_PS, masking the error (4th basic scenario). When the Normal component requests external services through I_N_RS, the Coordinator propagates the request to the Required through I_R_PS. After this, the Required requests the service for an external element through I_IFTE_RS and can receive two different responses: (i) a normal response through I_IFTE_RS (5th basic scenario); or (ii) an exception through I_IFTE_RE. In the last case, the external exception is propagated to the Abnormal (from I_R_PE to I_A_RE through the Coordinator), which tries to handle it. The Abnormal can provide either a failure exception through I_A_PE (6th basic scenario), or a normal response through I_A_PS, masking the external exception (7th basic scenario).

The other five scenarios where derived from the composition of the seven basic scenarios that were presented. Before the iFTE raises an internal exception, it could have successfully executed an external service (external request followed by an internal exception). In this case, the iFTE can either mask the exception (8th basic scenario), or fail (9th basic scenario). When the Normal requests an external service after it had masked an internal exception, it can receive an exceptional response (masked internal exception followed by an external exception). In this case, the Abnormal component tries to handle it. If the external exception is masked, it constitutes the 10th basic scenario, which masks both internal and external exceptions. If the external exception could not be successfully handled, the Abnormal component returns exceptionally and the iFTE crashes (11th basic scenario). Finally, the 12th basic scenario occurs when although the iFTE could mask an external exception (Scenario 7), it could not mask a following internal one.

5   Formal Specification and Verification of the iFTE

Although the iFTE abstraction has been partially verified in a previous work [17], this verification had used an extended timed automata notation, which has not the sufficient support for verifying the architectural elements in a specific architectural context, considering specific provided and required services and the respective exceptions. Besides, to support the development of component-based software systems, it is necessary to consider the behaviour of different iFTEs connected together into a fault-tolerant software architecture. In order to model and verify the fault-tolerant properties of a software architecture, we have used the combination of B-Method and CSP, supported by the ProB model checker.

As presented in Section 3.2, the combined use of B-Method and CSP provides a way for representing complex states and relationships among the internal elements of the iFTE. Since the internal elements were represented in B-Method through mathematical sets, the relationships among them were naturally represented through relations between sets. Although other formal notations, such as UPPAAL [2], represent internal states, most of them do not provide a way for representing neither types nor relationships among them, what is essential for specifying specific exceptional behaviours, depending on the type of the exception that was raised or propagated. Besides that, although other formalisms, such as SMV [18], reason about types and relations between types, they do not provide an intuitive way to represent specific execution scenarios, what reduces the state explosion necessary for verifying the formal model, and is essential for generating test cases.

5.1 Formal Specification of the iFTE

We have defined two models that can be instantiated for representing an iFTE element: the abstract model, which specify only the external behaviour of the iFTE [7], and the detailed model, which includes the internal elements of the iFTE. Both models are composed of a B-Method machine, which specifies the structural elements of the iFTE, and a CSP behaviour specification, which restricts the interaction among the elements defined in B-Method. Due to space limitations, this paper will present only the detailed model of the iFTE. The abstract model was specified in a similar way [7].

Detailed Model of the iFTE. Figure 3 presents part of the B-Method machine of the detailed model. As it can be seen, the machine explicitly represents the structural characteristic of the iFTE: its internal elements, through the `InternalElements` set (Line 4); its interfaces with the direction of the event (input/output), through the the `InterfaceParts` set (Line 5); the provided and required services of each internal component, through eight sets: a `<component>ProvidedServices` and a `<component>RequiredServices` for each component (Lines 7 to 14), and the respective provided and required exceptions (Lines 16 to 23). Beyond representing the exceptions themselves, it is necessary to relate the exceptions and the services that propagate them. This information is represented through relations from a service to a power set of exceptions (Lines 26 to 33). Finally, since the ProB model checker works through the execution of B-Method operations, the proposed model defines three operations for each normal interface (`I_<component>_PS` and `I_<component>_RS`): a service request, a normal response, and an exceptional response. Operations in Lines 39 to 41 represent a service request to the iFTE (via the Provided internal component) and the respective returns through `I_iFTE_PS` and `I_iFTE_PE` interfaces. Lines 45 to 47 refer to the `I_iFTE_RS` and `I_iFTE_RE` interfaces. Exactly the same occurs with each one of the internal interfaces, but for space limitations, this information was omitted from the figure. Beyond the structural information of the iFTE, the B-Method machine also defines other variables that stores valuable data for verification purpose, for example, the `sequenceHistory` variable stores the order that the B-Method operations where executed, what can be used for identifying the execution scenarios. In the B-Method notation, the types of the variables are represented through invariants. The verification of type violation is proceeded during the model-checking process. But due to space limitations, Figure 3 does not present the variants definition.

As can be seen in Figure 4, using an external choice operator (`[]`), the CSP model defines all the possible combination of executions. For example, Line 3 states that after executing the `IFTE_PS_req` operation for a specific provided service (`PS`), the next operation has to be either an exceptional return (interface

```
 1  MACHINE abstractModel
 2  /* ════════════════════════════════════ */
 3  SETS
 4      InternalElements = {provided, normal, coordinator, abnormal,
            required};
 5      InterfaceParts = {i_ifte_ps_i,i_ifte_ps_o,i_ifte_pe_o,i_p_rs_o,
            i_p_rs_i,i_p_re_i,i_n_ps_i,i_n_ps_o,i_n_pe_o,i_n_rs_o,i_n_rs_i,
            i_n_re_i,i_a_ps_i,i_a_ps_o,i_a_pe_o,i_a_rs_o,i_a_rs_i,i_a_re_i,
            i_r_ps_i,i_r_ps_o,i_r_pe_o,i_ifte_rs_o,i_ifte_rs_i,i_ifte_re_i};
 6
 7      IFTEProvidedServices = {iftePS1,iftePS2};
 8      ProvRequiredServices = {provRS1,provRS2};
 9      NorProvidedServices = {norPS1,norPS2};
10      NorRequiredServices = {norRS1,norRS2};
11      AbnProvidedServices = {abnPS1,abnPS2};
12      AbnRequiredServices = {abnRS1,abnRS2};
13      ReqProvidedServices = {reqPS1,reqPS2};
14      IFTERequiredServices = {ifteRS1,ifteRS2};
15
16      IFTEProvidedExceptions = {iftePE1,iftePE2};
17      ProvRequiredExceptions = {provRE1,provRE2};
18      NorProvidedExceptions = {norPE1,norPE2};
19      NorRequiredExceptions = {norRE1,norRE2};
20      AbnProvidedExceptions = {abnPE1,abnPE2};
21      AbnRequiredExceptions = {norRE1,abnRE2};
22      ReqProvidedExceptions = {reqPE1,reqPE2};
23      IFTERequiredExceptions = {ifteRE1,ifteRE2};
24  /* ════════════════════════════════════ */
25  VARIABLES
26      iftePServiceExceptions, /*relation: IFTEProvidedServices --->
            powerSet(IFTEProvidedExceptions)*/
27      provRServiceExceptions, /*relation: ProvRequiredServices --->
            powerSet(ProvRequiredExceptions)*/
28      norPServiceExceptions,  /*relation: ...*/
29      norRServiceExceptions,  /*relation: ...*/
30      abnPServiceExceptions,  /*relation: ...*/
31      abnRServiceExceptions,  /*relation: ...*/
32      reqPServiceExceptions,  /*relation: ...*/
33      ifteRServiceExceptions, /*relation: ...*/
34      ... /*other variables*/
35      ...
36  /* ════════════════════════════════════ */
37  OPERATIONS
38      /*I_IFTE_PS  &  I_IFTE_PE*/
39  IFTE_PS_req(service) = ...
40  resp <--- IFTE_PS_resp(service) = ...
41  resp <--- IFTE_PE_resp(service) = ...
42      /* INTERNAL INTERFACES*/
43  ... /*not represented*/
44      /*I_IFTE_RS  &  I_IFTE_RE*/
45  IFTE_RS_req(service) = ...
46  resp <--- IFTE_RS_resp(service) = ...
47  resp <--- IFTE_RE_resp(service) = ...
```

Fig. 3. B-Method machine of an iFTE

exception) (Lines 7 and 8 - Scenario 1) or a request for an internal service of the Normal component through the Coordinator connector (Lines 7 and 11). When the Normal receives a service request, it may behaves in three different ways (Line 14): (i) returns normally (Lines 14 and 15); (ii) raises an exception (Lines 14 and 16), or (iii) requests external services through the Coordinator connector (Lines 24 and 19).

```
 1 --SPECIFICATION:
 2 MAIN = Start -> CLIENT;;
 3 CLIENT = (IFTE_PS_req.PS -> PROVIDED(PS) [] Stop -> MAIN);;
 4
 5
 6 -- Client -> Provided
 7 PROVIDED(PS) = (INTERFACE_EXCEPTION [] (P_RS_req.RS ->
     PROVIDED_COORDINATOR(PS,RS)));;
 8 INTERFACE_EXCEPTION = IFTE_PE_resp.PS?E -> Stop -> MAIN;;
 9
10 -- Provided -> Coordinator
11 PROVIDED_COORDINATOR(PS1,RS1) = (N_PS_req.PS -> NORMAL(PS1,RS1,PS));;
12
13 -- Coordinator -> Normal
14 NORMAL(PS1,RS1,PS2) = (NORMAL_NORMAL_REPONSE(PS1,RS1,PS2) []
     NORMAL_RAISES_EXCEPTION(PS1,RS1,PS2) [] (N_RS_req.RS ->
     NORMAL_COORDINATOR(PS1,RS1,PS2,RS)));;
15 NORMAL_NORMAL_REPONSE(PS1,RS1,PS2) = N_PS_resp.PS2 -> P_RS_resp.RS2->
     PROVIDED_ADAPTER;;
16 NORMAL_RAISES_EXCEPTION(PS1,RS1,PS2) = N_PE_resp.PS2?E -> HANDLING_NOR(E
     );; --internal exception
17
18 -- Normal -> Coordinator
19 NORMAL_COORDINATOR = ...
20 ...
```

Fig. 4. CSP specification of an iFTE

After representing the iFTE elements using the detailed model (B-Method and CSP), it is necessary to contextualise these elements together, through the architectural model. This contextualised representation is outside the context of this paper. Details about the architectural models and the verification of exception flow in the software architecture are available elsewhere [7,14].

5.2   Verification Process

Intending to remove faults early in the software development, the verification process consists on two steps, executed sequentially: (i) generate all possible execution scenarios; and (ii) verify the dependability properties of each scenario. First, we extract the scenarios from the model with a specialised tool for this purpose. From the CSP specification and the B-Method machine of an architectural element, a set of other CSP files are generated, one CSP file per scenario. A scenario is a sequence of B-Method operations that starts with a request through the IFTE_PS_req operation, which corresponds to the I_IFTE_PS interface of the Provided internal component, and finishes with the respective response (normal or exceptional). The second step consists on using the ProB model checker for verifying some properties of interest related with fault tolerance. These properties, which are presented in Section 5.3, are verified for the B-Method machine of the software architecture, guided by each one of the CSP scenarios generated in the previous step. The verification of these properties in the ProB model checker consists on trying to find counter examples of scenarios, analysing the content of the sequenceHistory variable of the iFTE model. The sequenceHistory variable is a sequence of three-tuples (interfaceType, service, abnReturn), where interfaceType is determines both the interface and the type of the event (request or response), service is a service that is the objective of the execution, and abnReturn represents the exceptional response of the service request, if it occurs. In case of requests and normal responses, its value is represented as an empty set ({}). In other words, interfacePart ∈ InterfaceParts, service ∈ <component>ProvidedServices ⋃ <component>RequiredServices, and abnReturn ∈ <component>ProvidedExceptions ⋃ <component>RequiredExceptions.

5.3 Verified Properties of Interest

In order to verify the internal integrity of the iFTE, we have specified five general properties (Table 1), which are related to both general and detailed models, and other seven detailed properties (Table 2), which are related only to the detailed model and verify the consistency of the propagation of exceptions among the iFTE internal parts.

Table 1. General properties of an iFTE (both models)

#	Property
1	The instantiation of the iFTE has to be free of deadlocks.
2	All required exceptions (IFTERequiredExceptions) have to be handled by the iFTE.
3	An exception can only be masked, if it is explicitly declared as maskable by the iFTE.
4	For each exception which can be masked, there has to be a scenario that mask it.
5	The iFTE can only signal or propagate external exceptions.

As an example, the general property 2 is specified as follows: "$\forall re \in IFTERequiredExceptions, \exists rs \in IFTERequiredServices \bullet re \in ifteRServiceExceptions(rs)$". In a similar way, the detailed property 1, which states that if there is no exception in the scenario, the Abnormal component cannot participate on it, ratifying the separation of concerns, since the abnormal is only responsible for handling exceptions. Remembering that a_PS_i represents a request of handling to the Abnormal component; ifte_RE_i represents an incoming exception from an external server to the iFTE; and ifte_PE_o represents an outcome exception from the iFTE to an external client, this property was specified as follows: "$\forall s \in <component>ProvidedServices \bigcup <component>RequiredServices, e \in <component>ProvidedExceptions \bigcup <component>RequiredExceptions \bullet ((ifte\_RE\_i, s, e) \notin sequenceHistiry \wedge (ifte\_PE\_o, s, e) \notin sequenceHistory) \Rightarrow (a\_PS\_i, s, e) \notin sequenceHistory$".

Table 2. Detailed properties of an iFTE (detailed model)

#	Property
1	When no exception is caught or thrown by an iFTE, the state of the Abnormal component remains the same (it does not receive any request).
2	After receiving a request, the Coordinator connector does not interact with the Abnormal component before receiving some response from the Normal component.
3	If the Normal component raises an exception that the Abnormal cannot mask, either the iFTE propagates the exception, or converts it.
4	If the Required connector receives an exception that the Abnormal cannot mask, either the iFTE propagates the exception, or converts it.
5	If the Normal component raises an exception that the Abnormal can mask, then it is possible that the Abnormal returns normally to the Coordinator.
6	If the Required connector receives an exception that the Abnormal can mask, then it is possible that the Abnormal returns normally to the Coordinator.
7	Only the Abnormal component may mask or convert exceptions.

6   Test Cases Generation

Test cases generation follows the model-based approach [6,5], and most of which can be automated. All the testing artifacts can be reused each time the component is tested: during its development or each time it is reused. Because of this, the component testing can be performed in a black-box way, allowing test cases reuse even without component source code.

For generating test cases for a provided service of an iFTE, it is necessary to generate a sequence graph, which represents the execution of the internal and required services that the provided service requires, as well as the respective normal and abnormal returns. The graph consists on a graphical representation of the formal models of the iFTE (Section 5.1), which is constructed for each one of its provided services. The nodes of the graph are identified from the B-Method machine, while the edges are identified from the CSP specification. Besides identifying the graph itself (nodes and edges), the proposed approach aims to organise the position of their nodes according to the iFTE structure. For this, it is defined a partition[1] for each interface of the iFTE. Thus, four partitions are defined for the abstract model, and sixteen for the detailed one.

First of all, the provided service that the graph refers is represented as a node of the I_X_PS partition, where X depends on the element whose graph represents: P for Provided, N for Normal, A for Abnormal, R for Required, and IFTE for the abstraction itself. The provided service the root node, which is the starting point for covering the graph. In the same way, each required service that an element needs for executing a provided service is represented as a node of the I_X_RS partition. The subset of required services of a specific provided service is determined by the CSP model. The exceptional returns of these required services are represented as nodes of the I_X_RE partition. About the exceptional

---

[1] Known as swim lane in UML Activity Diagram nomenclature.

returns of the provided service, the nodes are positioned into the I_X_PE partition, and are considered leaf nodes, which is an end point for covering the graph. Because the Coordinator is a connector that refers only to the interfaces of the internal components (it does not define any new interface), after representing the sequence of execution among the four internal components, the behaviour of the Coordinator is immediately represented. Thus, the Coordinator's test cases are generated from the interaction between the I_X_RS and I_X_PS interfaces of the internal components of the iFTE: Provided, Normal, Abnormal, and Required. For example, the execution of a service from I_P_RS followed by a service from I_N_PS indicates that the Coordinator has to mediate the request from the Provided to the Normal component, converting data types when necessary. In the inverse order (I_N_PS → I_P_RS) it indicates that the Coordinator has to mediate a normal response from the Normal to the Provided. Analysing all the sequences between the required and provided services of the internal components, it is possible to generate the test cases of the Coordinator element.

In the sequence graph, the order among the nodes (service request, and the respective returns) is indicated through directional edges, which are derived from the CSP model.

After constructing this graph, we follow the MDCE+ [15] criteria, where each path from the start to a final node is considered a test-case. Besides the identification of the test cases (paths of the graph), this testing artifacts are also useful for deriving stub synchronisation commands, because they illustrate the sequence on which the required services are called, as well as the respective returns of these services. Stubs replace required elements, simulating their behaviour in a controlled way, and making it possible to observe component behaviour under test in normal and exceptional situations related to interactions with required services.

Besides the generation of the test cases, it is necessary to determine the best order for executing them. For this, it is generated other testing artifact: the execution flow graph, which is a dependency graph that illustrates the sequential dependencies among the provided services of an architectural element. Beyond its usefulness for determine the best order for proceeding the test, the execution flow graph also derives test drivers, which execute test cases.

About the testing activities, iFTEs are tested using test cases generated covering the graph presented in this section. In this way, the test cases can either take into consideration the internal elements of the iFTE (its detailed structure), or generate test cases for the abstraction itself, considering only the external interfaces of the iFTE (I_IFTE_PS, I_IFTE_PE, I_IFTE_RS, and I_IFTE_RE).

7   Case Study: Mining Control System

The running example taken into consideration is a simplified version of the control system for a mining environment [29]. The extraction of minerals from a mine produces water and releases methane gas to the air. In addition to extracting minerals, the mining control system is used to drain water from the sump, and to remove air from the mine when the methane level becomes high. The system is composed by three main sub-systems: MineralExtractorController, which controls the extraction of minerals; PumpController, which controls the level of water; and AirExtractorController, which controls the level of methane. When the water reaches a high level, the pump is turned on and the sump is drained until the water reaches a low level. A water flow sensor is able to detect the flow of water in the pipe. However, the pump is situated underground, and for safety reasons it must not start, or continue to run, when the amount of methane in the mine exceeds a safety limit. For controlling the level of methane, there is an air extractor controller that monitors the level of methane inside the mine, and when the level is high an air extractor is switched on to remove air from the mine. The whole system is also controlled from the surface via an operator console that should handle any emergencies raised by the automatic system.

7.1   Software Architecture Specification

Figure 5 presents the software architecture of the mining control system using the UML 2.0 notation; the links between the architectural elements are represented as dependencies. As can be seen, the architecture is composed of eleven components, four of them are sensors: (i) MethaneLevel, which detects the level of methane inside the mine; (ii) AirFlow, which detects the flow of air inside the pipes; (iii) WaterLevel, which detects the level of water inside the mine; and (iv) WaterFlow, which detects the flow of water inside the pipes.

To illustrate the structure of the iFTEs of the software architecture, Figure 6 presents the internal details of the PumpController and Pump architectural elements. As can be seen, in the Required component of the PumpController and the Provided component of the Pump are responsible for enabling the interaction, adapting the received service requests (Provided), and the respective return values (Required).

In this architectural configuration, it is assumed that all the architectural elements are iFTEs, except for the four sensors. The three controllers that were identified (MineralExtractorController, AirExtractorController, and PumpController), have the role of architectural connectors (≪iFTEConnectors≫). Each

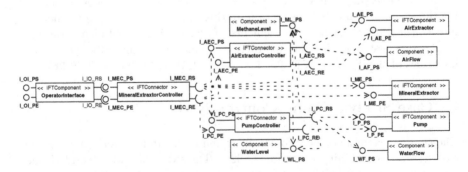

Fig. 5. Architectural Configuration of the Mining Control System

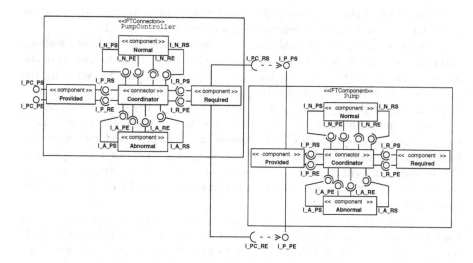

Fig. 6. Partially Detailed View of the Mining Control System Architecture

controller is responsible for dealing with the normal behaviour of the system, and handling any exceptions that are propagated by the components. Depending on the state of the sensors, one of the controllers will be always activated: (i) water low & methane low ⇒ MineralExtractorController; (ii) water high & methane low ⇒ PumpController; and (iii) methane high ⇒ AirExtractorController. In case there is a failure that cannot be handled by the system, this connector has to notify the OperatorInterface element.

It was specified a total of 13 architectural exceptions, which flows between architectural elements (iFTEs and non-iFTEs). For exemplifying the flow of exceptions, in the following, we consider the case in which the AirExtractor fails. When an error is detected inside the AirExtractor, an internal exception is raised and locally handled. If AirExtractor is not able to handle this exception, it propagates an exception to AirExtractorController. Again this component attempts to handle this exception at the role context, but if it fails, it propagates the exception to MileralExtractorController. Since the concentration of methane is high and the AirExtractor has failed, there is nothing that MileralExtractorController can do, except to propagate an exception among its collaborating architectural elements. Upon receiving this exception, the MineralExtractor, the PumpController and the AirExtractorController should shut down their activities, and the OperatorInterface should raise an alarm for the operator to take the appropriate measures.

7.2   Software Architecture Verification

The verification process of the software architecture consists on three activities: (i) verification of the architectural elements that are instantiations of the iFTE; (ii) verification of the software architecture in terms of exception propagation; and (iii) analyses of the results. In the context of this work, we shall detail only the verification of the iFTE elements. The verification of software architectures with many iFTEs connected together is presented elsewhere [7,14].

After instantiating the formal models of the application, we have identified approximately 25 scenarios for each one of the iFTE architectural elements. These scenarios were used to guide the B-Method machine for verifying the properties of interest using ProB. Regarding the software architecture, we have identified approximately 1,000 scenarios, which are not the focus of this paper.

During the verification of the PumpController iFTComponent, the model checker has detected a deadlock, caused by the non declaration of the MethaneLevelSensorFailureException, as an exception that can be propagated. One example of a violation of an exception propagation property was caused by the absence of two handlers (required exceptions) in the MineralExtractorController element.

The verification process took 14 seconds on average for each scenario, in an Intel Pentium 4 computer with 512 MB of RAM, totalising approximately 41 minutes for the seven iFTE architectural elements. After fixing all modelling faults, all properties were satisfied. The verification of the software architecture, with all the elements connected together, took approximately 6 hours [7].

7.3   Test Cases Generation

After modelling the software architecture, we have used the B-Method machine and the CSP specification of the software architecture for generating test cases for iFTEs through the procedure described in Section 6.

Figure 7 presents the execution sequence graph for the controlPumping() service of the PumpController connector. This graph represents only the external exceptions (provided and required) of the iFTE for generating test cases for a black-box testing. Analysing this graph, 22 paths are identified by a depth-first search algorithm, producing 22 test cases.

One of the test cases simulates the MethaneHighPumpOnException throwing. In this case, when the pump is turned on, the stub that simulates the getMethaneLevel() required service was prepared to return the highMethaneLevel. After that, for safety reasons the controller tries to turn off the pump. The stub of the turnOffPump() service was prepared to throw the PumpFailureException exception when the service were called. Because it indicates an emergency exception, the controller informs this warning to the MineralExtractorController connector through the MethaneHighPumpOnException. After executing this scenario, the test oracle has to proceed the contract verification, which checks exception class type and context.

Besides the generation of test cases for unit testing activities, the proposed approach also defines the right order for testing the various services of a component. For example, because the Pump component is initially turned off, its turnOnPump() service should be tested before the turnOffPump() one.

About the integration of the software architecture, it happened in four steps and for that, we have developed four integration graphs, one for each step. To exemplify the identification of integration test cases, for the interaction between the MineralExtractorController and the MineralExtractor elements, we have

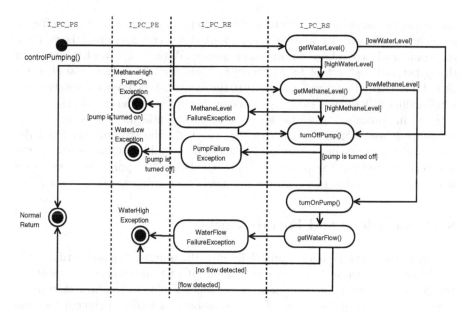

Fig. 7. Part of execution seuence graph for the controlPumping service

identified six test cases: three for the turnOnExtraction() service, and three for
the turnOffExtraction() service of the MineralExtractor component. Due to space
limitations, the interaction graph is not presented in this paper.

7.4   Case Study Evaluation

Above all, the case study has shown that the iFTE can be successfully used in the
specification of complex fault-tolerant systems. Simpler software architectures
can be obtained, first, by abstracting away from the actual system components,
and second, by enforcing a clear separation between the functionalities of the
application, and the exceptions and their respective handlers that are employed
for tolerating faults.

For specifying and verifying the architecture of the system, it was necessary
an effort of about 62.7 developers/hour. It was specified a total of eleven iFTE
elements, totalising eight B-Method machines (43 developers/hour) and a CSP
specification (19 developers/hour), and were spent about 0.7 hours operating
the scenarios tool and the ProB model checker.

During the verification of the software architecture, it was clear the rigorous
process has provided valuable information about the system properties, helping
to identify and correct specification faults of the architecture in earlier stages of
the software development. Although most of these problems are simple to correct,
failures to address them can result in problems that are harder to correct in later
phases of development.

For analysing the scalability of the proposed solution, we have compared it with
the Aereal framework (see Section 2). After generating the Alloy [21] specification of

the case study using Aereal, we have verified exception propagation in the software architecture using the Alloy Analyser [22] tool. However, with Aereal the verification could not be completed due to lack of memory. With the approach presented in this paper, although it took long to verify in ProB, the task was successfully completed. We attribute the best scalability to the scenario-based verification strategy, which sufficiently reduces the state explosion during the model checking activity.

Some limitations of the case study were also identified. First, since all the components were constructed during the case study, the assumptions about the easiness for reusing components to construct dependable software systems was not verified. Second, the proposed approach should be applied in a real case study, where the reuse of software components occurs in a systematic way.

8   Conclusions and Future Work

This paper has presented an approach for formally representing and verifying the idealised fault tolerant architectural element (iFTE), an architectural abstraction for structuring fault-tolerant systems, which is able to handle architectural mismatches in the presence of software component failures. Although the case study used for evaluating the overall approach was a snapshot of a real system, we were able to demonstrate nevertheless that compared with other similar approaches, this work supports an appropriate abstraction for modelling and analysing fault-tolerant software architectures.

Since a limitation of the proposed solution is the lack of concurrency within the architectural abstraction, as future work, we intend to deal with concurrent systems, which have more complex exception handling strategies and resolution of exceptions. The Required component, which is the boundary between an iFTE and its servers is the best place to plays this role. Besides that, because the instantiation of the formal model is an error prone activity, tool support for generating the formal models from a UML component diagram is still central to our work. We also intend to improve the tool support for facilitating the generation of the formal models. The same information used for constructing the sequence graphs of test cases generation can be used, for example, to automatically generate a more complete source code, thus preventing the introduction of faults. Finally, another line of research for a future work is to consider other architectural abstractions for supporting other fault models, for example crash failures.

References

1. Abrial, J.-R.: The B-book: assigning programs to meanings. Cambridge University Press, New York (1996)
2. Amnell, T., Behrmann, G., Bengtsson, J., D'Argenio, P.R., David, A., Fehnker, A., Hune, T., Jeannet, B., Larsen, K.G., Möller, M.O., Pettersson, P., Weise, C., Yi, W.: Uppaal - Now, Next, and Future. In: Cassez, F., Jard, C., Rozoy, B., Ryan, M. (eds.) MOVEP 2000. LNCS, vol. 2067, pp. 100–125. Springer, Heidelberg (2001)

3. Anderson, T., Lee, P.A.: Fault Tolerance: Principles and Practice. Prentice-Hall, Englewood Cliffs (1981)
4. Bass, L., Clements, P.C., Kazman, R.: Software Architecture in Practice, 2nd edn. Addison-Wesley, Reading (2003)
5. Bertolino, A., Marchetti, E., Muccini, H.: Introducing a reasonably complete and coherent approach for model-based testing. Electr. Notes Theor. Comput. Sci. 116, 85–97 (2005)
6. Binder, R.V.: Testing object-oriented systems: models, patterns, and tools. Addison-Wesley Longman Publishing Co., Inc., Redwood City, CA, USA (1999)
7. Brito, P.H.S., de Lemos, R., Martins, E., Rubira, C.M.F.: Verification and validation of a fault-tolerant architectural abstraction. In: DSN Workshop on Architecting Dependable Systems (WADS 2007), Edinburgh, Scotland - UK (Accepted for publication, 2007)
8. Brookes, S.D., Hoare, C.A.R., Roscoe, A.W.: A theory of communicating sequential processes. J. ACM 31(3), 560–599 (1984)
9. Castor Filho, F., Cacho, N., Figueiredo, E., Ferreira, R., Garcia, A., Rubira, C.M.F.: Exceptions and aspects: The devil is in the details. In: Proceedings of the 14th ACM SIGSOFT FSE, pp. 152–162 (November 2006)
10. Castor Filho, F., da Silva Brito, P.H., Rubira, C.M.F.: Specification of exception flow in software architectures. Journal of Systems and Software (October 2006)
11. Castor Filho, F., de Castro Guerra, P.A., Rubira, C.M.F.: An architectural-level exception-handling system for component-based applications. In: de Lemos, R., Weber, T.S., Camargo Jr., J.B. (eds.) LADC 2003. LNCS, vol. 2847, pp. 321–340. Springer, Heidelberg (2003)
12. Clements, P., et al.: Documenting Software Architectures: Views and Beyond. Addison-Wesley, Reading (2003)
13. Cristian, F.: Exception handling. In: Dependability of Resilient Computers, pp. 68–97. Blackwell (1989)
14. da Silva Brito, P.H., de Lemos, R., Filho, F.C., Rubira, C.M.F.: Architecture-centric fault tolerance with exception handling. Technical Report IC-07-04. State University of Campinas (February 2007)
15. Brito, P.H.S., Rocha, C.R., Castor Filho, F., Martins, E., Rubira, C.M.F.: A method for modeling and testing exceptions in component-based software development. In: Maziero, C.A., Silva, J.G., Andrade, A.M.S., Assis Silva, F.M.d. (eds.) LADC 2005. LNCS, vol. 3747, pp. 61–79. Springer, Heidelberg (2005)
16. de Castro Guerra, P.A., Rubira, C., de Lemos, R.: A fault-tolerant software architecture for component-based systems. In: de Lemos, R., Gacek, C., Romanovsky, A. (eds.) Architecting Dependable Systems. LNCS, vol. 2677, pp. 129–149. Springer, Heidelberg (2003)
17. de Lemos, R., de Castro Guerra, P.A., Rubira, C.M.F.: A fault-tolerant architectural approach for dependable system. IEEE Software 23(2), 80–87 (2006)
18. McMillan, K.L.: The SMV system. Technical Report CMU-CS-92-131, Carnegie Mellon University (1992)
19. Gray, J., Reuter, A.: Transaction Processing: Concepts and Techniques. Morgan Kaufmann, San Francisco (1993)
20. Issarny, V., Banatre, J.P.: Architecture-based exception handling. In: Proceedings of the 34th Annual Hawaii International Conference on System Sciences (2001)
21. Jackson, D.: Alloy: a lightweight object modelling notation. Software Engineering and Methodology 11(2), 256–290 (2002)

22. Jackson, D., Schechter, I., Shlyahter, H.: Alcoa: the alloy constraint analyzer. In: ICSE '00: Proceedings of the 22nd international conference on Software engineering, pp. 730–733. ACM Press, New York (2000)
23. Lee, P.A., Anderson, T.: Fault Tolerance: Principles and Practice. In: Dependable computing and fault-tolerant systems, 2nd edn., Springer, Berlin, New York (1990)
24. Leuschel, M., Butler, M.J.: Prob: A model checker for b. In: Araki, K., Gnesi, S., Mandrioli, D. (eds.) FME 2003. LNCS, vol. 2805, pp. 855–874. Springer, Heidelberg (2003)
25. Parnas, D.L., Würges, H.: Response to undesired events in software systems. In: Proceedings of the 2nd International Conference on Software Engineering, San Francisco, USA, pp. 437–446 (October 1976)
26. Randell, B.: System structure for software fault tolerance. IEEE Transactions on Software Engineering 1(2), 221–232 (1975)
27. Reimer, D., Srinivasan, H.: Analyzing exception usage in large java applications. In: Cardelli, L. (ed.) ECOOP 2003. LNCS, vol. 2743, Springer, Heidelberg (2003)
28. Schneider, S., Treharne, H.: Communicating b machines. In: Bert, D., Bowen, J.P., Henson, M.C., Robinson, K. (eds.) B 2002 and ZB 2002. LNCS, vol. 2272, pp. 416–435. Springer, Heidelberg (2002)
29. Sloman, M., Kramer, J.: Distributed systems and computer networks. Prentice Hall International (UK) Ltd, Hertfordshire, UK (1987)
30. Taylor, R.N., Medvidovic, N., Anderson, K., Whitehead, J.E.J., Robbins, J.: A component- and message- based architectural style for GUI software. In: Proceedings of the 17th International Conference on Software Engineering, pp. 295–304 (April 1995)
31. Weimer, W., Necula, G.: Finding and preventing run-time error handling mistakes. In: Proceedings of OOPSLA'2004, Vancouver, Canada, pp. 419–433 (October 2004)

Coverage-Oriented, Prioritized Testing – A Fuzzy Clustering Approach and Case Study

Fevzi Belli[1], Mubariz Eminov[2], and Nida Gökçe[2,3]

[1] Department of Computer Science, Electrical Engineering and Mathematics,
University of Paderborn, Germany
belli@upb.de
[2] Faculty of Arts and Sciences, Department of Statistics, Mugla University, Turkey
{gnida,meminov}@mu.edu.tr
[3] on leave at the Department of Computer Science, Electrical Engineering and Mathematics,
University of Paderborn, Germany

Abstract. Existing test techniques focus on particular, relevant aspects of the requirements of the system under test (SUT). Real-life SUTs have, however, numerous features to simultaneously be considered, often leading to a large number of tests. In such cases, because of time and cost constraints the entire set of tests cannot be run. It is then essential to prioritize the tests in sense of a ordering of the relevant events entailed in accordance with the importance of their numerous features. This paper proposes a graph-model-based approach to prioritizing the test process. Tests are ranked according to their preference degrees which are determined indirectly, i.e., through classifying the events. To construct the groups of events, Fuzzy c-Means (FCM) clustering algorithm is used. A case study demonstrates and validates the approach. Contrary to other approaches, no prior information is needed about the tests carried out before, e.g., as is case in regression testing.

Keywords: Software Testing, Test Prioritizing, Fuzzy Clustering.

1 Introduction: Motivation and Related Work

Testing is one of the important, traditional analytical techniques of quality assurance in the software industry. There is no justification, however, for any assessment of the correctness of software under test (SUT) based on the success (or failure) of a single test, because potentially there can be an infinite number of test cases. To overcome this principle shortcoming of testing concerning completeness of the validation, formal methods have been proposed. Those methods use models to visualize the relevant, desirable features of the SUT. The modeled features are either functional behavior or structural issues of the SUT, leading to *specification-oriented* testing or *implementation-oriented* testing, respectively. Once the model is established, it "guides" the test process to generate and select test cases, which form sets of test cases (also called *test suites*). The test selection is ruled by an *adequacy criterion*, which provides a measure of how effective a given set of test cases is in terms of its potential to reveal faults [1, 16]. Some of the existing adequacy criteria are

A. Bondavalli, F. Brasileiro, and S. Rajsbaum (Eds.): LADC 2007, LNCS 4746, pp. 95–110, 2007.

coverage-oriented. They use the ratio of the portion of the specification or code that is covered by the given test set in relation to the uncovered portion in order to determine the point in time at which to stop testing (*test termination problem*).

The test approach introduced in this paper is specification - and coverage - oriented. The underlying model graphically represents the system behavior interacting with the user's actions. In this context, *event sequence graphs* (*ESG*, [5-7]) are favored. ESG approach view the system's behavior and user's actions as events, more precisely, as *desirable events* if they are in accordance with the user expectations, otherwise they are *undesirable*. Mathematically speaking, a complementary view of the behavioral model is generated from the model given which explains the advantage of the ESG approach: The model will be exploited twice, i.e., once to validate the system behavior under regular conditions and a second time to test its robustness under irregular, unexpected conditions.

The costs of testing often tend to run out the limits of the test budget. In those cases, the tester may request a complete test suite and attempt to run as many tests as affordable, without running out the budget. Therefore, it is important to test the most important items first. This leads to the *Test Case Prioritization Problem* a formal definition of which is represented in [3] as follows:

> *Given:* A test suite T;
>
> The set PT of permutations of T;
>
> A function f from PT to the real numbers which represents the preference of the tester while testing.

Problem: Find $T' \in PT$ such that $(\forall T'') (T'' \neq T') [f(T') \geq f(T'')]$

Existing approaches to solving this problem usually suggest constructing a density covering array in which all pair-wise interactions are covered [2, 3]. Generally speaking, every n-tuple is then qualified by a number $n \in N$ (N : set of natural numbers) of values to each of which a *degree of importance* is assigned. In order to capture significant interactions among pairs of choices the importance of pairs is defined as the "benefit" of the tests. Every pair covered by the test contributes to the total benefit of a test suite by its individual benefit. Therefore, the tests given by a test suite are to be ordered according to the importance of corresponding pairs. However, such interaction-based, prioritized algorithms are computationally complex and thus mostly less effective [18, 19].

The ESG approach we favor in this paper generates test suites through a finite sequence of discrete events. The underlying optimization problem is a generalization of the *Chinese Postman Problem* (*CPP*) [8] and algorithms given in [5-7] differ from the well-known ones in that they satisfy not only the constraint that a minimum total length of test sequences is required, but also fulfill the coverage criterion with respect to converging of all event pairs represented graphically. This is substantial to solve the test termination problem and makes out a significant difference of this present paper from existing approaches. To overcome the problem that an exhaustive testing might be infeasible, the paper develops a *prioritized* version of the mentioned test generation and optimization algorithms, in sense of "divide and conquer" principle. This is the primary objective and the kernel of this paper which is novel and thus, to our knowledge, has not yet been worked out in previous work, including ours [5-7, 15].

The required prioritization has to schedule the test process, i.e., to meet the needs and preferences of test management how to spend the test budget. However, SUT and software objects, i.e., components, architecture, etc., usually have a great variety of features. Therefore, test prioritization entails the determination of order relation(s) for these features. Generally speaking, we have n objects, whereby each object has a number (p) of features that we call *dimension*. Test prioritization problem then represents the comparison of test objects with different, multiple dimensions. This is the further, important feature which differs the optimization approach presented in this paper, i.e., none of the existing approaches take the fact into account that SUT usually has a set of attributes and not a single one when prioritizing the test process. This is a tough, *np*-complete problem to solve in general.

The testing capacity of the algorithm developed in this paper is of less complexity than the ones known from literature and provides the ordering of the implementation of the tests to be run. To be more specific, to each of the tests generated a degree of its preference is assigned. This degree is indirectly determined through estimation of the events qualified by several attributes. These attributes depend on the features of the project and their values are justified by their significance to the user. We give some examples how to define such attributes and assign values to them, based on the ESG representation of corresponding events. We suggest to represent those events as an unstructured multidimensional data set and to divide them into groups which correspond to their importance. Beforehand, the optimal number of groups of events should be determined, in advance. For this aim, we use criterion V_{sv} *based cluster validity algorithm* [13, 14]. To derive the groups of events, Fuzzy c-Means (FCM) clustering algorithm is employed [12].

A last, but not least feature of the approach represented here is no prior information is needed about the tests carried out before, e.g., as is case in regression testing.

The paper is organized as follows. Section 2 explains the background of the approach, presenting also the definition of FCM to partition a data set into the different groups. Section 3 describes the proposed prioritized graph-based testing approach. Section 4 includes the case study. Section 5 summarizes the results, gives hints to further research and concludes the paper.

2 Modeling and Clustering

2.1 Event Sequence Graphs for Test Generation

Because the previous papers of the first author ([5-7, 15]) sufficiently explain the construction of ESG, test generation from ESGs, and test process optimization, only a brief introduction into ESG concept is given that is necessary and sufficient to understand the test prioritization approach represented in this paper.

Basically, an *event* is an externally observable phenomenon, such as an environmental or a user stimulus, or a system response, punctuating different stages of the system activity. A simple example of an ESG is given in Fig1. Mathematically, an ESG is a directed, labeled graph and may be thought of as an ordered pair $ESG = (\alpha, E)$, where α is a finite set of nodes (vertices) uniquely labeled by some input symbols of the alphabet Σ, denoting events, and $E: \alpha \rightarrow \alpha$, a precedence relation, possibly empty, on α. The elements of E represent directed arcs (edges) between the nodes in α. Given two nodes a and b in α, a directed arc ab from a to b signifies that event b can follow event a, defining an *event pair* (*EP*) ab (Fig. 1). The remaining pairs given by the alphabet Σ, but not in the ESG, form the set of *faulty event pairs* (*FEP*), e.g., ba.

As a convention, a dedicated, start vertex e.g., [, is the *entry* of the ESG whereas a final vertex e.g.,] represents the *exit*. These *pseudo vertices* are not included in Σ; therefore, the arcs from and to them form neither EP nor FEP; they are *pseudo arcs*.

The set of FEPs constitutes the *complement* of the given ESG ($\overline{ESG}$ in Fig 1).

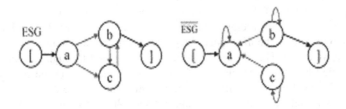

Fig.1. An event sequence graph ESG and $\overline{ESG}$ as the complement of the given ESG

Because the construction of ESG, test generation from ESG and $\overline{ESG}$, and test process optimization are sufficiently explained in the literature ([5-7, 15]), the present paper summarizes ESG concept and are informally introduces some definitions, as far as they are necessary and sufficient to understand the test prioritization approach represented in this paper.

A sequence of $n+1$ consecutive events that represents the sequence of n arcs is called an *event sequence* (*ES*) *of the length* $n+1$, e.g., an *EP* (*event pair*) is an ES of length 2. An ES is *complete* if it starts at the initial state of the ESG and ends at the final event; in this case it is called a *complete ES* (*CES*). Occasionally, we call CES also *walks* (or *paths*) through the ESG given. Accordingly, a *faulty event sequence* (*FES*) *of the length* n consists of $n-1$ subsequent events that form an ES of length $n-2$ plus a concluding, subsequent FEP. An FES is *complete* if it starts at the initial state of the ESG; in this case it is called *faulty complete ES*, abbreviated as *FCES*. A FCES must not necessarily end at the final event.

2.2 Fuzzy Cluster Analysis

Fuzzy cluster analysis is used for partitioning a given set of data or objects into clusters (subsets, group, and classes). This partition should be homogeneous within clusters and heterogeneous between clusters [21]. Since only crisp measurements are used, data would be vectors of real numbers, forming a set of objects $X = (x_1, x_2, \dots x_p) \in \mathbf{R}^p$. The Euclidean distance between data is used as a measure of the dissimilarity.

The set of objects X is partitioned into c fuzzy clusters. Non-exclusive fuzzy clusters are dealt as a fuzzy subset of the objects, i.e., the partition of a set of n objects (*patterns*) into c clusters $1 \leq i \leq c$ is represented by a n×c matrix U (or u_{ik}, where $u_{ik} \in$

[0,1] is the membership degree of datum x_k to cluster i, see [20]). This partition is referred to as *c-means fuzzy (probabilistic) clustering* with following feature:

$$\sum_{k=1}^{n} u_{ik} > 0 \quad \text{for all } i \in \{1,...,c\},$$

$$\sum_{i=1}^{c} u_{ik} = 1 \quad \text{for all } k \in \{1,...,n\} \tag{1}$$

Fuzzy c-means algorithm (FCM) as a fuzzy version of hard c-means as introduced in [9] and improved by "fuzzifier m" in [10]. FCM recognizes spherical clouds of points (datum) in p-dimensional space. Each cluster here is represented by its centre, called a *prototype*, as a representative of data assigned to the cluster.

Main issue in the fuzzy cluster analysis is to obtain the optimal assignment of data to clusters, in other words, the choice of the optimal prototypes for data given. This is usually carried out by means of the cluster algorithm for minimizing the objective function [22, 23]:

$$J (X, U, V) = \sum_{i=1}^{c} \sum_{k=1}^{n} (u_{ik})^m d^2 (v_i, x_k) \tag{2}$$

provided that no cluster is completely empty. Let X be the data with $X = \{x_1, x_2,... x_n\}$ $\in \mathbf{R}^p$, c be the number of fuzzy clusters, $u_{ik} \in [0,1]$ is membership degree of datum x_k to cluster i, $v_I \in \mathbf{R}^p$ be the prototype for cluster I, and d (v_i, x_k) be the Euclidian distance between prototype v_i and datum x_k. The parameter $1 < m$ is called *fuzziness index* which is usually chosen m = 2.

The quadratic distance of the data to the prototypes $d_{ik} = \| x_k - v_i \|$, weighted with their membership degrees, is used for minimizing (2). The prototypes of the cluster centers v_i, are calculated as, with the condition to have a local minimum.

$$v_i = \frac{\sum_{k=1}^{n} (u_{ik})^m x_k}{\sum_{k=1}^{n} (u_{ik})^m} \tag{3}$$

After randomly initialization of the partition matrix (u_{ik}), the prototypes v_i and new matrix (u_{ik}) are updated according to (3) at each optimization step as follows [11]:

$$u_{ik} = \frac{1}{\sum_{j=1}^{c} (d^2 (v_i, x_k) / d^2 (v_j, x_k))^{2/(m-1)}} \tag{4}$$

This procedure is iterated until successive approximation $\| v^{(t-1)} - v^{(t)} \| \leq \varepsilon$ is satisfied.

If the number of clusters (hence the number of classes) is not known in advance, the key problem is to determine the optimal number of clusters (unsupervised classification). In this case, for each $c \in \{2,3,..c_{max}\}$, the fuzzy cluster analysis has to find an optimal partition of data with respect to the new corresponding objective function according to (2) which is regarded as a validity function because it decreases by increasing c. The present approach uses the V_{sv} *index-based cluster validity algorithm* [14] for determining the optimal number c of groups in following steps:

> *Step 1.* Initialize U=[u_{ij}] matrix, $U^{(0)}$
> *Step 2.* Calculate the centers vectors $V^{(k)}$=[v_j] by (3)
> *Step 3.* Update $U^{(t)}$, $U^{(t+1)}$ by (4)
> *Step 4.* If $\| U^{(t+1)} - U^{(t)} \| < \varepsilon$ then Stop; otherwise return to Step 2.

Classification. After applying FCM algorithm, each data point belongs to all clusters with different membership degree, however, a unique assignment of data points is required for solving classification problem. A data point will be assigned to the cluster for which its membership value is maximal. This process is called *defuzzification* applying of which for all data points a class (group) S_i is constructed by following equation:

$$S_i = \left\{ \; x_k \Big| u_{ik} > u_{jk} , i \neq j \; \; i=1,...,c \right\} \tag{5}$$

Therefore, the fuzzy qualified groups S_i, i =1,..,c of events x_k, k=1,...,n, are obtained within which membership value of kth event will be

$$\mu_{S_i} (x_k) = \sup \left\{ u_{ik} \; i = 1, ..., c; k = 1, ..., n \; \right\} \tag{6}$$

To estimate groups on their importance degree, the length of center vectors v_1, v_2 , v_c are used that is based on the rule: the greater the value of attributes the more important the group.

Computational time for classification of events increases with the number n of the events and the number p of their attributes.

3   Prioritized ESG-Based Testing

Our approach is model-based; for test generation a set of ESGs are constructed which represent a discrete model of SUT. Those ESGs constitute the input to the test algorithms introduced in [5, 7] which use following coverage criteria for generating tests for the given set of ESG. In case other models are available, e.g., statecharts, which might have been produced in early stages of the software development process, they can be used accordingly to generate test cases as known from the literature. Thus, our test prioritization approach is applicable to any formal test generation technique. Following, we demonstrate our approach using ESG concept.

   a)   Cover all event pairs in the ESG.

   b)   Cover all faulty event pairs derived by the $\overline{ESG}$.

Note that a test suite which satisfies the first criterion consists of CESs while a test suite which satisfies the second consists of FCESs. These algorithms are able to provide the following constraints:

a) The sum of the lengths of the generated CESs should be minimal.
b) The sum of the lengths of the generated FCESs should be minimal.

The constraints on total lengths of the tests generated enable a considerable reduction in the cost of the test execution and thus the algorithms mentioned above can be referred to as the relatively efficient ones. However, as stated in Section 1 (Introduction), an entire test suite generated may not be executed due to limited project budget. Such circumstances entail ordering all tests to be checked and exercised as far as they do not exceed the test budget. To solve the test prioritizing problem, several algorithms have been introduced [1, 2]. Usually, during the test process for each *n-tuple* (in particular pair-wise) interaction a degree of importance is computationally determined and assigned to the corresponding test case. However, this kind of prioritized testing is computationally complex and hence restricted to deal with short test cases only. Our prioritized testing approach is based on the ESG-based testing algorithms mentioned above.

Note that our test suite consists of CESs which starts at the entry of the ESG and end of its exit, representing *walks (paths)* through the ESG under consideration. This assumption enables to order the generated tests, i.e., CESs. Test suites considered here consist of CESs which starts at the entry of the ESG and end of its exit, representing *walks (paths)* through the ESG. This assumption enables to order the generated tests, i.e., CESs. Test suites that cover $\overline{ESG}$ consists of FCESs are handled accordingly.

The ordering of the CESs is in accordance with their importance degree which is defined indirectly i.e., by estimation of events that are the nodes of ESG and represent objects (modules, components) of SUT. For this aim, firstly events are presented as a *multidimensional event vector* $x_i = (x_1, ..., x_p)$ where p is the *number of attributes*.

Then, a data set $X = \left\{ x_1, ..., x_n \right\} \subset R^p$ is constructed where n is the number of events, which being an unstructured one is divided into c groups The optimal number of groups are determined in advance by using the *cluster validity algorithm*, as described in [13,14]. The groups are constructed by using FCM clustering algorithm and then classification procedure as explained in the previous section 2.2. Afterwards, these groups are ordered on the importance degree according to length of their corresponding center vector. Finally, the CESs are ordered, scaling their preference degrees based on the events which incorporate the importance group(s). We assume that the behavior of the SUT is correctly specified, i.e., only CESs constructed are analyzed. Additionally, we deal with minimal length of the ES to be covered, i.e., pair-wise coverage is the termination criterion.

Importance (Imp(e)) of kth event in depending on importance degree of the group is defined as follows:

$$\text{Imp}(x_k) = c - \text{ImpD}(S_i) + 1 \tag{7}$$

where c is the optimal number of the groups; $ImpD(S_i)$ is defined by means of the importance degree of the group S_i the kth event belongs to.

Finally, choosing the events with their degree of membership from the ordered groups, a ranking of CESs (walks) is formed according to their descending preference degrees beginning from maximal one. The assignment of preference degrees to CESs is based on the rule that is given as follows:

a)   The CES under consideration has the highest degree if it contains the events which belong to the "top" group(s) with utmost importance degrees, i.e., that is placed within the highest part of group ordering.

b)   The CES under consideration has the lowest degree if it contains the events which belong to the group(s) that are within the lowest part of the "bottom" group(s) with least importance degree i.e., that is placed within the lowest part of group ordering.

Therefore, the preference degree of CES can be defined by taking into account both the importance of events (see 7) and the frequency of occurrence of   event(s) within them that is formulated as follows:

$$\text{PrefD}(CES_q) = \sum_{k=1}^{n} \text{Imp}(x_k)\, \mu_{s_i}(x_k)\, f_q(x_k) \quad i=1,..,c \quad q=1,...,r \quad i,q \in i \quad (8)$$

where r is the number of CESs, $Imp(x_k)$ is importance degree of the kth event (see (7)), $\mu_{s_i}(x_k)$ is membership degree of the kth event belonging to the group S_i, and $f_q(x_k)$ is frequency of occurrence of event k^{th} within CE_q.

Indirect Determination of the Preference:

Step 1. Construction of a set of events $X = \left\{ x_{ij} \right\}$ where $i = 1,...,n$; $i \in N$ is an event index, and $j = 1,..., p$; $j \in N$ is an attribute index.

Step 2. Clustering the events using FCM algorithm (see Section 2.2).

Step 3. Classification of the events into fuzzy qualified c groups (Section 2.2).

Step 4. Determination of importance degrees of groups according to length (ℓ) of center vectors,

*Step 5.*Determination of importance degrees of event in groups (see (7), this section)

Step 6. An ordering of the CESs for prioritizing the test process.

This order determines the *preference degree* $(PrefD(CES_q))$ of CESs as test cases (see (8), in present section).

Example for Qualifying and Quantifying the Attributes: To exemplify the approach for qualifying an event corresponding to a node in ESG, we introduce nine attributes ($p=9$) that determine the *dimension* of a data point represented in a data set.

x_1: The number of FEPs connected to the node under consideration (takes the number of all potential faulty events entailed by the event given into account).

x_2 :The number of nodes (events) which are directly and indirectly reachable from an event except entry and exit (indicates its "traffic" significance).

x_3 :The averaged frequencies of the usage of event ($Avrf(x)$) within the CESs (determines the averaged occurrence of each event within all CESs). This attribute is formulated as follows:

$$\text{Avrf}(x_k) = \frac{1}{d}\left(\sum_{q=1}^{r} \frac{f_q(x_k)}{l(CES_q)} \right) \quad q=1,...,r \in N \quad k=1,...,n \in N \quad d \in N \tag{9}$$

where $f_q(x_k)$ is frequency of occurrence of event k^{th} within CES_q and $l(CES_q)$ is length of qth CES_q, d is determined that events belonging to number of CESs as $d \leq r$.

x_4 : The *balancing degree* determines balancing a node as the sum of all incoming edges (as plus (+)) and outgoing edges (as minus (-)) for a given node.

x_5 : The number of incoming and outgoing edges (invokes usage density of a node, i.e., an event).

x_6: The number of nodes (events) of a sub-node as sub-menus that can be reached from this node (maximum number of sub-functions that can be invoked further).

x_7 : The total number of occurrences of an event (a node) within all CESs, i.e., walks (significance of an event).

x_8 : The maximum number of nodes to the entry [(its maximum distance in terms of events to the entry).

x_9 : The number of sub-windows to reach an event from the entry [(gives its distance to the beginning).

The attributes x1 to x9 listed above are arbitrarily chosen examples. Any user (i.e., tester) can extend, or reduce the list, in accordance with his or her preferences.

4 A Case Study

Based on the web-based system ISELTA (*Isik's System for Enterprise-Level Web-Centric Tourist Applications*), we now present a case study to validate the testing approach presented in the previous sections [15].

Both the construction of ESGs and generation of test cases from have been explained in the previous papers of the first author [5-7]. Therefore, the case study, which has not been published anywhere, concentrates on test prioritizing problem.

ISELTA has been developed by our group in cooperation with a commercial enterprise to market various tourist services for traveling, recreation and vacation. It can be used by hotel owners, travel agents, etc., but also by end consumers. A screenshot in Figure 2 demonstrates the process of definition and reservation of rooms of different

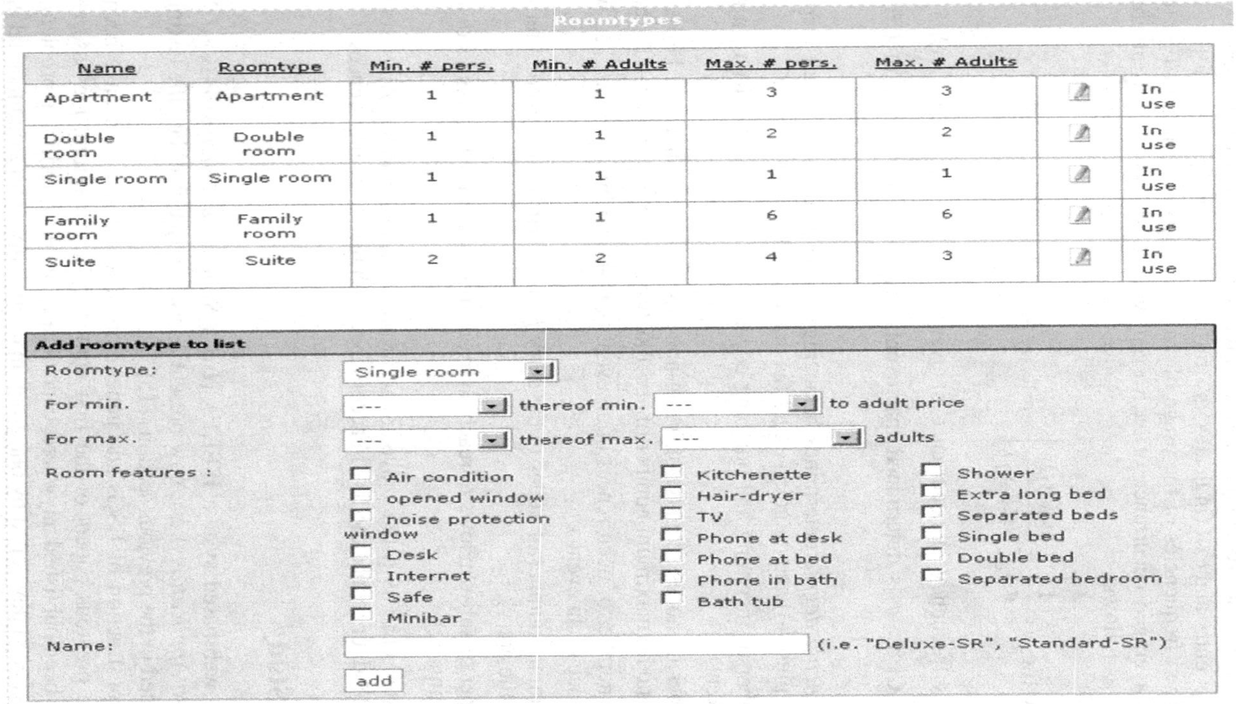

Fig. 2. Room definition/reservation process in ISELTA and ESG of this system

ESG

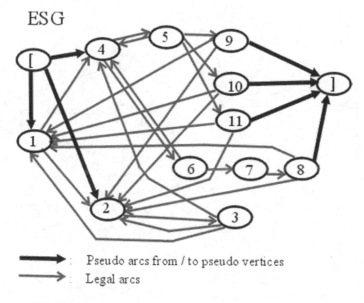

➤ : Pseudo arcs from / to pseudo vertices
→ : Legal arcs

Fig. 3. ESG of Room definition/reservation process in ISELTA

types. The bottom part of the screenshot defines different types of rooms, e.g., double room, single room, etc. and their features, e.g., air condition, kitchenette, etc. The top portion (in this example: two lines at the top, the second of which is highlighted) displays the status and steps of the working process. As an example, the first line summarizes the situation that a double room has already been selected for two adults with no (0, zero) children. The high-lighted, second line represents the ongoing booking process: A single room for one person has just been selected. In any case, a minimum of one person is required to continue the process.

ESG of the ISELTA Application and its Complement: Fig.3 depicts the ESG of the scenario described room definition/reservation process in ISELTA. The complement of this ESG is given in Fig.4.

The identifiers of the nodes of the Fig.3 and Fig.4 are abbreviated by numbers; these numbers and their meanings are given in the following list.

Legend of the Fig.3 and 4 (the inscriptions of the nodes, in order of their numbering)

1: Click on "Starting"
2: Click on "Registering"
3: Registering carried out
4: Click on "log in"
5: Logged in
6: Click on "Pass word forgotten"

7: Pass word forgotten
8: Click on "Request"
9: Indicate service(s) offered
10: Indicate administrator
11: Indicate agent

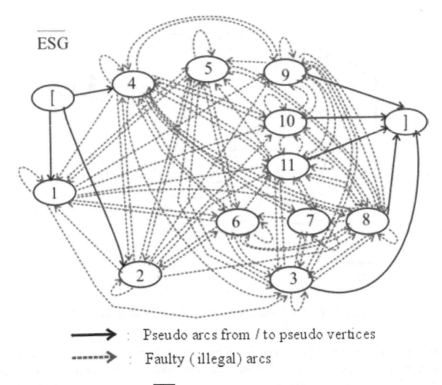

ESG

$\longrightarrow$: Pseudo arcs from / to pseudo vertices

$\dashrightarrow$: Faulty (illegal) arcs

Fig. 4. $\overline{ESG}$ as the complement of ESG of Fig.3.

Derivation of the Test Cases: Test cases can now be generated using the algorithms mentioned in Section 3 and described in [6, 7] in detail. For the lack of space, reference is made to these papers and the CESs generated are listed below:

Table 1. List of CESs

CES₁	CES₂	CES₃	CES₄	CES₅
[4 5 4 5 9 1 4 5 10 1 4 5 11 1 4 5 9 2 3 4 5 10 2 3 2 3 1 4 5 11 2 3 4 6 4 6 7 8 1 2 3]	[1 4 5 9]	[2 3 4 6 7 8 2 3 4 5 10]	[4 5 11]	[4 6 7 8]

Determination of Attributes of Events: As a follow-on step, each event, i.e., the corresponding node in the ESG, is represented as a multidimensional data point using the values of all nine attributes as defined in the previous section. Estimating by means of the ESG and $\overline{ESG}$, the values of attributes for all events are determined and the data set is constructed as follows in Table 2.

Construction of the Groups of Events: For the data set gained from the case study (Fig.2,3), the optimal number c of the groups is determined to be 5 which leads to the groups S_i, i=1,…,5. Importance degrees ($ImpD(S_i)$) of obtained groups are determined by comparing the length of their center vectors (ℓ), and all $ImpD(S_i)$ values that are presented in Table 3.

Table 2. Data set of events

Event No & Attributes	1	2	3	4	5	6	7	8	9	10	11
x_1	8	9	11	7	9	7	9	10	9	9	9
x_2	10	10	10	10	10	10	10	10	10	10	10
x_3	0,19	0,15	0,15	0,25	0,21	0,22	0,12	0,12	0,15	0,07	0,19
x_4	4	6	-3	3	-3	-1	0	-2	-2	-2	-2
x_5	8	8	5	7	5	3	2	4	4	4	4
x_6	0	0	6	0	0	0	0	0	30	0	0
x_7	6	7	7	14	10	4	3	3	3	3	3
x_8	39	40	41	35	29	36	37	38	17	22	30
x_9	1	1	2	1	2	2	3	4	3	3	3

Table 3. Obtained groups of events

	Groups			*Length of Center Vectors* (ℓ)
No	*Importance Degrees*	*Events*	*Membership Degrees*	
S_1	1	8	0,9948	3,4112
S_2	3	3	0,3036	1,896
		5	0,9589	
S_3	4	6	0,4896	1,4313
		7	0,5728	
		11	0,6769	
S_4	2	1	0,9414	3,132
		2	0,8781	
		4	0,4056	
S_5	5	9	0,7918	0,8819
		10	0,8297	

Indirect Determination of the Preference Degrees: As mentioned in the previous section, the preference degree of the CESs is determined indirectly by (7) that depends on the importance degree of the event (see (8)), membership degree of the kth event belonging to the group S_i and frequency of event(s) within CES. The ranking of the CESs (walks) is represented in Table 4.

Exercising the test cases (CESs, or walks) in this order ensure that the most important tests will be carried out first. In the case when the test budget is exhausted before all tests are done, i.e., after the performance of the CES_3, the tester can be sure that the tests performed up to that test CES_3 are more significant than the remaining ones, i.e., CES_4 and CES_5, subject to the attributes x_1 to x_9.

Table 4. Ranking of CESs (walks)

Preference		CESs	
Degree	PrefD(CES_q) (8)	No	Walks
1	11,1183	CES_1	[4 5 4 5 9 1 4 5 10 1 4 5 11 1 4 5 9 2 3 4 5 10 2 3 2 3 1 4 5 11 2 3 4 6 4 6 7 8 1 2 3]
2	8,0061	CES_3	[2 3 4 6 7 8 2 3 4 5 10]
3	1,9504	CES_5	[4 6 7 8]
4	0,7894	CES_2	[1 4 5 9]
5	0,7251	CES_4	[4 5 11]

Moreover, the achieved ranking of CESs complies with the tester's view. Thus, an ordering of the complete set of CESs (walks) is determined using the test suite generated by the test process, i.e., we now have a ranking of test cases to make the decision which test cases are to be primarily tested.

Undesirable events can be handled in a similar way; therefore, we skip the construction of ranking of the FCES.

5 Conclusions and Future Work

Graph-based testing algorithms are popular to generate software test suites to fulfill various criteria, e.g., concerning minimal total length of the test sequences required for a complete coverage to minimize test costs. In this paper, test capacity of these algorithms is improved by prioritizing the test process.

The model-based, coverage-and specification-oriented approach described in this paper provides a novel and effective algorithm for ordering the test cases according to their degree of preference. Such degrees are determined indirectly through the use of the events specified by several attributes, and not a single one. Furthermore, no prior knowledge about the tests carried out before is needed. Those are important issues and consequently, the approach introduced radically differs from the existing ones.

The relevant attributes are visualized by means of graphical representation (here, given as a set of both ESGs, their complements (FESGs), and complemented ESGs (CESGs)). The events (nodes of ESG) are classified by using FCM clustering algorithm and applying defuzzification procedure. The approach is useful when an ordering of the tests due to restricted budget and time is required. Run-time complexity of this approach is of $o(n^2)$, assuming that the number of events (n) greater than the number of attributes (p), otherwise it is $o(p^2)$.

The deployment of ESGs is not strictly necessary to apply our prioritizing approach. We used here this event-based modeling because we observed that event-based thinking is often favored by testers in industrial practice: They wish to reach a desirable event, or exclude that an undesirable one occurs, or v.v.

We plan to apply our prioritization approach to a more general class of testing problems, e.g., to multiple-metrics-based testing where a family of software measures is used to generate tests [17]. Generally speaking, the approach can be applied to prioritize the testing process if the SUT is modeled by a graph the nodes of which represent events or sub-systems of various granularities (modules and functions, or objects, methods, classes, packages, etc.).

Next work planned is to extend the approach to cases where n-tuple events coverage (with n=3, 4, ...) is required instead of the pair-wise one (n=2) as studied in this paper. Additionally, the fuzzy-event-based prioritized testing will be considered as an alternative the ordinary-event-based one with the usage of fuzzy clustering and classification procedure presented in present paper and then will be compared their prioritizing performance. Finally, more applications and case studies are planned to also empirically validate and to extend the results achieved in this paper formally.

References

1. Binder, R.V.: Testing Object-Oriented Systems. Addison-Wesley, Reading (2000)
2. Bryce, R.C., Colbourn, Ch.C.: Prioritized Interaction Testing for Pair-wise Coverage with Seeding and Constraints. Information and Software Technolog 48, 960–970 (2006)
3. Elbaum, S., Malishevsky, A., Rothermel, G.: Test Case Prioritization: A Family of Empirical Studies. IEEE Transactions on Software Engineering 28(2), 182–191 (2002)
4. Cohen, D.M., Dalal, S.R., Freedman, M.L., Patton, G.C.: The AETG System: An Approach to Testing Based on Combinatorial Design. IEEE Trans. Software Engineering 23(7), 437–444 (1997)
5. Belli, F.: Finite-State Testing and analysis of Graphical User Interfaces. In: Proc. 12th Int'l. Symp. Softw. Reliability Eng (ISSRE'01), p. 43 (2001)
6. Belli, F., Budnik, C.J., White, L.: Event-Based Modeling, Analysis and Testing of User Interactions - Approach and Case Study. J. Software Testing, Verification & Reliability 16(1), 3–32 (2006)
7. Belli, F., Budnik, F.C.J.: Test Minimization for Human-Computer Interaction. J. Applied Intelligence 7(2) (2007) (to appear)
8. Edmonds, J., Johnson, E.L.: Matching: Euler Tours and the Chinese Postman, Math. Programming, pp. 88-124 (1973)
9. Bezdek, J.C.: Pattern Recognition with Fuzzy Objective Function Algorithms. Plenum Press, New York (1981)
10. Dunn, J.C.: A Fuzzy Relative of the ISODATA Process and Its Use in Detecting Compact Well-Separated Clusters. Journal of Cybernetics 3, 32–57 (1973)
11. Eminov, M.: Rule-Based Fuzzy Classification Using Query Processing. Int. J. Mathematical & Computational Applications (2003)
12. Eminov, M., Gokce, N.: Neural Network Clustering Using Competitive Learning Algorithm, Proc. TAINN 2005. In: Savacı, F.A. (ed.) TAINN 2005. LNCS (LNAI), vol. 3949, pp. 161–168. Springer, Heidelberg (2006)

13. Eminov, M.E.: Fuzzy c-Means Based Adaptive Neural Network Clustering. Proc. TAINN-2003, Int. J. Computational Intelligence, 338-343 (2003)
14. Kim, D.J., Park, Y.W., Park, D.J.: A Novel Validity Index for Clusters. IEICE Trans. Inf. & System, 282–285 (2001)
15. Belli, F., Budnik, Ch.J., Linschulte, M., Schieferdecker, I.: Testing Web-Based Systems with Structured, Graphic Models - Comparison through a Case Study (in German). In: Proc. Annual German National Conf. for Informatics, GI-Jahrestagung, 2006 (to appear)
16. Gerhart, S., Goodenough, J.B.: Toward a Theory of Test Data Selection. IEEE Trans. On Softw. Eng., 156–173 (1975)
17. Neate, B., Warwick, I., Churcher, N.: CodeRank: A New Family of Software Metrics. In: Proc. Australian Software Engineering Conference - ASWEC 2006, pp. 369–377. IEEE Comp. Press, Los Alamitos (2006)
18. Jeffrey, D., Gu, N.: Test Case Prioritization Using Relevant Slices. ICSE (2002)
19. Kim, J.-M., Porter, A.: A History-Based Test Prioritization Technique for Regression Testing in Resource Constrained Environments, COMPSAC (2006)
20. Bezdek, J.C., Keller, J., Krisnapuram, R., Pal, N.R.: Fuzzy Models and Algorithms for Pattern Recognition and Image Processing. Kluwer Academic Publishers, Dordrecht (1999)
21. Hoppner, F., Klawonn, F., Kruse, R., Runkler, T.: Fuzzy Cluster Analysis, John Wiley, Chichester, New York (1999)
22. Klawonn, F., Kruse, R.: Derivation of Fuzzy Classification Rules from Multidimensional Data. In: The International Institute for Advanced Studies in System Research and Cybernetics, Windsor, Ontario, pp. 90–94 (1995)
23. Eminov, M.: Querying a Database by Fuzzification of Attribute Values, 5.National Econometrics and Statistics Symposium, Adana (19-22 September, 2001)

Error Propagation Monitoring
on Windows Mobile-Based Devices

José Carlos Bregieiro Ribeiro[1], Bruno Miguel Luís[2], Mário Zenha-Rela[2]

[1] Polytechnic Institute of Leiria (IPL), Morro do Lena, Alto do Vieiro,
Leiria, Portugal
jose.ribeiro@estg.ipleiria.pt
[2] University of Coimbra (UC), CISUC, DEI, 3030-290,
Coimbra, Portugal
mzrela@dei.uc.pt

Abstract. Mobile devices, such as Smartphones, are being used virtually by every modern individual. Such devices are expected to work continuously and flawlessly for years, despite having been designed without criticality requirements. However, the requirements of mobility, digital identification and authentication lead to an increasing dependence of societies on the correct behaviour of these 'proxies for the individual'. The Windows Mobile 5.0 release has delivered a new set of internal state monitoring services, centralized into the State and Notifications Broker. This API was designed to be used by context-aware applications, providing a comprehensive monitoring of the internal state and resources of mobile devices. In this paper we propose using this service to increase the dependability of mobile applications by showing, through a series of fault-injection campaigns, that this novel API is very effective for error propagation profiling and monitoring.

Keywords: Robustness Testing, Dependability Evaluation, State and Notifications Broker, Windows Mobile, COTS.

1 Introduction

The philosophy for mobile devices has been evolving towards the 'wallet' paradigm: they contain important personal information, and virtually every adult carries one. They are true "proxies for the individual" [1]. Additionally, people are getting used to take care of their business affairs on these pervasive devices, since they are becoming increasingly more sophisticated and are able to handle most basic tasks. But not all mobile devices were designed with enterprise class security in mind, and even components which were specifically designed for mission-critical applications may prove to have problems if used in a different context. Retrofitting trust in any technology is considerably harder than building it in from the start [1], especially when users have already perceived it as invasive, intrusive, or dangerous.

Software behaviour is a combination of many factors: which particular data states are created, what paths are exercised, how long execution takes, what outputs are produced, and so forth [2]. An operating system is, itself, a dynamic entity [3], as different services have diverse robustness properties; the way in which software

A. Bondavalli, F. Brasileiro, and S. Rajsbaum (Eds.): LADC 2007, LNCS 4746, pp. 111–122, 2007.

makes use of those services will have impact on the robustness of their operations. What's more, mobile devices – such as Pocket PCs and Smartphones – are expected to work continuously and flawlessly for years, with varying energy and in harsh environmental conditions; this requires stringent internal state and resource monitoring. One of the major problems in dependability evaluation is the difficulty of observing what happens inside the system that is submitted to stress. This problem is exacerbated when the source code of the system under evaluation is unavailable; alas, this is the most common situation.

The Windows Mobile 5.0 release has delivered a new API with a set of services targeting context-aware applications, the State and Notifications Broker (SNB) [4], which aims to provide comprehensive monitoring of resources. This service, while not providing true white-box testing tools, makes the system transparent enough to allow for a semantically-oriented monitoring of relevant state-variables.

One of the key ideas presented in this paper is to use the internal monitoring services provided by the State and Notifications Broker for error propagation profiling and monitoring. Although most of the information provided by the State and Notifications Broker could be obtained by other means, this tool enables the monitoring of a standard set of relevant system variables defined by the API itself, in a straightforward manner. We also aim to contribute to the issue of interpreting the raw data produced into useful information, into insight. It is clear that automated testing of black-box components requires (or, at least, can be greatly improved by) built-in system support.

2 Background

Computer dependability can be defined as the trustworthiness of a computing system, which allows reliance to be justifiably placed on the service it delivers [5]. The applications envisaged by our approach, however, are not mission-critical – actually, this is not the target of the Windows Mobile platform. This work's focus is trustworthiness – i.e. reliable and secure behaviour of standard personal applications – such as those used by mobile devices for e-commerce or personal identification. In fact, the key dependability attribute we are interested in is the robustness of software, formally defined as the degree to which a software component functions correctly in the presence of exceptional inputs or stressful environmental conditions [6]. The robustness of software is tested by exercising it with a tailored workload. Black-box or behavioural testing [7] is the preferred approach whenever the source code is not available – as is the case of a proprietary operating system. There are several research works on the evaluation of the robustness of operating systems [8-13]. Drivers were identified as a major source of OS failures, and its effects were studied in [2, 14, 15].

The works based on the Ballista methodology [16-18] interested us particularly, due to the possibility of automating the testing of component interfaces. Its main contribution was the proposal of an object-oriented approach based on parameter data types instead of component functionality, thus eliminating the need for function-specific test scaffolding. Since we are emulating software errors, we focus on data level errors flowing through the different module interfaces and on the evaluation of the impact of these errors on the overall system dependability. This is also the approach followed in [2, 19-21]; however, in [20] the study of the impact of data errors is focused on the consequences of error propagation in control applications. The experiments presented in this paper closely follow the line of the work presented in [2] by extending the observability; while in their work the error propagation analysis is limited by the observation at the interface between components, we delve deeper into the system internals, as this was made feasible by the State and Notifications Broker of the Windows Mobile 5.0 platform. Johansson and Suri's work has the added interest in that they present a case study based on Windows CE.net, the platform from which Windows Mobile (our testbed) derives.

Thus, the main focus of this paper is on presenting, employing, and discussing the usefulness of this service to increase the dependability of mobile applications by showing, through a series of fault-injection campaigns, that this novel API is very effective for error propagation profiling and monitoring. The rationale behind this study falls into the 'callee interface fault injection' as defined in [22].

3   State and Notifications Broker Overview

The recent Windows Mobile 5.0 operating system has centralised its state information into a single entity, the State and Notifications Broker[1] – whether that information is related to the device itself or to the standard Windows Mobile 5.0 applications. It provides a standard architecture for monitoring state values for changes and for distributing change notifications to the interested parties using a publish-subscribe model, thus making it unnecessary to hunt down a separate function or API for each individual state value. Also, prior to the introduction of the State and Notifications Broker API, determining a specific state value often required several function calls and additional logic.

Each state value is available either through native or managed code: native code provides direct access to the behaviours and capabilities of the platform using the C or C++ language, but the developer is responsible for handling the details involved in interacting with the platform; managed code puts a greater focus on development productivity by encapsulating details within class libraries. For the managed code developers, the .NET Compact framework includes more than a hundred pre-defined static *base State and Notification Properties*[2] that represent the available state values; in addition, original equipment manufacturers (OEMs) are free to add more values, as the underlying implementation of the State and Notifications Broker uses the registry as the data store. The base State and Notification Properties encompass information on the system state, phone, user, tasks and appointments, connections, messages, media player and time. To access the present value of a given property, managed-code developers simply access the SystemState property that corresponds to the state value of their interests: to receive state value change notifications, an application must simply create an instance of the SystemState class and pass the appropriate SystemProperty enumeration that identifies the value of interest, and attach a delegate to the new SystemState instance's Changed event.

---

[1] http://msdn2.microsoft.com/en-us/library/aa455748.aspx [cited: 2007/03/03].

[2] http://msdn2.microsoft.com/en-us/library/aa455750.aspx [cited: 2007/04/03].

Still, some problems persist. Firstly, there is no standard way for third-party software companies to expose their own properties in the State and Notifications Broker. Secondly, not all the device's properties are exposed, although registry-based custom-made states can be implemented to extend the default functionality. Thirdly, even though C# managed code is easier to use, it includes reduced functionality when compared to native C++ code.

4 Framework Description

In order to access the usefulness of the State and Notifications Broker for error propagation monitoring and profiling, we've developed a prototype general-purpose software testing tool – ^{m}Crash – that allowed us to automate the testing process. This section describes this framework and contextualizes the use of the State and Notifications Broker API.

Presently, ^{m}Crash allows automatic testing of classes, methods, parameters and objects in the .NET framework. In order to achieve this, several .NET framework APIs were employed, such as the `System.Reflection` and `System.CodeDom` namespaces, and the Microsoft Excel Object Library. This tool is meant to dynamically generate a test script, compile it into a .NET assembly, and invoke the test process. Many ideas of this approach were inspired by previous work of others and ourselves. This tool was first presented in [23], and its design closely follows the guidelines proposed by [3, 24].

Four fundamental modules embody our tool: the Faultload Database; the Input Generation and Fault Injection Module; the Postcondition Checker; and the Execution Manager. These modules are schematically represented in Figure 1, and will be discussed in further detail in the following subsections.

4.1 Faultload Database

The process of building the Faultload Database precedes the actual testing phase, as a set of test cases must be created for each unique public constructor, method and property of each class made available by the Module Under Test (MUT). The first step is to catalogue all the MUTs information – including input and output parameters, their data types and error codes. Most of these tasks are achieved automatically by means of the Reflection API; alas, some of the information (e.g. the expected return values) must be manually defined by the software tester.

The following step involves performing a domain analysis for each individual data type in order to establish the faultload. Test cases encompass valid, boundary and invalid conditions for the different data types; this allows the coverage of a vast array of erroneous inputs, and also enables the tester to obtain a reference execution (i.e. the *gold run*).

Finally, all this information is inserted in an Excel spreadsheet – using Excel API Programming in the case of the automated tasks, and manually in the case of the values that must be defined by the software tester. This spreadsheet holds an ordered list of the API calls that will be used to test the MUT.

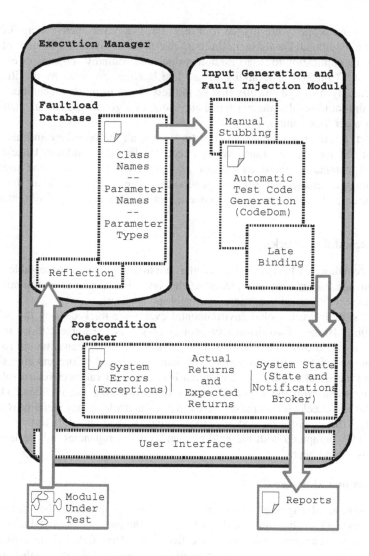

Fig. 1. Framework scheme

4.2   Input Generation and Fault Injection Module

The Input Generation component dynamically generates test cases for a given set of constructors, methods and properties; the Fault Injection component automatically executes the test cases, and collects the information returned by a particular function call.

The test cases' source code is generated using the CodeDom API, and is based on the parameters defined in the Excel spreadsheet during the Faultload Database building process. Additionally, the necessary code for logging any events detected by State and Notifications Broker is included in the test cases' source code. Any changes to a monitored property are logged to a text file. If any parameters were left blank during the Faultload Database definition, the user is given the option of either allowing the application to insert random values and "dummy" objects, or entering a "manual stub" himself. The ability to use late binding, provided by the Reflection API, is employed to dynamically invoke the test cases; using this technique enables the ^{m}Crash tool to resolve the existence and name of a given type and its members at runtime (rather than compile time).

In short, a reference execution is run first; then, all the boundary and invalid test cases defined for a given function are executed. The Postcondition Checker is in charge of comparing these executions and presenting reports to the user. This methodology automates the test case generation process, hence avoiding the need to write source code, and it even allows for a considerable amount of system state to be set.

4.3 Postcondition Checker

The Postcondition Checker monitors the environment for unacceptable events. Assertions are put in two main places: at the system level and at the output. All of these values are recorded in a Microsoft Excel spreadsheet.

At the system level, global environmental events are tracked using the State and Notifications Broker. Two distinct categories of values are logged: those incoming from the notifications received, and those of the properties being monitored – the Base State and Notification Properties. The latter are logged before and after the fault injection process takes place. At the output level, the tool validates return values (by comparing them with the expected returns defined during the Faultload Database definition) and checks if exceptions were thrown – and where they were thrown.

Finally, the results yielded by the boundary and invalid test values are automatically compared with the gold run, and any discrepancies will be inserted in the results spreadsheet.

4.4 Execution Manager

The Execution Manager provides the visual interface between the user and the software testing tool. It allows for the definition of the parameters used during a given software testing campaign, such as the location of the .NET IDE and of the MUT. It is also responsible for dealing with the complexity of creating the three other modules, and for feeding each one of them with the necessary incoming data.

Until now, this tool was only tested using Microsoft Visual Studio 2005 as the IDE. During the fault injection process, the IDE is automatically started and the code produced by the Fault Injection component is executed.

At the end of the software testing campaign, the results spreadsheet, containing all the results gathered by the Postcondition Checker, is presented to the user.

5 Experimental Observations

In the experiment described in this paper, we employed the ^{m}Crash tool to conduct a software testing campaign with the purpose of accessing Windows Mobile 5.0's trustworthiness properties and uncovering faults.

5.1 Targets and Methodology

The targets of this experiment were the public properties made available by the Microsoft Windows Mobile 5 `Microsoft.WindowsMobile.PocketOutlook` namespace. We chose to target the `PocketOutlook` namespace in this study because it is a productivity package used, essentially, by programmers that develop mobile and context-aware applications, and also because its complexity is adequate for research and demonstration purposes. The rationale for focusing our study on the public properties is related with the extended insight that the State and Notifications Broker allows.

We started by using ^{m}Crash to extract the list of public properties available in all the classes made available by the `PocketOutlook` namespace. During the Faultload Database building process, 9 distinct classes, including 96 distinct public properties, were identified and catalogued. These 96 distinct public properties encompassed 13 different data types, including primitive data types (`bool`, `int`, `string`), enumerations (`WeekOfMonth`, `TimeSpan`, `Sensitivity`, `RecurrenceType`, `Month`, `Importance`, `DaysOfWeek`, `DateTime`, `BusyStatus`) and objects (`Uri`).

The methodology fallowed was that of performing fault-injection by changing the target public properties' values. Valid, boundary and invalid test values were defined for each of the data types, except for `bool` properties, to which only true or false values can be assigned. Manual stubbing was employed to instantiate an object and to set the minimum amount of state needed for each individual test case. In the majority of the cases, creating a "dummy" object sufficed but, in some situations, additional complexity was required; these special situations were individually addressed in order to create the state needed.

Preliminary experiments showed that some errors were only uncovered by the operating system when the object carrying the faulty property was used as an input parameter in a method call. In order to pinpoint such situations, we tested all of the abovementioned objects as input parameters in a method belonging to the same class.

Finally, we analysed the results collected by ^{m}Crash in order to draw conclusions. The logs generated by the Postcondition Checker were automatically compared to the previously recorded *gold run*; all the exceptions thrown (and the phase of the testing process in which they were thrown) were annotated; the values the properties assumed (in the cases in which no exception was thrown) after the fault injection process were compared to those that were expected. The results of this comparison were thoroughly analysed, and will be discussed in the following subsection.

5.2 Results and Observations

As a result of our experiments, we were able to categorize the exceptions thrown during the fault injection procedure in two types, according to their *latency*:

- if the exception is thrown during the process of assigning an erroneous value to a property (i.e. if the assertion is located in the property's setter method) the exception is considered to be *immediate*;
- if the exception is thrown by the method that receives the object containing the faulty property as an input parameter (i.e. the assertion is located in the method called) the exception is considered to be *late*.

Table 1. Data Types and corresponding Test Cases that threw late exceptions. Late Exception Types and corresponding number of occurrences.

Late Exceptions	
Data Types	Test Cases
`string`	`string with 4096 characters;` `"\\\u0066\n"; string.Empty; null`
`DateTime`	`DateTime.MaxValue`
`EmailMessage.Importance`	`(Importance)1000; (Importance)(-1);` `Importance.Low; Importance.High`
`EmailMessage.Sensitivity`	`(Sensitivity)int.MaxValue;` `(Sensitivity)(-1);` `Sensitivity.Confidential; 0`

Exception types	Ocurrences
`System.ComponentModel.Win32Exception`	60
`System.InvalidCastException`	17

Late exceptions are more problematic, due to the high probability of error propagation. In fact, objects containing "faulty" properties could linger in the system indefinitely, until they are used as an input parameter and the exception is triggered. Late exception statistics are depicted in Table 1.

The vast majority of the test values that threw late exceptions were of the string data type; the property can be assigned an invalid value, but when the object is used as an input in a method an assertion existed to make sure that the string could not exceed the maximum length. Actually, the maximum length of these strings is defined in the documentation, but nothing is mentioned on when the check is made. What's more, this limit is documented in the property's entry; hence the programmer has no reason to assume that the check won't be done immediately. The `DateTime` data type is also problematic in terms of latency; the `DateTime.MaxValue` test value (which we considered to be a boundary value) often generated a late exception. Such was also the case of some of the enumeration types associated to the `EmailMessage` class.

Immediate exceptions included null, range and format exceptions. Table 2 resumes the data for these categories of exceptions. The analysis of the exceptions' data doesn't allow us to typify the data types according to category of exception generated – there is no coherent behaviour or pattern that allows us to conclude that a particular data type or a particular test case always have the same exception latency. Similar invalid test values generate both immediate and late exceptions, which can only be explained by the API's internal structure (of which no source code is available).

It is at this point that the extended insight provided by the State and Notifications Broker can prove to be invaluable; this API can be used to monitor properties continuously. The software tester will thus be able to assert properties' values all the way through – and early on – the software testing process.

Table 2. Data Types and corresponding Test Cases that threw immediate exceptions. Immediate Exception Types and corresponding number of occurrences.

Immediate Exceptions	
Data Types	Test Cases
`string`	`String with 4096 characters`

`DateTime`	`DateTime.MaxValue;`
	`DateTime.MinValue;`
	`new DateTime(int.MaxValue,`
	`int.MaxValue, int.MaxValue);`
	`new DateTime(int.MinValue,`
	`int.MinValue, int.MinValue)`

`TimeSpan`	`TimeSpan.MaxValue;`
	`new TimeSpan(int.MaxValue,`
	`int.MaxValue, int.MaxValue)`

`Uri`	`new Uri(null); new Uri("dei.uc.pt")`
`EmailMessage.Importance`	`(Importance)1000; (Importance)(-1)`
`EmailMessage.Sensitivity`	`(Sensitivity)int.MaxValue;` `(Sensitivity)(-1)`
`Appointment.BusyStatus`	`(BusyStatus)(-1)`

Exception types	Ocurrences
`System.ArgumentOutOfRangeException`	23
`System.ComponentModel.Win32Exception`	16
`System.UriFormatException`	1
`System.NullReferenceException`	1
`System.ArgumentNullException`	1

With this in mind, we devoted special attention to the time frame between the contamination of the property with an erroneous value and the usage of the "faulty" object as an input parameter in a method (error latency). The measurements made to the `Appointment` class were especially interesting, since the State and Notifications Broker monitors an extensive set of properties regarding Task and Appointment information. For instance, we observed that when the `Appointment.Start` property was set to a value below the allowed range, an immediate "Argument Out Of Range" exception was thrown; nevertheless the Postcondition Checker received a notification of the property being set to its lower bound – i.e. some of the properties values are changed even though an exception is thrown. What's more, in a similar situation – when the `Appointment.Start` property was set to a value above its upper bound – an immediate exception of the type `System.ComponentModel.Win32Exception` was thrown, and the property kept its previous value. This irregular behaviour requires distinct handling of similar situations.

Other anomalous behaviour observed using the State and Notifications Broker included receiving notifications of changes to properties other than those directly disturbed. The following observations are typical of this situation:

- when the `Appointment.Start` property was set to an invalid value, the `Appointment.End` property was set to its default value;
- when the `Appointment.End` property was set to an invalid value the `Appointment.Start` property was set to its default value.

Although this behaviour is not completely unreasonable – the `Start` and `End` properties of the `Appointment` class are obviously related – it does constitute a means for error propagation. It also provides a clear sign that to increase the effectiveness of the postcondition checking the system must me monitored as a whole. In some circumstances, we were also able to detect the contamination of objects before the errors were detected by the runtime environment. For instance, in the `Appointment.Subject` property, the "String with 4096 characters" boundary test case (the documentation explicitly refers that an appointment's subject is limited to 4096 characters) generated a late exception when the object was used as an argument in a method call. Nevertheless, by means of the State and Notification Broker, it was possible to observe that this property assumed a null value immediately after the erroneous value was assigned to the property; it issued a notification for the change of the base State and Notification Property `CalendarAppointmentSubject`, and the logs also showed that the property was reset to null – its default value.

It must be stressed that this anomalous behaviour was unveiled by the State and Notifications Broker – it published a notification of the property change – before the runtime environment threw an exception.

6 Conclusions and Future Work

This paper proposes using a custom-tailored framework for accessing Windows Mobile 5.0's trustworthiness properties. For this, we employed the State and Notifications Broker API for error monitoring and propagation profiling, and presented an experimental study illustrating the feasibility of the approach.

The State and Notifications Broker centralizes system state information in documented locations, and distributes change notifications to interested parties using a publish-subscribe model. It provides built-in monitoring services to internal system variables, which constitutes a means for keeping an eye on undesirable state value modifications.

The experimental observations show that system built-in assertions are sparsely distributed and less than thoroughly documented, and that errors can remain dormant in the system until they are detected and dealt with e.g. by throwing an exception. This behaviour renders the State and Notifications Broker particularly useful for detecting erroneous internal states. Interesting observations include:

- receiving notifications of changes to properties other than those disturbed;
- receiving notification of a property being changed, even though an exception was immediately thrown after an invalid value was assigned to it;

- receiving notification of invalid values being assigned to a property; an exception was only triggered when the faulty property's instance was used as an argument in a method call.

Even thought this API is not enough to prevent the contamination of internal objects with erroneous values, we believe it represents an opportunity for enhancing dependability in large-scale, not limited to mission-critical applications.

Our work so far was limited to the base State and Notification Properties defined by default; nevertheless, these are clearly insufficient to cover the system as a whole. Future work includes extending the set of properties exposed, with the purpose of broadening the range of relevant system variables being monitored by our tool.

Along this work, we realized that the current fault-injection paradigm is still much too centred on the stimulus-response functional model. However, a growing number of real-world mission-critical applications are now based on the object-oriented model; nonetheless, tools for dependability evaluation are seldom used in this context.

References

1. Langheinrich, M.: Privacy by Design - Principles of Privacy-Aware Ubiquitous Systems. In: ACM UbiComp., ACM Press, New York (2001)
2. Johansson, A., Suri, N.: Error Propagation Profiling of Operating Systems, presented at DSN (2005)
3. Voas, J.M., McGraw, G.: Software fault injection: inoculating programs against errors. Wiley Computer Pub., New York (1998)
4. Wilson, J.: The State and Notifications Broker Part I, MSDN Library (2006)
5. Avizienis, A., Laprie, J.-C., Randell, B.: Fundamental Concepts of Dependability, LAAS-CNRS N01145 (2001)
6. IEEE Standard Glossary of Software Engineering Terminology (IEEE Std610.12-1990) (1990)
7. Beizer, B.: Black-box testing: techniques for functional testing of software and systems. Wiley, New York, Chichester (1995)
8. Gu, W.N., Kalbarczyk, Z., Lyer, R.K., Yang, Z.Y.: Characterization of Linux kernel behavior under errors, presented at DSN (2003)
9. Murphy, B., Levidow, B.: Windows 2000 Dependability. In: Workshop on Dependable Networks and OS (2000)
10. Chou, A., Yang, J., Chelf, B., Hallem, S., Engler, D.: An Empirical Study of Operating System Errors, presented at SOSP (2001)
11. Arlat, J., Fabre, J.-C., Rodriguez, M., Salles, F.: Dependability of COTS Microkernel-Based Systems. IEEE Trans. on Computers 51, 138–163 (2002)
12. Swift, M.M., Bershad, B.N., Levy, H.M.: Improving the Reliability of Commodity OS's. Operating Systems Review 37, 207–222 (2003)
13. Jun, X., Zbigniew, K., Ravishankar, K.I.: Networked Windows NT System Field Failure Data Analysis (1999)
14. Albinet, A., Arlat, J., Fabre, J.-C.: Characterization of the Impact of Faulty Drivers on the Robustness of the Linux Kernel, presented at DSN (2004)
15. Durães, J., Madeira, H.: Multidimensional Characterization of the Impact of Faulty Drivers on the OS Behavior. IEICE , 2563–2570 (2003)

16. Kropp, N.P., Koopman, P.J., Siewiorek, D.P.: Automated Robustness Testing of Off the Shelf Software Components. FTCS 98, IEEE (1998)
17. Koopman, P., DeVale, J.: Comparing the robustness of POSIX operating systems, presented at FTCS 99 (1999)
18. Shelton, C.P., Koopman, P., Devale, K.: Robustness testing of the Microsoft Win32 API, presented at DSN (2000)
19. Hiller, M., Jhumka, A., Suri, N.: PROPANE: An environment for examining the propagation of errors in software. In: Proceedings of the ACM SIGSOFT 2002 International Symposium on Software Testing and Analysis, p. 81 (2002)
20. Askerdal, Ö., Gafvert, M., Hiller, M., Suri, N.: Analyzing the Impact of Data Errors in Safety-Critical Control Systems. IEEE Trans. Inf. Syst. (2003)
21. Hiller, M., Jhumka, A., Suri, N.: EPIC: Profiling the propagation and effect of data errors in software. IEEE Trans. on Computers 53, 512–530 (2004)
22. Koopman, P.: What's Wrong With Fault Injection As A Benchmarking Tool?, presented at DSN, Washington (2002)
23. Ribeiro, J., -Rela, M. Z.: mCrash: a Framework for the Evaluation of Mobile Devices Trustworthiness Properties, presented at CMUS, Portugal (2006)
24. Li, K., Wu, M.: Effective software test automation: developing an automated software testing tool. Sybex, London (2004)

Gossiping: Adaptive and Reliable Broadcasting in MANETs*

Abdelmajid Khelil and Neeraj Suri

Technische Universität Darmstadt,
Dependable, Embedded Systems and Software Group,
Hochschulstr. 10, 64289 Darmstadt, Germany
Tel: (+49) 6151-16-3414, Fax: (+49)6151-16-4310
{khelil,suri}@informatik.tu-darmstadt.de

Abstract. Given the frequent topology changes in Mobile Ad Hoc Networks (MANET), the choice of appropriate broadcasting techniques is crucial to ensure reliable delivery of messages. The spreading of broadcast messages has a strong similarity with the spreading of infectious diseases. Applying epidemiological models to broadcasting allows an easy evaluation of such strategies depending on the MANET characteristics, e.g. the node density. In this paper, we develop an epidemic model for gossiping, which is a flooding-based probabilistic broadcasting technique. We analytically investigate the impact of node density and forwarding probability on the quality of gossiping. The result of our investigation is to enable mobile nodes for dynamically adapting their forwarding probability depending on the local node density. Simulation results in ns-2 show the reliability, efficiency and scalability of adaptive gossiping.

Keywords: MANET, Broadcasting, Gossiping, Reliability, Epidemic Models, Analytical Modeling.

1 Introduction

Mobile Ad Hoc Networks (MANETs) are composed by mobile devices equipped with short range radios. Communication is possible between devices within each other's radio range. The mobility leads to frequent network topology changes, which complicates classical networking tasks such as broadcasting.

Network-wide *broadcasting* aims at distributing messages from the source node to all other nodes in the network. It is a major communication primitive required by many applications and protocols in MANETs. Broadcast protocols present a fundamental building block to realize principal middleware functionalities such as replication [1] and group communication [2]. Furthermore, broadcasting is frequently used to distribute information and discover or advertise resources.

Flooding is a common approach to realize broadcasting in MANETs because of its topology independency. In flooding-based approaches nodes forward a received message to all their neighbors. Subsequently, all nodes within the network should receive the message. Even though flooding might expose some unnecessary message overhead

---

* Research supported in part by EC DECOS, NoE ReSIST and DFG GRK 1362 (TUD GKMM).

A. Bondavalli, F. Brasileiro, and S. Rajsbaum (Eds.): LADC 2007, LNCS 4746, pp. 123–141, 2007.

it should provide a robust basic strategy for broadcasting in networks with an unknown or changing topology. However, the characteristics of MANETs prohibit that a flooding process reaches every node. If the *node density*, i.e. the number of nodes operating in a given area, is too high the radio transmission will block out messages if too many nodes are rebroadcasting the received messages as it is in blind flooding. This problem is referred to as *broadcast storms* [3]. Here flooding shows a worse performance than selecting a smaller number of nodes to forward the message.

Node spatial distribution is therefore a key issue for the performance of broadcast protocols, since it determines the connectivity of the MANET. The investigation of potential MANET application scenarios shows a wide range of possible node spatial distributions and node mobilities. Therefore, a MANET generally shows a continuously changing network connectivity over space and time. Consequently, an adaptive solution for broadcasting that accounts for the heterogeneous and evolving node spatial distribution and mobility is a major contribution.

Most of the research conducted on broadcasting in MANETs has primarily focused only on carefully selected application and evaluation scenarios. Consequently, the developed broadcasting schemes do not yield good performance for other scenarios. Different comparative studies [4, 5] show that the existing broadcasting techniques are tailored to only one class of MANETs with respect to node density and node mobility, and are unfortunately not likely to operate well in other classes.

Our main objective is to provide an adaptive broadcast algorithm for a wide range of MANET operation conditions. The main contribution of this paper is *reliable gossiping*, a frugal and adaptive broadcasting technique. Reliable gossiping provides a simple mechanism for tuning the forwarding probability of gossiping depending on the local density of a node, reflected by the number of its neighbors. Reliability is a key descriptor of correctly delivered broadcast messages. Using intensive simulations in ns-2 we show that reliable gossiping can be deployed in a wide spectrum of MANETs with respect to node density, node mobility and communication range.

The remainder of this paper is organized as follows. In Section 2, we define the system model and the fault model, and outline the requirements on broadcasting in MANETs. Section 3 discusses the related work. Then, we detail the paper's objectives in Section 4. Section 5 shows how to adopt a simple mathematical compartmental model from epidemiology to analytically investigate gossiping. Using this model we show how to adapt the forwarding probability of gossiping to the local node density. In Section 6, we evaluate adaptive gossiping and compare it to related work. We conclude the paper in Section 7.

2   Preliminaries

2.1   System Model and Fault Model

In this work, we consider a MANET that is formed by N autonomous mobile nodes of similar communication capabilities (communication range R and bandwidth r). We assume that nodes may have no knowledge about their position or speed. The MANET may show a very *heterogeneous* spatial distribution of nodes, from locally very sparse to very dense, and very heterogeneous node mobility patterns, from low mobile to highly mobile. We assume that nodes acquire neighborhood information by means of HELLO beaconing.

The broadcast messages are uniquely identified, e.g. through the Media Access Control (MAC) address of the source and a locally unique sequence number. Nodes are required to store the list of IDs of messages received or originated, in a so-called *broadcast_table*. Thus nodes are able to decide, whether a received copy of a given message is the first one.

In our fault model, we consider the following communication failures: Collision, contention, frequent link breakage and network partitioning. We define network partitioning as the split of the network into two (or more) disjoint groups of nodes that can not communicate with each other. Tolerating these failures is a key issue to ensure the reliability of broadcasting.

2.2 Requirements

As node density heavily influences the performance of broadcasting, and MANETs may show a wide range of node densities, the first requirement on a broadcasting technique for MANETs is to adapt to the node density, in order to reduce broadcast storms. Global state in MANETs is hard to obtain and spatial distribution of nodes may change continuously, therefore, the second requirement on such a strategy is that nodes *independently* adapt to *local* MANET characteristics.

Furthermore, we identify two basic requirements of the applications on a broadcasting protocol, i.e. delivery reliability and delivery timeliness. In this work, we consider delay-critical applications. These applications require to efficiently reach all nodes belonging to the network partition, where the source node is located, while minimizing the message delay.

3 Related Work

The design of broadcasting is a fundamental problem in MANETs and several broadcast strategies have been proposed in the literature. In [4, 5], the authors provide two comparative studies for the existing broadcasting techniques. [4] classifies broadcasting schemes into heuristic-based and topology-based. [5] subclassifies heuristic-based class into probability-based and area-based. We categorize all these protocols into adaptive and non-adaptive protocols.

Non-adaptive heuristic-based protocols use heuristics with predefined fixed parameters to reduce broadcast storms. They do not adapt to the time-varying MANET situations that show quite different levels of broadcast storms. Examples of non-adaptive probability-based schemes are gossiping [6,3] and counter-based [3]. Examples of non-adaptive area-based schemes are location-based [3] and distance-based schemes [3]. Non-adaptive topology-based protocols (e.g. Multipoint Relaying Broadcasting [7], Connected Dominating Set Based [8], Minimum Forwarding Set Based [9], and Deterministic Broadcast [10]) require an accurate topology information which is hard to

acquire in highly mobile environments and due to collisions. That is why the performance of these protocols drops for highly mobile scenarios [5] or highly congested
ones.

The common drawback of all these non-adaptive broadcasting techniques is that they
are optimized for specific scenarios and do not support a broader range of MANET
situations [5]. In order to suit non-adaptive broadcast schemes to a broader range of
operation conditions, some of them are adapted to local MANET characteristics.

In [11] the authors proposed two adaptive heuristic-based schemes, called adaptive
counter-based (ACB) and adaptive location-based (ALB), and one adaptive topology-
based scheme, called neighbor-coverage scheme (NC). Using a simulation-based approach the authors derived the best appropriate counter-threshold and coverage-threshold
as a function of the number of neighbors for ACB and ALB respectively. The authors
adapted the NC scheme by adjusting dynamically the HELLO interval to node mobility
reflected by neighborhood variation, so that the needed 2-hop topology information gets
more accurate. Despite this optimization, the NC scheme still has the main drawback
that neighborhood information may be inaccurate in congested networks. The authors
showed that these adaptive schemes outperform the non-adaptive schemes and recom-
mend ACB if location information is unavailable and simplicity is required. We will
compare our strategy to ACB in Section 6.5. [12] introduced the density-aware stochastic flooding (STOCH-FLOOD). Nodes forward messages with the following probability:
$p = min\{1, 11/n\}$, where n is the number of neighbors. In [13], the authors proposed a
similar scheme to STOCH-FLOOD. However, they use the counter of the message's
copies received as an estimation for node density, which is obviously less accurate than
the number of neighbors. Therefore, we compare our strategy to STOCH-FLOOD.

4   Objectives

With respect to broadcasting, protocol designers are interested in understanding the
nature of the spreading depending on the *protocol parameters* and on the *MANET properties*. The quality of broadcasting can be expressed in the spreading progress, both in
time and in space. In this work, we focus on the spreading progress in time. We define
for a given message the *spreading ratio* at time t as the ratio of the number of nodes
that received the message up to time t to the total number of nodes N. We denote the
spreading ratio at time t by $i(t)$, with $0 \leq i(t) \leq 1$. The most relevant factors which
affect the characteristics of message spreading are the parameters of the broadcast protocol and the network connectivity over space and time. The network connectivity over
space and time is mainly determined by the node spatial distribution, node mobility,
communication parameters (e.g., transmission range and rate), and number of nodes N.

To obtain the spreading ratio i over time t for a given broadcast protocol and a given
MANET configuration, *simulations* can be used. *Analytical models* however provide
the spreading ratio as a mathematical expression, e.g. *spreading_ratio* $= i(t)$, which
represents an elegant method to describe the spreading ratio over time. Our approach
for analytically modeling broadcast protocols in MANETs consists in adjusting existing
mathematical models from the epidemiology to MANET broadcasting.

Existing mathematical models that describe the spreading of epidemics can be as useful for network designers as they are for medical researchers. Medical researchers use epidemic models both to describe the spread of disease within a population and to take preventive or treatment measures. We use epidemic models both to *describe* and to *adapt* broadcasting in MANETs.

5   Modeling and Adaptation of Gossiping

In this section, we demonstrate the utility of epidemic models to adapt broadcast protocols in MANETs. For this we first detail the gossiping protocol and model it with the SI epidemic model. Then, we adapt its core parameter, the forwarding probability, to the local node density using the model.

5.1   The Gossiping Protocol

Gossiping in MANETs is simply defined as probabilistic flooding. On receiving the first copy of a given message, a node forwards the message with a fixed probability p to all nodes in its communication range using the broadcast primitive of the MAC layer. In order to reduce the collision probability, nodes delay forwarding for a random time between 0 and *fDelay*. The pseudo-code for gossiping is given by Algorithm 1. We denote by *random(x)*, a function that returns a random float value $\in [0,x]$.

Algorithm 1. Gossiping (p)

```
 1:  Var: p, fDelay
 2:  List: broadcast_table
 3:  # On receiving a DATA message M
 4:  if M.ID ∉ broadcast_table then
 5:      # M is received for the first time
 6:      deliver M to the application
 7:      add {M.ID} to broadcast_table
 8:      if random(1.0) ≤ p then
 9:          wait (random(fDelay))
10:          broadcast M to all neighbors
11:      end if
12:  else
13:      discard M
14:  end if
```

According to this protocol, on average, only $p*N$ nodes forward the message. Thus the number of saved forwards is $(1-p)*N$. To maximize the number of saved forwards, we have to reduce the probability p. But how much can we reduce it? [6] and [14] investigated gossiping, where every node forwards a message based on a fixed probability p. In [6], the authors showed that gossiping exhibits a bimodal behavior. There is a threshold value p_0 such that, in sufficiently large random networks, the gossiping quickly dies out if $p < p_0$ and the gossiping message spreads to the entire network if $p > p_0$. Thus, ideally we would set p close to p_0 (slightly higher), and therefore save approximately a ratio of $(1 - p_0)$ forwards compared to blind flooding. [14] investigated the phase transition of gossiping in more details.

The authors in [6] identified an optimum value of $p_0 = 0.65$ for their test scenarios. Intuitively, an optimal probability for one node density may be suboptimal for other densities, so this value is not likely to be globally optimal. Furthermore, since the node density varies over time and space, we have to adjust the probability p to the local density.

Deviating from [12] [13], we do not rely on pure simulations but we use an epidemic model to determine the appropriate forwarding probability of gossiping depending on the local node density.

5.2 Epidemic Model for Gossiping

In a previous work [15] we adopted the simple epidemic SI-model to the SPIN-based broadcast protocol. In this section, we briefly summarize the main results of [15] and adopt the SI-model to the gossiping protocol.

In the SI-model, a node follows a two-state *compartmental model*: It either carries the message or not, and once "infected" by the message, a node remains infectious. The message delay of gossiping is usually in the range of milliseconds or rarely a few seconds, depending on the current network parameters and load. During this small time interval we can assume that "infected" nodes remain infectious. Consequently, we can model gossiping using the SI-model.

Let $S(t)$ denote the number of *susceptible* nodes, and $I(t)$ the number of *infected* nodes at time t. The two-state mathematical SI-model is shown in Fig. 1. Each letter in a rectangle refers to a compartment in which a node can reside.

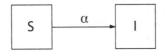

Fig. 1. Compartment diagram for the SI-model

Hereby, α is the broadcast force in the MANET. This parameter indicates the strength of the broadcasting process and has the dimension $1/time$. To develop the solution, we need to write the mass balance equations for each compartment:

$$\begin{cases} \frac{dS(t)}{dt} = -\alpha * S(t) \\ \frac{dI(t)}{dt} = \alpha * S(t) \end{cases} \tag{1}$$

The value of α is not constant, but depends on the number of susceptible and infectious nodes and the probability of transmitting the message upon encounter. We say that two nodes encounter each other if they are in each other's communication range. We define the encounter rate e as the average number of encounters per node and per unit of time. Therefore, each susceptible node makes e encounters per unit of time. Thus in total, all the susceptible nodes make $e * S(t)$ encounters per unit of time. Since we assume that nodes move autonomously, the encounters are at random with members of the total population ($N = S(t) + I(t)$). Then, only the fraction $I(t)/N$ of the encounters are with infectious individuals. Let β be the probability of message transmission in an encounter between an infectious node and a susceptible node. Then the rate of susceptible nodes that become infectious is $\beta(e * S(t))\frac{I(t)}{N}$. Thus the broadcast force is $\alpha = \frac{\beta * e}{N}I(t)$. We substitute

$$a = \frac{\beta * e}{N} \qquad (2)$$

and call a the *infection rate*. As discussed in [15] with details, the solution of the system of differential equations (1) results in that the spreading ratio is:

$$i(t) = \frac{I(t)}{N} = \frac{1}{1 + (N-1) * \exp(-a * N * t)} \qquad (3)$$

Eq. (2) shows that the infection rate a depends on the total number of nodes N, the encounter rate e, and the probability β of message transmission, given an adequate encounter. We note here that the encounter rate e depends on the node spatial distribution, node mobility and communication properties. β captures the impact of the communication properties and broadcast protocol parameters on the message propagation. This shows that our modeling approach is *hierarchical* which allows us to proceed *modularly* to further develop the analytical model by providing an analytical expression for a depending on the MANET properties and the broadcast protocol parameters. The calculation of a can be reduced to the determination of e from the mobility and communication models, and the determination of β from the broadcast algorithm and the communication model.

In [16], we investigated encounters between nodes in more details. We defined a set of mobility metrics based on node encounters and presented a detailed statistical and analytical analysis of these metrics for the widely used random waypoint mobility model [17] as example. In [16], we provided an analytical expression of the encounter rate (e) for the random waypoint mobility model assuming that nodes can communicate if their geographical distance is lower than the communication range: $e = R * (v_{max} - v_{min}) * d$, where R, v_{max}, v_{min} and d are the communication range in m, the maximum node speed in m/s, the minimum node speed in m/s and the node density in $1/m^2$ respectively. The analytical computation of e depends on the complexity of the considered mobility and network models.

The probability of message transmission given an adequate encounter (β) is a function of the gossiping probability (p) and the the message transmission reliability, which could be easily calculated given an appropriate analytical model for the MAC layer. In this work, we will not further consider the analytical computation. Instead of that, we use an empirical approach to calibrate our analytical model.

We proceed similarly to the epidemiologists who assume the availability of some experimental data that roughly describe the spreading of the infectious disease to calibrate the corresponding epidemic model. We rely on a few simulations to calibrate the epidemic model for gossiping. First of all, we determine the spreading ratio of gossiping for the considered MANET scenario using simulations. Afterwards, we use the *least squares method* to fit the simulation results to Eq. (3). We use the software package mathematica [18] to perform this fitting procedure. If the network is partitioned, we set the delay for unreachable nodes to be ∞. Therefore, the infection rate is approximately 0 for highly partitioned MANETs.

5.3   Adaptation of Gossiping

The goal of adapting gossiping is to achieve higher efficiency by reducing the number of forwarders, but without sacrificing the reliability or experiencing any significant degradation. Since the intensity of the broadcast storm depends on the local node density and may vary over time and space, we should adapt the gossiping probability p to the node's current number of neighbors, which reduces forward redundancy, contention, and collisions. In this section, we adapt gossiping to the local node density by determining the appropriate gossiping probability as a function of the number of neighbors.

Simulation Model. We use ns-2 [19] for the simulation-based performance analysis. We generate N mobile nodes in a $1km$ x $1km$ two-dimensional field, where nodes move according to the random waypoint model [17]. We vary the node speed between 0 m/s and a maximum speed value v_{max} m/s, and select a pause time uniformly between 0 and $2s$. The simulation parameters are summarized in Table 1.

Table 1. Simulation parameters

Parameters	Value(s)
Simulation area	1000m x 1000m
Number of nodes	$N \in [50, 1000]$
Comm. range	$R \in \{50, 100, 200, 300\}$m
Bandwidth	$r = 1$ Mbps
Message size	280 bytes
Mobility model	Random waypoint
- Max speed	- $v_{max} \in [0,30]$ m/s
- Pause	- Uniform between 0 and 2s
fDelay	10ms

We use the following traffic model. At the beginning of the simulation (namely random between first and second sec) each of the S senders sends a single message. The simulation time selected for all scenarios in this paper is $20s$. For the adaptation process, we set $S = 1$, $R = 100m$ and $v_{max} = 3m/s$.

The random waypoint model shows an almost uniform node spatial distribution. This property simplifies the conversion of node density to number of neighbors and vice versa. Given n the number of neighbors and R the communication range, a node easily computes its local density by:

$$d = \frac{n+1}{\pi R^2} \Leftrightarrow n = \pi R^2 d - 1 \tag{4}$$

As mentioned before, nodes acquire neighborhood information by means of HELLO beaconing. For all simulations in this work we use a random beaconing period between $0.75s$ and $1.25s$. A node removes a neighbor from its neighbor list, if during 2s no beacon is received from this neighbor.

Adaptation Using the Epidemic Model. The infection rate a clearly depends on the gossiping probability p. If this probability is 0, the infection rate will also be 0. If p increases, the infection rate also increases. However, if the network is very dense and all nodes forward every newly received message, contention and collisions increase, so that delay increases, and subsequently the overall infection rate will decrease. Hence, we investigate the impact of both node density and gossiping probability on the infection rate in more details. This investigation allows the selection of the appropriate probability depending on node density.

According to the SI-model, the infection rate determines the spreading ratio and therefore it is a measure for delivery reliability and timeliness. The higher the infection rate, the lower the mean delay. In the following we show how we used these results to adapt gossiping. In order to adapt the forwarding probability to the node density, we should select the probability that maximizes the infection rate. We vary node density and the forwarding probability p and compute the corresponding infection rate for some combinations. Fig. 2 (a) shows the measured infection rates and their interpolation. Fig. 2 (b) shows the optimal probability, which should be used for gossiping depending on the MANET node density.

Consistent with our second requirement on a broadcasting technique, we let every node set the gossiping probability *locally* and *independently*. A node j can easily estimate its local node density d_j using Eq. (4), given its number of neighbors n_j. According to the value of d_j the node sets on-the-fly the forwarding probability p_j for gossiping.

To avoid the computation of local node density, which also assumes that nodes know their communication range R, we propose that nodes select the gossiping probability

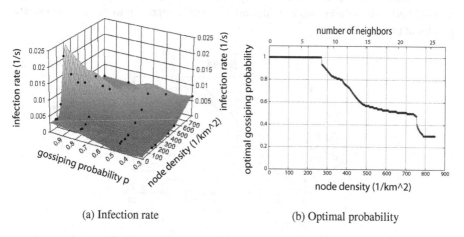

(a) Infection rate   (b) Optimal probability

Fig. 2. Adaptation of gossiping using the infection rate

depending on the current number of neighbors n. By scaling the x-axis of Fig. 2 (b) using Eq. (4), we get the optimal gossiping probability p as a function of n. We could now provide the discrete values of this curve as a lookup table that maps the number of neighbors to the probability values. At run-time, nodes could then access this lookup table in order to set the gossiping probability dynamically, depending on their current number of neighbors.

Nevertheless, in order to elegantly present our adaptation results for the community, we analytically express the gossiping probability depending on the number of neighbors. To ensure adaptation for higher dense networks, we extrapolate the gossiping probability value to higher number of neighbors. We use the following series expansion ansatz: $p(n) = a + b/n$. The fitting process using the least squares method, recommends $a = 0.175$ and $b = 6.050$. The fitting standard error is about 4.75%. The result of the adaptation is a simple function that nodes can easily use to calculate the appropriate gossiping probability (p) for the current number of neighbors (n). The function is given by Eq. (5) or simply Eq. (6):

$$\begin{cases} p = 1.0, & \text{if } n \leq 7 \\ p = 0.175 + 6.05/n & \text{if } n \geq 8 \end{cases} \tag{5}$$

$$p = min\left(1.0, 0.175 + \frac{6.05}{n}\right) \tag{6}$$

Relevance of Epidemic Models for Protocol Adaptation. We show the relevance of the analytical epidemic models for the adaptation of broadcast protocols through investigating alternative approaches for the adaptation.

Fig. 3 shows the spreading ratio of gossiping over time for 500 nodes and different forwarding probabilities. We conclude that only probabilities higher than 0.6 provide a delivery reliability close to 100%. We also conclude that the forwarding probability 0.6 provides faster propagation than higher probabilities. This is due to broadcast storms if more than 60% of nodes forward the packet. Thus, investigating the spreading ratio obtained from simulations provides an alternative approach to fix the appropriate gossiping probability.

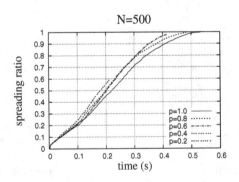

Fig. 3. Adaptation of forwarding probability (Simulation-based approach)

However, the selection of the probability is achieved manually and therefore it is not practical and error-prone. Furthermore, the approach requires running simulations for probability values as fine as possible to increase the accuracy of adaptation. Comparing the simulation-based approach with the approach relying on the epidemic model we note the simplicity of the last approach, which provides an automated method for the selection of the appropriate forwarding probability depending on node density, using only fewer simulations. The use of the SI-model for adaptation of key protocol parameters to relevant network properties can be easily repeated for further adaptation needs.

6   Evaluation of Reliable Gossiping

We now evaluate the adaptive gossiping protocol with scenarios that show a wide range of node densities and node speeds. Additionally, we study the impact of communication range on the performance of adaptive gossiping. We also compare adaptive gossiping with STOCH-FLOOD [12] and ACB [11]. Our evaluation approach is simulation-based.

We use the same simulation model as in Section 5.3. We set the number of senders to $S = 25$. Since the knowledge of the partitioning of the MANET is important for understanding the performance of adaptive gossiping, we computed the average number of partitions for the different scenarios that we consider in this section (Fig. 4). For this computation we use our own framework presented in [20].

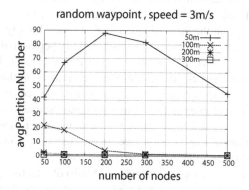

Fig. 4. Average number of partitions

6.1   Performance Metrics

In order to evaluate broadcast protocols with respect to delivery reliability and timeliness, the performance metrics reachability and delay respectively are commonly used in the broadcast community. In the following we define these both metrics. With respect to a given broadcast message, we denote by *#Forwd* the number of nodes that forwarded the message and by *#Reach* the number of nodes that received the message after the termination of the protocol.

REachability (RE): The ratio of nodes receiving the message to the total number of nodes, i.e. $RE = \frac{\#Reach}{N}$ ($\in [0,1]$). The reachability metric measures the delivery reliability.

Delay: Average end-to-end delay over all receivers. Denoting by t_s the origination time of the message and by t_j the arrival time of the message at node j, we calculate the delay as follows: $delay = \frac{1}{\#Reach} \sum_{reachedNode_j} (t_j - t_s)$.

To evaluate the efficiency of broadcast protocols the message complexity is a key factor. The common efficiency metric for broadcast protocols is:

MNF: Mean Number of Forwards per node and message. $MNF = \frac{\#Forwd}{N}$.

As we used the spreading ratio for describing the quality of a broadcast protocol, we differentiate the above metrics from the spreading ratio. Both metrics *RE* and *delay* are easily gained from the spreading ratio. Given the spreading ratio as a time function $i(t) \in [0,1]$. The RE is the the maximum value of the spreading ratio (reached when the broadcast protocol terminates), or $RE = \max(i(t))$. The delay is calculated as follows: $\frac{1}{RE} \int_0^{RE} i^{-1}(t)\,dt$, where $i^{-1}(t)$ is the inverse function of $i(t)$.

6.2   Impact of Node Density and Node Mobility

For this study, we vary the node density by tuning the total number of nodes and keeping the area unmodified. From Fig. 5 (a), we observe that the reachability of adaptive gossiping first increases with node density, reaches a maximum and then starts to decrease. We qualitatively explain this effect as follows: Obviously, gossiping can only reach nodes that belong to the partition, which contains the source node. For random waypoint, the mean number of partitions decreases with the increasing number of nodes (Fig. 4, 100m range). This means that the average partition size is increasing. Therefore, reachability increases with the increasing number of nodes. For high number of nodes, collision probability becomes higher and the reachability begins to decline slightly.

The impact of node speed is marginal. However, we present three observations. Firstly, for very sparse networks the mobility has no impact on the reachability. Secondly, for scenarios that are neither very sparse nor connected (e.g. 200 nodes), the mobility may help to overcome network partitioning and the reachability increases with higher speeds. Thirdly, for dense scenarios, reachability decreases with higher speeds. The reason is that a node may sense a free carrier and starts to transmit; but while moving very fast it disturbs other ongoing transmissions.

In Fig. 5 (b), we show the message overhead (MNF) of adaptive gossiping. For random waypoint, we can assume a uniform node distribution, and therefore estimate the MNF of gossiping as follows: $MNF \approx p * RE$. This explains the behavior of MNF, which shows a strong similarity to that of reachability. For lower number of nodes, The forwarding probability p is frequently set to 1.0 and $MNF \approx RE$. For higher number of nodes, nodes use lower forwarding probabilities, thus increasing the number of saved forwards, and therefore $MNF < RE$. The delivery delay increases with increasing number of nodes since the number of traversed hops to the destination and the buffering time of messages at the MAC layer increase (Fig. 5 (c)).

6.3   Impact of Transmission Range

In this study, we investigate the performance of gossiping for different communication ranges $\in \{50, 100, 200, 300\}m$. We note that an increase in communication range can be interpreted as an increase of node density.

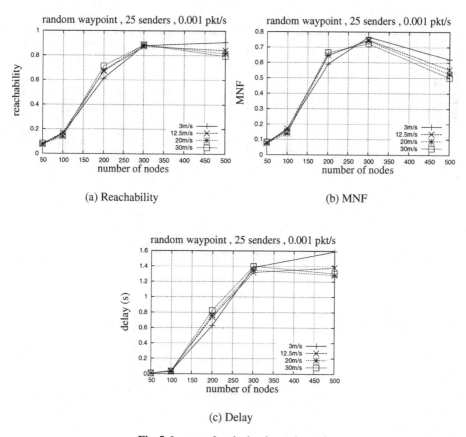

(a) Reachability   (b) MNF

(c) Delay

Fig. 5. Impact of node density and speed

The reachability of gossiping increases with the communication range (Fig. 6 (a)). For low communication ranges, the reachability decreases with increasing number of nodes and reaches a minimum (by $N = 200$ and for $R = 50m$), and increases for higher numbers of nodes. We explain this decrease of reachability as follows. For highly sparse MANETs, an increase of number of nodes, leads to a decrease in the ratio of partition size to the total number of nodes. Consider the extreme case, where nodes are isolated and the reachability of gossiping is $1/N$. If we increase the number of nodes by δN and all nodes remain isolated, the reachability of gossiping is $1/(N + \delta N)$. Therefore, the reachability of gossiping decreases with increasing number of nodes in highly sparse MANETs.

For higher communication ranges, the curve of reachability however shows a maximum. The reachability slightly decreases for higher numbers of nodes due to the increasing number of collisions. The number of collisions increases since most of source nodes are within each other's communication range. Therefore, one broadcast has more impact on the other broadcasts taking place almost simultaneously. Gossiping has not been adapted to network load. Consequently, for higher network loads the reachability of gossiping is likely to decrease.

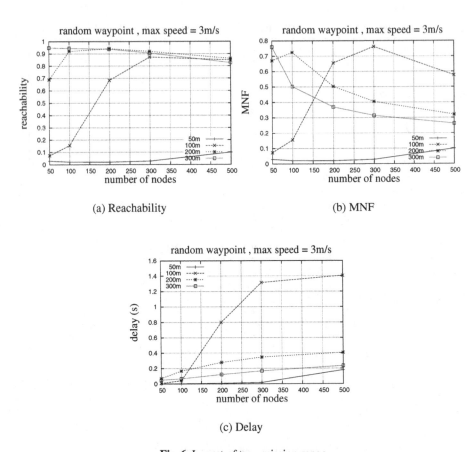

(a) Reachability   (b) MNF

(c) Delay

Fig. 6. Impact of transmission range

For discussing the message overhead, we first consider the communication range 100m (Fig. 6 (b)). MNF first increases with the number of nodes, reaches a maximum and then decreases. The maximum is reached, when almost all nodes forward broadcast messages, i.e. gossiping goes into blind flooding. MNF reaches its maximum, when the MANET starts to be constituted of one large partition and a few small partitions. If the MANET node density increases, adaptation of gossiping runs and saves a number of forwards, which is reflected by the decrease of MNF. For the 200m communication range, the maximum is reached for 100 nodes. For a 300m communication range the maximum moves to the left of 50 nodes and is no longer observed for our experiment settings. For a 50m range, MNF is very close to reachability, since the node density is very low and almost all receivers forward messages. The maximum is reached for a number of nodes that is higher than 500 nodes.

We note that the performed delay should be interpreted relatively to the achieved reachability. Fig. 6 (c) shows that the delay decreases with an increasing communication range (except for 50m). The explanation is that: If the communication range gets higher, a transmission is more likely to reach more nodes, which decreases average delay.

We observe however that the delay for 50m is lower than that for higher communication ranges. This is due to the fact that, for 50m the MANET is highly partitioned (Fig. 4) and a network partition is composed of few nodes. Gossiping reaches these few nodes in a few transmissions, i.e. very fast. Similarly, we explain the low delay values for 100m range and number of nodes less than 100.

6.4 Comparison of Reliable Gossiping to the Optimal Case

From the above studies, we realize the strong need for a global view with respect to network partitioning in the MANET for a better understanding of the protocol performance. In [20], we presented the utilities required for ns-2 users, in order to simplify the access to this global view. In the following, we present the global evaluation of reliable gossiping.

Reliable gossiping aims to efficiently reach all nodes in the partition where the broadcast source is located. In this section, we aim to investigate in more details the delivery reliability of gossiping. In particular, we define the optimal gossiping reachability (OG_RE) as the ratio of the size of the partition containing the gossiping source node to the total number of nodes: $OG\_RE = \frac{partition\_size}{N}$.

The reachability of adaptive gossiping should correlate with the partition size. Fig. 7 (a) shows that the gossiping reachability is lower than the optimal gossiping reachability and that the difference is more important for higher number of nodes. This is due to collisions, which prohibit gossiping from progressing, and become more frequent with increasing number of nodes. Fig. 7 (b) shows the frequency histogram of the ratio of the number of nodes reached by gossiping to the sender's partition size. We observe that in most of cases gossiping reaches either more than 90% of the partition nodes or less than 10% of nodes, which proves the transitional behavior discussed in [6] [14].

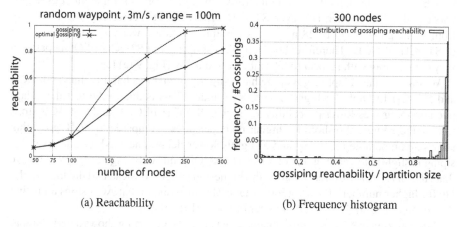

(a) Reachability   (b) Frequency histogram

Fig. 7. Comparison of reliable gossiping to the optimal case

6.5   Comparison to Related Work

We compare the performance of our adaptive scheme to that of the Adaptive Counter Based scheme (ACB) [11] and of stochastic flooding (STOCH-FLOOD) [12]. We arbitrarily fix v_{max} to 3 m/s. However, we vary the total number of nodes N.

The ACB scheme uses a random time span to count redundant packet receptions and forwards the message after this span, only if the counter value is below a threshold value. This time period is comparable to the random forwarding delay of gossiping ($fDelay$) and STOCH-FLOOD. Therefore, we choose the same value for all three protocols, i.e. 10ms, which is also used in [5]. The adaptive thresholds for all three protocols are shown in Fig. 8.

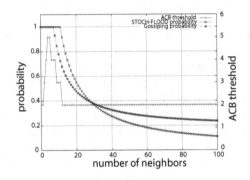

Fig. 8. Adaptive thresholds

The comparison of reliable gossiping to STOCH-FLOOD can be intuitively undertaken based on the comparison of probability functions used by each protocol (Fig. 8). Reliable gossiping starts decreasing the forwarding probability for a number of neighbors equal to 8 or higher. However, STOCH-FLOOD starts decreasing the probability from 11 neighbors. Up to 28 neighbors gossiping uses a lower probability than that of STOCH-FLOOD. Therefore, both reliable gossiping and STOCH-FLOOD perform very comparably with respect to reachability and delay (Fig. 9 (a) (c)).

We observe that adaptive gossiping has a slightly higher reachability than both ACB and STOCH-FLOOD for higher numbers of nodes. This is due to the fact that adaptive gossiping uses lower probability value than STOCH-FLOOD and that ACB stops to tune the counter threshold for higher node densities. Compared to ACB, gossiping shows a comparable reliability and a slightly lower delay. The MNF of adaptive gossiping is slightly lower than that of STOCH-FLOOD and ACB (Fig. 9 (b)). We observe that ACB has the lowest reachability, the highest message overhead and the highest delay for higher number of nodes (500 nodes). This also due to that ACB stops adjusting the counter threshold for higher number of nodes (Fig. 8).

Summarizing, we can roughly conclude that adaptive gossiping shows a very comparable overall performance to STOCH-FLOOD and that both protocols outperform ACB and particularly in highly dense scenarios. Between adaptive gossiping and STOCH-FLOOD, we identify the following marginal differences. In extremely dense networks,

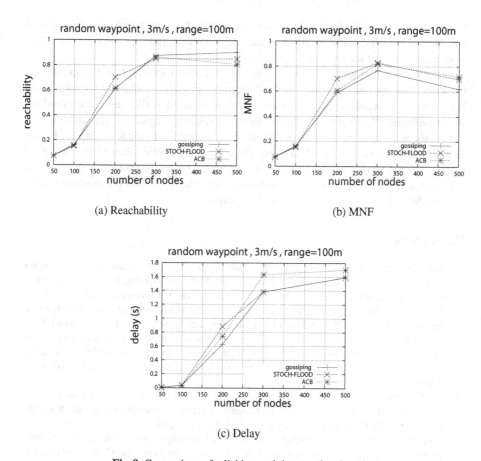

(a) Reachability

(b) MNF

(c) Delay

Fig. 9. Comparison of reliable gossiping to related work

STOCH-FLOOD saves more forwards and reaches slightly more nodes than adaptive gossiping. However, in less dense scenarios adaptive gossiping saves more forwards and reaches slightly less nodes than STOCH-FLOOD.

Simulation results that we do not include here show that the three protocols achieve a very comparable performance for further mobility models such as the reference-point group mobility model [21] and the graph-based mobility model [22], which show quite different node spatial distributions.

7 Conclusions

We showed at the example of gossiping, how to use epidemic models to adapt broadcasting strategies in MANETs. We used the analytical epidemic model developed for gossiping to adapt the main parameter of gossiping, i.e. the forwarding probability, to the most relevant MANET property, i.e. node density. The result is a reliable broadcast protocol that adapts locally to the continuously changing node spatial distribution.

Gossiping dynamically adjusts the forwarding probability only based on the number of neighbors, a locally available information, and without requiring any particular information, such as distance, position, or velocity.

Intensive simulations show the near-optimal reliability of adaptive gossiping. Furthermore, the dynamic selection of the forwarding probability reduces the total number of nodes forwarding a certain message, thus effectively alleviating the broadcast storm problem. We additionally highlight the simplicity, frugalness and scalability of our protocol. Adaptive gossiping performs very comparably to the few adaptive broadcast schemes known from the literature. This shows the applicability of the analytical platform we developed for the adaptation of MANET broadcast protocols. Particularly, we emphasize that the use of the SI-model for adaptation of further protocols to further relevant MANET properties can be easily repeated.

References

1. Bellavista, P., Corradi, A., Magistretti, E.: Redman: An optimistic replication middleware for read-only resources in dense manets. Pervasive and Mobile Computing 1(3), 279–310 (2005)
2. Pleisch, S., Clouser, T., Nesterenko, M., Schiper, A.: Drift: Efficient message ordering in ad hoc networks using virtual flooding. In: Proc. of the IEEE Symposium on Reliable Distributed Systems (SRDS), pp. 119–131. IEEE Computer Society Press, Los Alamitos (2006)
3. Ni, S., Tseng, Y., Chen, Y., Sheu, J.: The broadcast storm problem in a mobile ad hoc network. In: Proc. of the Annual ACM/IEEE International Conference on Mobile Computing and Networking (MOBICOM), pp. 151–162. IEEE Computer Society Press, Los Alamitos (1999)
4. Yi, Y., Gerla, M., Kwon, T.: Efficient flooding in ad hoc networks: A comparative performance study. In: Proc. of the IEEE International Conference on Communications (ICC), pp. 1059–1063. IEEE Computer Society Press, Los Alamitos (2003)
5. Williams, B., Camp, T.: Comparison of broadcasting techniques for mobile ad hoc networks. In: Proc. of the ACM Symposium on Mobile Ad Hoc Networking and Computing (MOBIHOC), pp. 194–205. ACM Press, New York (2002)
6. Haas, Z., Halpern, J., Li, L.: Gossip-based ad hoc routing. In: Proc. of the IEEE Joint Conference of Computer and Communication Societies (INFOCOM), pp. 1707–1716. IEEE Computer Society Press, Los Alamitos (2002)
7. Qayyum, A., Viennot, L., Laouiti, A.: Multipoint relaying for flooding broadcast messages in mobile wireless networks. In: Proc. of the 35th Annual Hawaii International Conference on System Sciences (HICSS), pp. 3866–3875 (2002)
8. Stojmenovic, I., Seddigh, M., Zunic, J.: Dominating sets and neighbor elimination-based broadcasting algorithms in wireless networks. IEEE Transactions on Parallel and Distributed Systems 13(1), 14–25 (2002)
9. Calinescu, G., Mandoiu, I., Wan, P., Zelikovsky, A.: Selecting forwarding neighbors in wireless ad hoc networks. In: Proc. of the 5th International Workshop on Discrete Algorithms and Methods for Mobile Computing and Communications (DIAL-M), pp. 34–43 (2001)
10. Basagni, S., Bruschi, D., Chlamtac, I.: A mobility transparent deterministic broadcast mechanism for ad hoc networks. ACM/IEEE Transactions on Networking 7(6), 799–807 (1999)
11. Tseng, Y., Ni, S., Shih, E.: Adaptive approaches to relieving broadcast storms in a wireless multihop mobile ad hoc networks. IEEE Transactions on Computers 52(5), 545–557 (2003)
12. Cartigny, J., Simplot, D.: Border node retransmission based probabilistic broadcast protocols in ad-hoc networks. In: Proc. of the Annual Hawaii International Conference on System Sciences (HICSS), 303 (2003)

13. Zhang, Q., Agrawal, D.: Dynamic probabilistic broadcasting in manets. Journal of Parallel and Distributed Computing 65(2), 220–233 (2005)
14. Sasson, Y., Cavin, D., Schiper, A.: Probabilistic broadcast for flooding in wireless mobile ad hoc networks. In: Proc. of The IEEE Wireless Communications and Networking Conference (WCNC), pp. 1124–1130. IEEE Computer Society Press, Los Alamitos (2003)
15. Khelil, A., Becker, C., Tian, J., Rothermel, K.: An epidemic model for information diffusion in manets. In: Proc. of the ACM international workshop on Modeling, analysis and simulation of wireless and mobile systems (MSWiM), pp. 54–60. ACM Press, New York (2002)
16. Khelil, A., Marrón, P., Rothermel, K.: Contact-based mobility metrics for delay-tolerant ad hoc networking. In: Proc. of The 13th IEEE/ACM International Symposium on Modeling, Analysis, and Simulation of Computer and Telecommunication Systems (MASCOTS), pp. 435–444. ACM Press, New York (2005)
17. Broch, J., Maltz, D., Johnson, D., Hu, Y., Jetcheva, J.: A performance comparison of multi-hop wireless ad hoc network routing protocols. In: Proc. of the Fourth Annual ACM/IEEE International Conference on Mobile Computing and Networking (MOBICOM), IEEE Computer Society Press, Los Alamitos (1998)
18. Wolfram-Research-Inc.: Mathematica, version 4.0 (1999)
19. McCanne, S., Floyd, S.: Ns network simulator, http://www.isi.edu/nsnam/ns/
20. Khelil, A., Marrón, P., Dietrich, R., Rothermel, K.: Evaluation of partition-aware manet protocols and applications with ns-2. In: Proc. of the 2005 International Symposium on Performance Evaluation of Computer and Telecommunication Systems (SPECTS) (2005)
21. Hong, X., Gerla, M., Bagrodia, R., Pei, G.: A group mobility model for ad hoc wireless networks. In: Proceedings of the 2nd ACM international workshop on Modeling, analysis and simulation of wireless and mobile systems (MSWiM), pp. 53–60. ACM Press, New York (1999)
22. Tian, J., Hähner, J., Becker, C., Stepanov, I., Rothermel, K.: Graph-based mobility model for mobile ad hoc network simulation. In: Proceedings of the 35th Annual Simulation Symposium (ANSS), pp. 337–344 (2002)

On the Behavior of Broadcasting Protocols for MANETs Under Omission Faults Scenarios*

Talmai Brandão de Oliveira, Victor Franco Costa, and Fabíola Greve

Federal University of Bahia,
Computer Science Department,
Mechatronics Graduate Program
Salvador BA 40.170-110, Brazil
talmai@ufba.br, vfcosta@dcc.ufba.br, fabiola@dcc.ufba.br

Abstract. Ensuring reliable communication between nodes is a major challenge in mobile ad-hoc networks due to wireless signal propagation that can be significantly affected by terrain, obstacles, battery exhaustion and node mobility. Existing broadcasting protocols for MANETs are able to deal with mobility, as well as congestion and collision, but only when under a fail-stop failure model. However, this model is not a good representative of the real scenarios of faults frequent in MANETs such as link failures, temporary network partitions, topology changes and momentary node failures. In this work we evaluate – through the aid of simulation experiments – how well MANET broadcasting protocols behave when under a more realistic failure model, which are characterized by omission faults. We also discuss their properties and behaviors when taking reliability into consideration. The study conducted here show that most protocols are highly impacted by node failures and are not capable of maintaining high delivery rate. Some even exhibit coverage levels that are unreasonable to expect from broadcasting protocols when placed in a real world scenario.

Keywords: Mobile Ad-Hoc Networks, Broadcasting, Fault-Tolerant Wireless Communication, Reliable Broadcasting.

1 Introduction

A mobile ad hoc network (MANET) is a special kind of network where the mobile hosts (also called nodes) are capable of communication restricted to their wireless transmission range. Thus they are only able to communicate directly with neighboring nodes. The lack of fixed and wired gateways (base stations) forces cooperation between the nodes every time a packet has to be forwarded. Moreover, because of the shared transmission channels, nodes are not able to selectively transmit: whenever it sends a message, all of its neighbors receive it. Whenever messages overlap, collisions may occur, preventing correct reception [1].

---

* This work is supported by grants from CNPQ - Brazil and FAPESB - Bahia/Brazil.

A. Bondavalli, F. Brasileiro, and S. Rajsbaum (Eds.): LADC 2007, LNCS 4746, pp. 142–159, 2007.

Broadcasting refers to the process by which one node sends messages to all other nodes in the network. It is an essential operation in all kind of networks since it may be used to collect global information, to support addressing algorithms, to implement multicasting and, particularly in MANETs, to help routing protocols to propagate routing-related information [2]. Broadcasting is an active research topic and the most significant challenge in its development is compensating between the number of messages broadcast and the number of nodes reached [3].

A large number of algorithms for broadcasting in MANETs exist. Most of them assume that during the process of broadcasting there happens none or very little topology change and that the network remains connected. But in a real scenario, this cannot always be guaranteed. This is what motivates our work. We propose to study how well existing MANET broadcasting protocols behave when under a realistic scenario. It is well known that wireless signal propagation is significantly affected by terrain, obstacles, unanticipated interference and unpredictable fading, causing constant link failures and fluctuating communication channels [4,5]. Many other factors also impede correct message transmission and reception as well, including hardware failure, battery exhaustion and node mobility [6,7].

Previous studies on the impact of faults in broadcasting protocols have limited themselves on analyzing the impact of mobility, collisions and network congestion on the delivery rate (reliability) and on the number of gateway nodes (efficiency) [2,8]. Although these three factors can be considered as faults, they are not sufficient to denote all the possible fault scenarios that affect MANETs such as link failures, temporary network partitions, topology change during broadcasts and momentary node failures. Existing works consider fail-stop failures and most broadcasting protocols are tolerant to these types of failures. Furthermore, this failure model provides a simple abstraction for reasoning about failure-prone environments and system reliability, but in real systems this is not always the case. In our opinion it is the omission failure model[1] that appropriately represents real fault scenarios.

We propose to study six significant broadcasting protocols. The protocols are: Simple Flooding, Dynamic Probabilistic Protocol [3], Wu and Li's protocol's [9], Scalable Broadcasting Algorithm [10], Dominant Pruning [11] and Double-Covered Broadcast [12]. For each one of these, we discuss their properties and behaviors when taking reliability into consideration, and evaluate the impact of omission faults on their performance. Our simulation studies consist of measuring the reliability, the forwarding ratio and the end-to-end delay of the protocols when 0%, 5%, 10%, 20%, 30% and 50% of the nodes fail using an omissive failure model. As far as we know, no performance study about the impact of omission faults in broadcasting protocols has ever been done.

Although previous simulated studies show that the broadcast protocols are very mobile resilient and support well congestion and collisions, the study

---

[1] In the omission model, nodes fails by crashing (prematurely halting) or by sending/receiving only a subset of the messages that it actually attempts to send/receive.

conducted here show that these protocols are not fault tolerant when omission failures are taken into account. They are not capable of maintaining high delivery rate when placed in a real world scenario. The choice of the protocols leads us to believe that this conclusion can be extended to most, if not all, broadcasting protocols for MANETs which are based on the same reliability mechanisms. Based on the study conducted, we investigate the source of existing broadcasting problems and list the lessons learned as a step towards enhancing the capability of broadcasting algorithms to deal with omission faults in scalable scenarios.

This paper is organized as follows. Section 2 describes the protocols in study. Section 3 presents the simulation model, the results and lessons learned with the study. Finally, Section 4 concludes the paper and presents future works.

2   Broadcasting in MANETs

Since MANETs are dynamic in nature, global information exchange are no longer reasonable to expect and support. Nodes must then somehow limit themselves to local information on topology in order to broadcast. Broadcasting protocols must also be able to adapt to a wide range of MANETs including partition-less scenarios, eventually disconnected scenarios (where partitions occur rarely but reconnect quickly) and eventually connected scenarios (where partitions occur most of the time, eventually reconnect, but quickly partition once again). Broadcasting protocols are commonly classified based on their delivery guarantees, and they can either be probabilistic or deterministic. *Probabilistic broadcasting* protocols are those that guarantee delivery with a certain probability. Probabilistic protocols have less constraints and assumptions when compared to deterministic protocols; are usually simpler to implement; and normally have little memory requirements. *Deterministic protocols* on the other hand are those which assume non-probabilistic delivery guarantees. Deterministic broadcasting protocols can be further classified as either self-pruning or neighborhood designating. In self-pruning algorithms a node that receives a message decides by itself whether it is a forwarding node (also known as gateway). While in neighborhood designating algorithms it is the sending node who selects the neighboring nodes that should become gateways by piggy-backing this list in the broadcast message.

If the topology of the network is known and static, it is possible to calculate the *minimum connected dominating set* (namely, MCDS) [13] in order to select the set of gateways with which the smallest overhead of retransmissions can achieve the highest delivery rate. A MCDS is the smallest set of forwarding nodes such that every node in the set is connected, and all nodes which are not in the set are within transmission range of at least one node in the MCDS. Once found, the process of forwarding messages can be handled by the nodes within the set. Unfortunately, the problem of finding a MCDS has been proven to be NP-complete [3,13], thus the use of efficient approximation algorithms is necessary. Among various alternative approximation approaches, many protocols utilizes 2-hop neighborhood information to reduce redundant transmission. Updated local topology information comes at a small price since by periodically sending *"Hello"* messages, nodes are able to construct a local view of their neighbors. But this information can be imprecise and inconsistent, since between any two *"Hello"* messages, a node may move, its neighbors may crash, a link may become unstable or many other situations may arise.

2.1   Description of Chosen Protocols

In the following paragraphs we will describe each of the chosen protocols. Among such a large number of existing broadcasting protocols for MANETs, it has been no easy task to choose the few which will be used in our study. We later justify our choices.

Simple Flooding. This is one of the simplest solutions to broadcasting. In this approach every message received by a node is forwarded. In fact, flooding (and all probabilistic protocols) are seen as an option to tackle the lack of determinism of MANETs by applying a non-deterministic solution. While there exists many papers that use this naive approach, it has been shown in [14,15] that it leads to unreasonable high contention, collision and redundancy problems, which may possibly interfere in the coverage (number of individual nodes that received a specific message) and increase latency of the broadcast. This is known as the *broadcast storm* problem [14]. Although for a more static scenario it is not re-commended, many extremely mobile and dynamic scenarios can only rely on this approach to broadcast. Actually, flooding is used by many existing broadcasting protocols as a last resort when "all else fails"[16].

Dynamic Probabilistic Approach. In order to reduce the number of forward nodes in the flooding approach, one alternative probabilistic solution proposed in [14] is that each node be allowed to re-transmit based on a probability P. Clearly, when $P = 1$ it will behave as flooding. Most approaches to probabilistic broadcasting assume a fixed probability [2,14]. Depending on the value chosen a high ratio of delivery can be obtained. Another option proposed in [14] was to use a counter to keep track on the number of times a message has been recei-ved. If after a random delay the counter equals an internal counter threshold, it is assumed that the message has been received by all neighbors and the node will not re-transmit. Thus, in a dense area of the network, some nodes will not rebroadcast, while in sparse areas of the network, all nodes rebroadcast. Zhang and Agrawal proposed the dynamic probabilistic approach [3] by combining the probabilistic approach with the counter based approach [14] and adjusting the value of P according to the density of the network. The re-transmission proba-bility P is lowered whenever a node is positioned in a high-density area, while it is raised when in sparser areas. Network density is estimated by using an in-ternal counter that increases whenever a node detects a neighbor and decreases periodically.

Wu and Li. Wu and Li [9] proposed a deterministic self-pruning algorithm to calculate a set of forward nodes that form a connected dominating set. Their solution reduces the number of forwarding nodes while maintaining a high delivery ratio, and is scalable to many diverse network scenarios. Their marking process is simple and relies on constant neighborhood set exchange between nodes: a node is marked as a gateway if it has two neighbors that are not directly connected. Clearly, after neighborhood set exchange, each node knows its 2-hop neighbors. The algorithm uses a constant number of rounds to calculate the connected dominating set, which is directly related to the number of neighbors each node has. Additionally, it also uses pruning rules to reduce even further the set of gateway nodes. Their solution establishes priorities between nodes by using individual node IDs and degree (number of 1-hop neighboring nodes). The priority values are used in order to establish a total order among all nodes of the MANET. Wu and Li´s protocol is well known and has been used and extended by many others [8,17,18]. But these works where all inspired on reducing the number of gateways nodes and on increasing broadcasting efficiency; not necessarily on achieving high message delivery ratio. Simulation results clearly show that although older, the original protocol still ensures higher message coverage [8]. This is why we chose it over the newer protocols.

Scalable Broadcast Algorithm (SBA). The main idea of the deterministic self-pruning scalable broadcasting algorithm proposed by Peng and Lu (namely, SBA) [10] is that a node does not need to rebroadcast a message that already has been received by neighboring nodes. In order to determine this, each node needs to have knowledge of local 2-hop topology and of duplicate messages. Their algorithm works in 2 steps: local neighborhood discovery and data broadcasting. Local neighborhood discovery consists of exchanging neighborhood sets between local nodes in order to learn 2-hop topology information (exactly like Wu and Li's protocol). For data broadcasting, whenever a node t receives a message m from his neighbor v, before forwarding the message it checks which nodes belong to v's neighborhood. Since v transmitted, node t knows all the nodes that should have received the message. By looking at its own neighborhood set, t can determine if there are still any other neighbors which have not received m. Only when there exists neighbors in this situation will t schedule a re-transmission. Instead of immediately re-transmitting, the authors proposed a random backoff delay based on the density of the neighborhood. Nodes with more neighbors will have a higher priority and will rebroadcast earlier, thus raising the chances of a single transmission reaching a greater number of nodes.

Dominant Pruning (DP). The dominant pruning algorithm (namely, DP) [11] is a deterministic neighborhood designating broadcasting protocol that uses 2-hop neighborhood information to reduce redundant transmissions. In DP, whenever a node receives a message, it selects the smallest number of forwarding nodes that can cover all nodes in a 2-hop distance. That is, when node j receives a message from node k, it selects from the set $N(j)$ the minimum number of nodes that should act as gateways to reach all nodes in $N(N(j))$. The DP protocol assumes that when node k first transmitted the message, all of its 1-hop neighbors (which is the set $N(k)$) correctly received the message. It also assumes that when node j forwards the message, all of its 1-hop neighbors $(N(j))$ will correctly receive the message as well. Thus, node j will then just try to determine $N(N(j)) - N(j) - N(k)$ (which *supposedly* will be the remaining nodes who, after node j forwards, will not have received the message yet). By determining this, it will then loop through $N(j)$ and select the smallest number of nodes that are able to guarantee coverage. These nodes will become forwarding nodes. Since it is a neighborhood designating protocol, it piggybacks this list in the broadcast message. Although there exist newer algorithms that extend DP, such as [19] where simulation results show that neighborhood information is more effectively used (lower number of gateway nodes) and even more redundant messages are eliminated, they unfortunately seem to produce results which have lower delivery rates. This obviously makes sense since it is the redundant messages that help raise message coverage. Once again we prefer the original protocol with higher coverage for this work.

Double-Covered Broadcast (DCB). Lou and Wu's goal when proposing the double-covered broadcasting protocol (namely, DCB) [12] was to reduce the number of forwarding nodes (increase efficiency) without sacrificing the broadcast delivery ratio (reliability). It is classified as a neighborhood designating protocol, much like dominant pruning. By selecting a set of gateway nodes where not only every 2-hop node is covered, but also where all 1-hop nodes are covered by at least 2 forwarding neighbors (the sender itself and one of the selected gateway nodes), it benefits from the broadcast redundancy to improve reliability. Additionally, in DCB the re-transmission of the message by the gateways node serves as an ack of correct message reception to the original sending node. This scheme avoids the ACK implosion problem [20]. The sender will wait during a pre-determined time to overhear the re-transmissions by every chosen gateway node. If it fails to detect all of the re-transmissions it assumes that a transmission failure occurred. The sender will keep re-sending the message until all forward nodes have re-transmitted or until a threshold is reached. By double-covering, DCB assumes that at least two transmissions will reach the nodes, therefore this redundancy prevents a single transmission error from interfering on message transmission and reception.

Justifications. Simple flooding and Dynamic Probabilistic protocol are, in our opinion, good representations of the probabilistic approach and were chosen for their high redundancy. Simple flooding seemed a natural choice for its simplicity while Dynamic Probabilistic for its novel approach for dynamically setting the re-broadcast probability. As representatives of self-pruning protocols we chose Wu and Li's protocol and Scalable Broadcasting Algorithm for their efficient use of neighborhood information and for their good simulation results (regarding message delivery rate). Dominant Pruning was chosen for similar reasons, but rather as the representative of neighborhood designating protocols. The Double-Covered Broadcast protocol can be considered a reliable broadcasting since it tries to ensure message delivery beyond best-effort guarantees. It was chosen not only for its' novelty, but also for applying multiple reliability mechanisms.

3   Performance Evaluation

In order to evaluate the performance and behavior of the broadcasting protocols when in an omission-fault injected environment, we ran simulations using the NS-2 network simulator [21].

3.1   Simulation Model

The Scenario. Motivated by findings that simplistic mobility and radio propagation models had a significant impact on the behavior of MANET broadcasting protocols [5] and, in order to attest that our simulation results were valid, we chose more realistic parameters with which to simulate. The simulation parameters are listed in Table 1. During the simulation the nodes were confined within $1300 \times 1300\ m^2$. Each of them had a constant transmission range of $250\ m$. For the radio propagation model we used the *Two-Ray Ground Reflection* model as implemented in the simulator, while the MAC layer followed the IEEE 802.11 specification with no RTS/CTS/ACK for all message transmissions. We used BonnMotion v1.3a [22] as our mobility scenario generator. The movement pattern of each node follows the Gauss-Markov mobility model as defined by BonnMotion. Up to an 18 *second* pause time can occur before a node moves to a new location.

To allow for proper initialization and settling, we allow 3000 *seconds* of node movement without any kind of message exchange. Each simulation then ran for a total of 500 *seconds*. In the first 100 *seconds* only *"Hello"* type messages are sent to allow for updated local topology information to be exchanged throughout the network. It is during the next 100 *seconds* that we configure nodes to broadcast

Table 1. Simulation Parameters

Simulation Parameters	
Simulator	NS-2 (2.30)
Network Area	$1300 \times 1300\ m^2$
Transmission Range	$250\ m$
Simulation Time	$500\ s$
# of Trials	20
Mobility Model	Gauss-Markov
Broadcast Rate	$10\ msg/s$
Node Speed	$1\ m/s$
Confidence Interval	95 %

data messages as well. For the last 300 *seconds* no *new* data messages are broadcasted, but nodes still exchange *"Hello"* messages, retransmit buffered messages as needed and move. This is to allow for proper message delivery termination, such as unsent queued messages, as well as possible re-transmission attempts. Each simulation was repeated 20 times to achieve at least a 95% confidence interval for the results.

Values used for the simulation such as broadcast rate and node speed were determined based on results obtained through a previous work [23]. Although well known that mobility is a major cause of delivery failure [19,24,25], in the cited work node speeds where varied between $1m/s$ and $160m/s$. The choice of $1m/s$ reduces the negative effects of mobility on the protocols. In the same manner, the broadcast rate value of 10 *packets/s* was determined after simulation runs varying between 1 *packet/s* and 111 *packets/s*. This value was chosen since, on average, even when taking node failure in consideration, had the best overall effect on every metric measured and permitted the most stable and reliable communication. We refer the reader to [23] for more details.

The Metrics. We have defined three metrics with which we have divided the simulation studies. The metrics are *reliability, forwarding ratio* and *end-to-end delay*. Since our main priority is analyzing the reliability of the protocols, both energy concerns and protocol overhead-related metrics (such as "hello" message exchange) were not taken into consideration. All of the values listed below are available through logs generated by the simulator.

• Reliability. A high delivery ratio is the primary goal of any broadcast protocol, thus reliability is the most significant metric. It will demonstrate not only if the broadcast protocol in question does what it is supposed to do, but will help to show how each protocol deals with failure. Since the number of nodes participating in the simulation is known by the simulator, we are able to extract and analyze the percentage of nodes that received any given message.

• Forwarding Ratio. Protocol efficiency is given by the number of gateway nodes that re-transmit and take an active role in the broadcast. Therefore, an efficient broadcast protocol is one that uses the lowest number of gateways to reach the highest number of nodes, which in turn will lead to a lower number of packets and consequently to less congestion and collision. But with the induced failure of nodes, efficiency is better measured as a ratio of the number of nodes that received a packet to the number of nodes that acted as gateways. We denominate this the forwarding ratio.

• End-to-End Delay. Finally, end-to-end delay is a metric normally used in conjunction with the others to help understand how congestion has affected the protocols, since it measures how long it takes any given packet to reach every node.

Fault Model. Most deterministic broadcasting protocols are resilient to fail-stop failures due to the fact that these protocols use constant neighborhood set exchange between nodes. Thus, a faulty node can only interfere for a short time during the broadcasting process. Shortly after the failure, all neighboring nodes will detect the fault and in future broadcasts, the node (which has now crashed), will no longer be involved in any broadcast. Using a fail-stop failure model is, in our opinion, inadequate to analyze faults when simulating deterministic broadcasting protocols. Thus, unlike any other work we have seen before, we have implemented an omission fault model in order to simulate a real world scenario characterized by interference introduced by the environment, link instability and transmission failure due to node movement. This model is also applicable to probabilistic broadcasting protocols.

In our implementation, during each one of the runs, an uniformly random selected set of nodes will fail to send and receive any kind of messages for 10 seconds. When this period is over, a new group of randomly selected nodes will be chosen to fail. The exact number of nodes chosen depends on the percentage of failed nodes which can be 0% (failure free), 5%, 10%, 20%, 30% and 50%. When defining this fault model, we had in mind the importance of randomly choosing faulty nodes, instead of selecting a static groups of nodes. But, since the number of failures is fixed, to help better spread the failure and to represent omission faults such as the ones listed above, we periodically pick another group of nodes throughout the network.

This implements an omission fault model and also helps to stress those protocols that assume a correct behavior on the reception and transmission during a broadcast, specially by some special set of nodes such as the gateway nodes. On the other hand, this fault model will favor those protocols that use additional mechanisms to properly identify message reception by neighboring nodes. It is important to note that, in parallel with the omission faults simulated by our model, other failures still keep occurring during the execution. For example, transmitted messages frequently are dropped since, after all, the radio propagation model used (in NS-2) allows for transmission errors. Nodes are also mobile, so they may even move out of transmission range.

In order to correctly compare the protocols, all were simulated under the same set of mobility and fault patterns, including the exact same broadcast message sending times.

3.2   Simulation Results

We present now the simulation results for each of the defined metric. We individually compared each of the protocols with themselves in order to be able to identify how each of them behaved when under different failure scenarios, ranging from 0% to 50%. Then we compared the protocols with each other under the same scenarios of faults. Note that all specific values used in the next paragraphs are mean values, but the results in the graphs have confidence intervals of 95% plotted as well, although these are extremely small and when plotted on a full scale graph, can hardly be seen.

Reliability Results. Figure 1 clearly shows what was expected: the reliability of all broadcasting protocols simulated lowers as the number of node failure

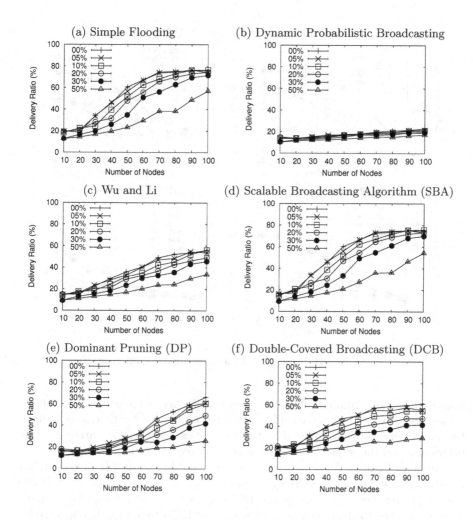

Fig. 1. The Effects of Node Failure on Reliability (Individual View)

increases. This conclusion is true to both deterministic and probabilistic approaches. In no scenario was any protocol able to deliver messages to more than 80% of the network. Flooding and SBA where the ones with the highest delivery ratios, reaching almost 80% of the network on a fail-free run (0% of node failure) in a dense network scenario. Even when failure rates raised to 30% both protocols remained pretty stable, decreasing an average of 5% in delivery rates. On the other hand, in the worst-case scenario, where 50% of the nodes failed, even in a dense network the delivery ratio barely reached 57%. In Figure 2 we can realize how similar both protocols behave. In simple flooding, both reliability and fault-tolerance is *assumed* because of the high redundancy [26]. Unfortunately, this does not guarantee message delivery to all nodes and only relies on the inherent redundancy to obtain coverage. SBA's drawback is that it requires up-to-date

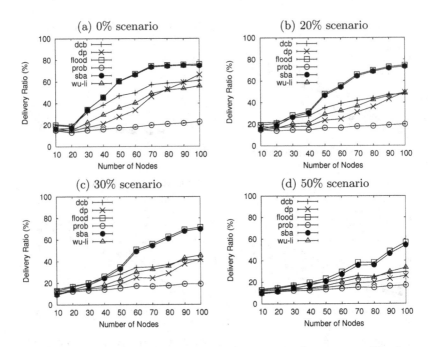

Fig. 2. The Effects of Node Failure on Reliability (Comparison View)

neighborhood information. Without it, unfortunately, a node that is receiving a message will erroneously calculate its forward status. Furthermore, a node has absolutely no guarantees that the same message correctly arrived at its neighbors, and therefore cannot just assume correct reception.

Dominant Pruning, Double-Covered and Wu and Li's protocols all had similar results regarding message delivery when in a dense fail-free network (with 100 nodes). DP reached 66% of the nodes, DCB 61% and Wu 56%. But, when failures were introduced to the simulation, both DP and DCB were rapidly impacted by node failures, delivering messages to less than 50% of the network with as little as 20% node failure, and barely reaching 41% when 30% of the nodes failed. In the worst case (50% failure) neither were able to reach more than 29% of the network. Wu and Li's, on the other hand, was capable of delivering messages to 56% of the network as long as node failures remained below 10%. This value decreases to about 45% when node failures increase to 30%. The delivery ratio only drops to 33% when in a worst-case scenario. We can appreciate direct comparisons through the graphs of Figure 2.

The authors of DP inherently assume that no errors occur during message transmission, by accepting that when a node transmits a message, all of its 1-hop neighbors correctly received the message and that, when a neighboring node forwards the message, all of its 1-hop neighbors correctly receive the message as well. But, in a fault-enabled environment this is, most often, not the case and simulations result corroborate with this as perceptible consequences to message delivery can be seen. Double-Covered's approach to broadcasting, unfortunately, relies on the reception of the acknowledgment by the sender node, but this does not ensure that the 2-hop neighbors received the message as well. Both the exposed terminal problem – where an outgoing transmission collides with an incoming transmission – and the hidden terminal problem – where two incoming transmissions collide with one another – can defeat the reliability mechanism inherent in DCB.

According to Wu and Li, in their protocol the resultant dominating set includes nodes of the shortest path. But, in an ad hoc environment, where the nodes are free to move, the shortest path tends to be the most unstable and prone to link failure [27]. This is not taken into consideration and no guarantees are ever made that a gateway is forwarding the messages nor is the delivery of any message ensured.

Dynamic Probabilistic delivery ratios' had the lowest values of all protocols, and were all between 25% and 17%. The highest value when in a fail-free scenario, and the lowest in the worst-case. It is assumed by the protocol that the network topology does not change drastically, so that the probability calculated can be a reasonable approximation of the optional probability for the next packet transmission. This, unfortunately, is only the case for networks where movement speed is low. Furthermore, while the probability of broadcasting is dynamically adjusted, it becomes dependent upon other fixed parameters that need also be carefully selected (like for example, the exact value of timeouts).

Forwarding Ratio Results. As already stated, forwarding ratio is defined as a ratio of the number of nodes that received a packet (#*receptions*) to the number of nodes that acted as gateways (#*gateways*). That is, #*gateways*/#*receptions*. The higher the forwarding ratio, the greater the number of nodes that had to forward the message. A low forwarding ratio then means that the protocol is efficient, since it uses the lowest number of gateways to reach the highest number of nodes. However, this does not mean that an efficient protocol is also reliable. In Figure 3 we can note how the forwarding ratio of all protocols is lowered as failures are introduced to the scenarios. That is, as more nodes fail, the smaller the number of nodes involved in the forwarding process. Flooding is the most inefficient protocol, as it needs to involve almost all receiving nodes in the forwarding process. Note how in the fail-free scenario it involves 100% of the nodes that receive a message in the forwarding process. Double-Covered Broadcasting also involves a large number of nodes in the forwarding process, and while it is more efficient than flooding, it is not much. Dynamic probabilistic obtains higher efficiency, since it compromises at most 50% of the nodes, but this drops to as low as 25% when in a 50% failure scenario. In an increasing scale, dominant pruning is the next most efficient protocol, as it also maintains node participation in the 25% – 40% range, but unlike dynamic probabilistic, this happens most of the time. In the worst-case scenario (50% node failure) this lowers to 18%. Both Wu and Li's protocol, as well as SBA, have high efficiency values when in a sparse and fault-enabled scenario, involving between 16% – 25% of the network on average, but reaching values as low as 10%. But similarities

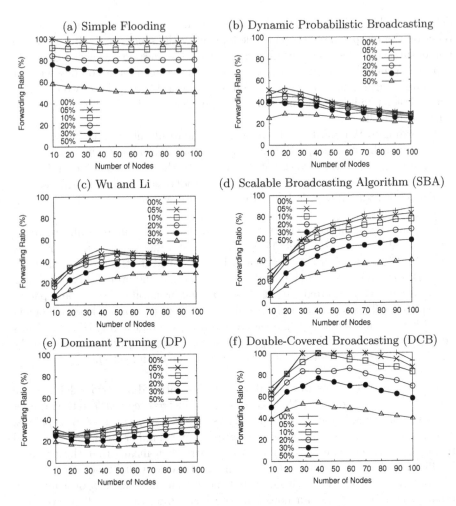

Fig. 3. The Effects of Node Failure on Forwarding Ratio (Individual View)

stop there. SBA's efficiency then drops sharply, involving between 60% – 80% of the network. While Wu and Li's behavior settle between 25% – 40%. Through Figure 4 we are able to directly compare the protocols.

End-to-End Delay Results. All protocols, as can be seen in Figure 5, have a slight drop in the end-to-end delay as more nodes failed. This was the expected behavior since the node re-transmission activity ceased on all faulty nodes. Overall, DCB had the highest end-to-end delay, mostly due to the re-transmission attempts when no acknowledgement is overheard. SBA's backoff delay (to reduce congestion and collisions) produced a longer overall delay to transmit messages. Flooding, on the other hand, causes the broadcast storm problem which also increases latency of the broadcast. The remaining protocols all had

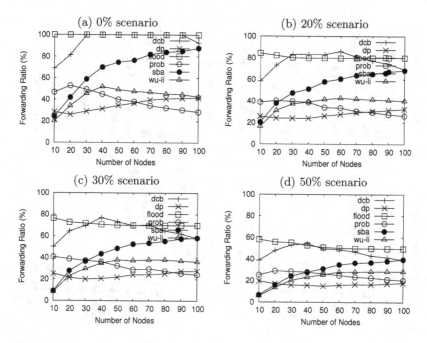

Fig. 4. The Effects of Node Failure on Forwarding Ratio (Comparison View)

low delays, with both Wu and Li and DP needing some time to update 2-hop neighborhood information, while dynamic probabilistic's simpler approach to broadcasting maintains latency to a minimum.

3.3 Lessons Learned

The biggest challenge behind broadcasting in MANETs still lies in finding the balance between message overhead (i.e. redundancy) and reliability. On one hand, a large number of re-transmissions will result in a larger number of nodes reached, but so will the chances of collisions and possibly transmission delays rise as well. On the other hand, when too small of a number of re-transmissions is chosen there is a potential risk of not all nodes being reached. The results here presented allows us to list a few lessons learned:

1. While probabilistic protocols are seen as a way to handle the lack of determinism of MANETs, improperly adjusting this class of protocols in order to inhibit redundant retransmissions can cause more loss than gains. While flooding had high delivery ratios, dynamic probabilistic broadcasts hardly reached the intended nodes.

2. Most deterministic algorithms rely on correctly updated neighborhood knowledge in order to calculate forward status. But in a fail-prone scenario this information may be misleading. This seems to affect much more neighborhood designating protocols than self-prunning ones.

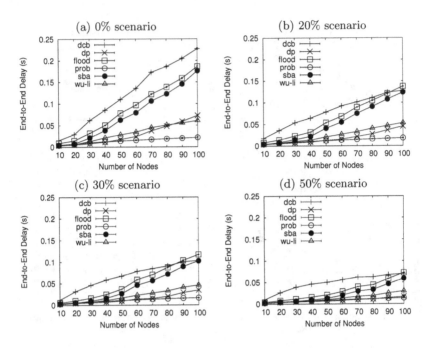

Fig. 5. The Effects of Node Failure on End-to-End Delay (Comparison View)

3. Additional mechanisms to properly identify message reception is recommended to determine if all 1-hop and 2-hop neighbors received a message. Nodes must not just assume correct reception. While simply overhearing a retransmission by a neighboring node is one possible solution, its use should be limited to self-pruning algorithms where more nodes can possibly detect incorrect forwarding-related decisions.

4. Most protocols handled failures up to 10% of the network without a large impact on delivery rates. This information should be used by algorithms, especially when adjusting dynamic thresholds.

5. For reliability to be ensured, redundancy is a must. Simulations result indicate that when 60% of the network received a message, at least 25% of the network acted as gateways. And to reach 80% of the network, at least 60% of the nodes forwarded the message. Efficiency, albeit important, must not be the primary focus of a broadcasting protocol that intends to reach all correct nodes of the network.

4 Conclusion

In order to evaluate the impact of faults on the performance of significant broadcasting protocols, we have conducted simulations under various network scenarios and situations. The simulation studies consisted of measuring the reliability, the forwarding ratio and the end-to-end delay of the protocols when in an omission fault injected environment. It is interesting to note that the protocols are unable to cope well with failures under the realistic model proposed. Regarding message delivery ratio, all protocols suffer a somewhat performance degradation, but a few reach levels of coverage that is unacceptable for broadcasting protocols. Based on the study conducted, we investigated the source of existing broadcasting problems and list the lessons learned as a step towards enhancing the capability of broadcasting algorithms to deal with omission faults in scalable scenarios.

Our future work includes researching possible extensions to broadcasting algorithms in order to provide efficient mechanisms to deal with faults. We also plan on extending our fault model to reflect an even more realistic environment. The current definition of our fault model takes into consideration the importance of randomly choosing faulty nodes throughout the network and represent failures characterized by interference introduced by the environment, link instability and transmission failure due to node movement. Nevertheless, it still represents a rather peculiar failure model where a certain number of nodes fail (and then start working correctly) at exactly the same time. Despite this fact, the results presented in this work are valid since they still model a scenario much more realistic than the simpler fail-stop model.

Acknowledgement

The authors would like to thank all the anonymous referees whose insightful comments helped us to improve the paper presentation.

References

1. Ray, S., Carruthers, J., Starobinski, D.: Evaluation of the masked node problem in ad hoc wireless lans. IEEE Trans. on Mobile Computing 4(5), 430–442 (2005)
2. Williams, B., Camp, T.: Comparison of broadcasting techniques for mobile ad hoc networks. In: Proc. of the 3rd ACM Int. Symp. on Mob. Ad Hoc Networking & Computing, pp. 194–205. ACM Press, New York (2002)
3. Zhang, Q., Agrawal, D.P.: Dynamic probabilistic broadcasting in manets. Journal of Parallel and Distributed Computing 65(2), 220–233 (2005)
4. Basile, C., Killijian, M., Powell, D.: A survey of dependability issues in mobile wireless networks. Technical report, LAAS CNRS Toulouse, France (2003)
5. Kotz, D., Newport, C., Gray, R.S., Liu, J., Yuan, Y., Elliott, C.: Experimental evaluation of wireless simulation assumptions. In: Proc. of the 7th ACM Int. Symp. on Modeling, Snalysis and Simulation of Wireless and Mobile Systems (MSWiM '04), pp. 78–82. ACM Press, New York, NY, USA (2004)
6. Huang, Q., Julien, C., Roman, G.: Relying on safe distance to achieve strong partionable group membership in ad hoc networks. IEEE Transactions on Mobile Computing 3(2), 192–205 (2004)
7. Stankovic, J.A., Abdelzaher, T., Lu, C., Sha, L., Hou, J.: Real-time communication and coordination in embedded sensor networks. In: Proceedings of the IEEE, IEEE Computer Society Press, Los Alamitos (2003)

8. Dai, F., Wu, J.: Performance analysis of broadcast protocols in ad hoc networks based on self-prunning. IEEE Transactions on Parallel and Distributed Systems 15(11), 1027–1040 (2004)

9. Wu, J., Li, H.: On calculating connected dominating set for efficient routing in ad hoc wireless networks. In: DIALM '99: Proc. of the 3rd Int. Workshop on Discrete algorithms and Methods for Mobile Computing and Comm., pp. 7–14. ACM Press, New York, NY, USA (1999)

10. Peng, W., Lu, X.-C.: On the reduction of broadcast redundancy in mobile ad hoc networks. In: Proc. 1st ACM international symp. on Mobile ad hoc networking & computing (Mobihoc), pp. 129–130. IEEE Press, Piscataway, NJ, USA (2000)

11. Lim, H., Kim, C.: Flooding in wireless ad hoc networks. Computer Comm. 24(3–4), 353–363 (2001)

12. Lou, W., Wu, J.: Toward broadcast reliability in mobile ad hoc networks with double coverage. IEEE Trans. on Mobile Computing 6(2), 148–163 (2007)

13. Lim, H., Kim, C.: Multicast tree construction and flooding in wireless ad hoc networks. In: Proc. of the 3rd ACM Int. Workshop on Modeling, Analysis and Simul. of Wireless And Mob. Sys (MSWIM '00), pp. 61–68. ACM Press, New York (2000)

14. Ni, S.-Y., Tseng, Y.-C., Chen, Y.-S., Sheu, J.-P.: The broadcast storm problem in a mobile ad hoc network. In: Proc. 5th ACM/IEEE Int. Conf. on Mobile Computing and Networking, pp. 151–162. ACM Press, New York (1999)

15. Tseng, Y.-C., Ni, S.-Y., Shih, E.-Y.: Adaptive approaches to relieving broadcast storms in a wireless multihop mobile ad hoc network. IEEE Transactions on Computers 52(5), 545–557 (2003)

16. Obraczka, K., Viswanath, K., Tsudik, G.: Flooding for reliable multicast in multihop ad hoc networks. Wireless Networks 7(6), 627–634 (2001)

17. Dai, F., Wu, J.: Distributed dominant pruning in ad hoc networks. In: Proceedings of the IEEE 2003 International Conference on Communications (ICC 2003), vol. 1, pp. 353–357. IEEE Computer Society Press, Los Alamitos (2003)

18. Wu, J., Dai, F.: A generic distributed broadcast scheme in ad hoc wireless networks. IEEE Trans. Computers 53(10), 1343–1354 (2004)

19. Lou, W., Wu, J.: On reducing broadcast redundancy in ad hoc wireless networks. IEEE Trans. on Mobile Computing 1(2), 111–123 (2002)

20. Impett, M., Corson, M.S., Park, V.: A receiver-oriented approach to reliable broadcast in ad hoc networks. In: Proc. of Wireless Comm. and Networking Conf (WCNC), September 2000, vol. 1, pp. 117–122 (2000)

21. NS-2: The network simulator (2007), http://www.isi.edu/nsnam/ns/

22. de Waal, C.: A mobility scenario generation and analysis tool (2007), www.informatik.uni-bonn.de/IV/BonnMotion/

23. de Oliveira, T.B., Costa, V.F., Greve, F., Schnitman, L.: Evaluating the impact of faults on broadcasting protocols for manets. In: VII Workshop on Fault-Tolerant Computing, with (SBRC) Symp. on Computer Networks, Curitiba, Brazil, May 2006, pp. 49–60 (2006)

24. Wu, J., Dai, F.: Efficient broadcasting with guaranteed coverage in mobile ad hoc networks. IEEE Transactions on Mobile Computing 4(2), 259–270 (2005)

25. Pagani, E., Rossi, G.P.: Providing reliable and fault tolerant broadcast delivery in mobile ad-hoc networks. Mob. Netw. Appl. 4(3), 175–192 (1999)
26. Kermarrec, A.-M., Massoulié, L., Ganesh, A.J.: Probabilistic reliable dissemination in large-scale systems. IEEE Trans. Parallel Distrib. Syst. 14(3), 248–258 (2003)
27. Lim, G., Shin, K., Lee, S., Yoon, H., Ma, J.S.: Link stability and route lifetime in ad-hoc wireless networks. In: Proc. of the 2002 Int. Conf. on Parallel Processing Workshops (ICPPW '02), Washington, DC, USA, p. 116. IEEE Computer Society Press, Los Alamitos (2002)

Failure Boundedness in Discrete Applications

João Muranho[1], Paula Prata[1], Mário Zenha-Rela[2], and João Gabriel Silva[2]

[1] Department of Informatics, Universidade da Beira Interior,
P 6201-001 Covilhã, Portugal
[2] University of Coimbra (UC),
CISUC, Department of Informatics Engineering, P 3030-290 Coimbra, Portugal
{muranho,pprata}@di.ubi.pt, {mzrela,jgabriel}@dei.uc.pt

Abstract. Computer control of discrete applications present a challenging dependability problem since any wrong output may lead the system to a completely anomalous state. This is in contrast with continuous feedback systems where wrong outputs can only gradually deviate the system under control from its intended set point. Transient errors may even be filtered by the latency inherent to the physical application. In this paper we extend our previous experimental research on the use of the fail-bounded model in continuous feedback systems into discrete control applications in order to evaluate whether it could be applied to this kind of problems. The reset-driven approach was used as the basic error detection and recovery mechanism complemented by assertions based on the Petri Net modeling of the problem, thus taking advantage of the discrete nature of the applications. The well-known semaphore control problem is used as testbed for experimental evaluation by fault-injection in the controller. The main contribution of this paper is to present experimental data showing that effectively the fail-bounded model can be applied to discrete applications whenever a continuous physical system exists in the control loop.

Keywords: Failure avoidance, Discrete applications, Fail-bounded model, Petri nets, Experimental Dependability Evaluation.

1 Introduction

The control of discrete applications is one of the most common uses of computer control in industry. Applications range from a multitude of manufacturing equipment to specialized markets such as traffic light controllers. There are specific tools and techniques to guarantee an adequate description, modeling and development of discrete control applications since they cannot be properly handled by the common approaches used in continuous feedback control systems (e.g. PID controllers). The modeling of such systems, namely the most critical ones, is often based on Petri Nets due to its boundedness, reachability and liveness properties that are well adapted to this type of real world problems. Of particular interest for this class of problems are timed and stochastic Petri Nets[1]. Such systems are mostly based on state transitions, so that they expect the occurrence of events from sensors (e.g. an empty bottle entered

A. Bondavalli, F. Brasileiro, and S. Rajsbaum (Eds.): LADC 2007, LNCS 4746, pp. 160–169, 2007.

into a filling area, a button pressed), determine the following state and generate the related output (e.g. turn on/off the filling valve, turn on/off a red light).

In such applications fault tolerance is normally considered to be an hardware issue, so control engineers simply assume that controllers don't fail. To meet these expectations, a common approach is to use fail-silent controllers, which either produce correct results or do not output any value at all [2]. Since standard simplex hardware fails far from silently [3], such systems are usually built by pairing two computers and continuously comparing their outputs. In fields such as avionics, nuclear power plants, medical life support systems and similar critical applications the cost of that replication may be acceptable but there is a very large number of applications where such redundancy is not economically viable. For that reason, most low cost Programmable Logic Controllers (PLCs) use a conservative fault avoidance design approach, rather than dedicated fault tolerance. Typically, the only standard provisions for error detection in such systems are a watchdog timer that detects crashes and resets the processor, and periodic self-check routines that detect permanent faults. No guarantees are given as to what happens when these mechanisms are not effective, which is the case of transient faults. This is unfortunate, because transients generally occur much more frequently than permanent faults, due to electromagnetic interference, power brownouts, or other environmental disturbances. Although significant variations result from different designs and operating conditions, in average about 80% of hardware faults are transient [4], and as VLSI implementations use smaller geometries and lower power levels, the importance of transients increases.

To address this problem in [5],[6] it was shown that feedback algorithms can compensate for many computer malfunctions, not just disturbances in the controlled system. We have shown that the fail-silent model may be inadequate since it would flag as failures many situations where the system in fact does not suffer any negative impact at all. The point is that the fail-silent model lacks the notion of time –a single erroneous controller output is not significant, only a sequence of erroneous outputs is– and fails to take into account the fact that the natural inertia of the controlled system filters out short lived disturbances. Those observations confirm a well-known concept in industry, that of grace-time [7] (the time that an application can run without control, exhibiting irrelevant or even null consequences). In our research we claim that the Fail-Bounded model is more appropriate to describe the behavior of those systems than the Fail-Silent model. As introduced in [8], a system is said to be *Fail-Bounded* if it either:

i.   Produces correct outputs;
ii.   Stops producing outputs after detecting some error;
iii. Produces wrong outputs, but these are not arbitrary, the deviation from the correct output having an upper bound.

That upper bound can be enforced by means of assertions that, if implemented according the Robust Assertions method [9] guarantee with very high probability that the Fail-Bounded model is satisfied.

In this paper, we extend our previous research into discrete applications. The major problem in this kind of systems is that while in continuous feedback control an error may generate a gradual deviation from the correct output, in discrete systems errors may lead to state transitions completely distinct from what would be the correct path. The fundamental observation here is that while the erroneous output may not be bounded in the value domain since the state reached may be definitely erroneous, *it may be bounded in the time domain*, thus if there is a physical (continuous) system in the control loop and a correct output is resumed within the application's grace time, the whole system can benefit from the application's physical inertia (i.e. we must break the dichotomy controller/controlled and consider the system as a whole.

A most relevant point is that if the system crashes this time-boundedness cannot be guaranteed. Thus, the effective adoption of the fail-bounded model in discrete systems requires a dedicated effort to avoid the occurrence of system crashes and/or recover from them on time to prevent the violation of the application's grace-time.

The experimental evaluation described in this paper was performed by means of software fault-injection, using RT-Xception [10], a real-time version of the Xception tool described in [11], which is able to emulate hardware transients, introducing a predictable and negligible overhead. Faults were inserted in the controller computer running a traffic semaphore control algorithm, a life critical discrete application.

The paper is organized as follows: in the next section we present the system model and how the fail-bounded model can be applied to discrete applications. The reset-driven fault tolerance technique is described as it is used as the error detection and recovery mechanism to support the fail-bounded approach. Since discrete applications have specific properties that differentiate it from continuous applications, assertions derived from these properties are also used for error detection. In section 3 the testbed and the target application is described. In section 4 we present and discuss the experimental observations. Section 5 closes the paper with a discussion on the most relevant observations and conclusions.

2   System Model

2.1   Fail-Boundedness and Fault-Tolerance

In a continuous system the state-space variables assume values in a metric space. On the contrary, in a discrete system the state variables assume values in a countable space. From the controller system design perspective a continuous system follows a continuous smooth trajectory, and a feedback control action is applied periodically. In a discrete system we don't have such smoothness to follow and the control actions often don't have such regularity even if the control action is a numeric value.

For the evaluation of the effectiveness of using the fail-bounded model in discrete applications we assume that such systems can be modeled as a state-machine with event-driven state transitions such that the correct state sequence is derived from the application model: events arrive, a new state is computed, and the related outputs updated. The physical system under test (SUT) is a non-replicated (simplex) computer controlling a physical system through its sensors and actuators.

In the experimental evaluation presented in this paper the application is the well-known traffic-light control. The controlled system is another computer running a model of the application (traffic lights), in fact collecting the SUT behavior. For simplicity sake we considered only the occurrence of single transient faults.

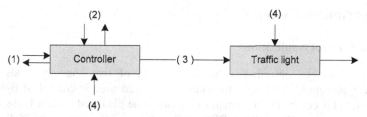

1) User interface 2) Comunication interface 3) Process interface 4) Disturbances

Fig. 1. Controller computer and controlled system (traffic light)

Nevertheless, a transient fault may cause long-lasting or even permanent errors if it affects the controller's internal state.

The assertions supporting the fail-bounded approach evaluated in this paper are based on state awareness: when some erroneous state is detected the controller 'falls back' and corrects the erroneous output by resuming its correct transition path. While this may be an impossibility in some applications, any engineer in the field is well aware that the physical world is intrinsically continuous, and resilient to failure: thus, even if a process is described in state-transition terms, if there is a physical (continuous) system in the control loop we can always associate a cost to an erroneous state transition and 'fall back'. If the recovery time is short enough the real world application may not even be aware of the erroneous transition (e.g. the conveyor belt will not stop, the gate in the production line will not turn left, the green light on a semaphore will not turn on,...). This a fundamental requirement: the discrete application in the control loop must have a quantifiable grace time. Even in a life critical application such as traffic light control this time is defined as 80 milliseconds, the time to conscious reaction to a visual stimulus.

Using the available idle time of the controller computer, a model the controlled system based on its state transitions is checked for correctness. It takes into account the system's present state, previous state and sequence of input events. If an erroneous transition is detected the system just corrects its output. This type of error detection and recovery can be obtained either by re-execution on the same hardware (if only transient faults are considered) or by substitution by a backup controller (if additional tolerance to permanent faults is envisaged).

The proper modeling of a discrete-state application involves the use of a state-machine approach, in some cases based on the corresponding Petri Net. We adopted this model not only for the development of the solution, but also as a tool to support error detection. By using the state transition model we can determine the of correct path. Thus, as a transition is performed, its validity is checked. Notice that this is a means of using the very effective technique of control flow checking [12] but at a more abstract level, rather than at the basic assembly-block level.

As shell be shown later, we also used reset-driven fault-tolerance [13], an error removal approach based on resetting systematically the system between two consecutive outputs, so that any latent error is flushed by the programmed reset.

3 Experimental Setup

3.1 The Control Application

The system to be controlled, is an intersection of two one-way roads without pedestrian passages. The right to access the shared area is controlled by a timed controller. This controller implements only one time plan, and cyclically displays the light sequence ...→GR →YR →RR →RG →RY →RR →... (Green/Yellow/Red). The low-level meaning of these states can be found in Table 1 which also shows the nominal time and design time tolerance for each lamp set. This time tolerance for the transition to a new lamp set was defined as 80 milliseconds, a typical figure.

Table 1. Nominal time for each lamp set stay on

Lamps On	GR	YR	RR	RG	RY	RR
Binary	001 100	010 100	100 100	100 001	100 010	100 100
Hex	000c	0014	0024	0021	0022	0024
Decimal	12	20	36	33	34	36
Time (ms)	1500	1000	500	1500	1000	500
Tolerance (ms)	80	80	80	80	80	80

The traffic light system is a discrete application where the controller outputs are integer values representing the bit patterns of the target signals (e.g. for a pedestrian signal the control action '10' means power the "walk" bulb and cut the power to the "don't walk" bulb). The controller mission is to send meaningful messages to the traffic signal control equipment in order to regulate the system users. Despite being a discrete application, the whole system has some components that react in a continuous way: the main sources of grace-time are the electrical equipment (a tungsten-filament bulb lamp takes approximately 50-70 milliseconds to generate light) and the users (pedestrians and drivers). The human being takes approximately 100 milliseconds to detect a stimulus (lamp energized) and conscious reaction to them [14]. The U.S.A. traffic controller's models NEMA and Model 170 [15] also assume time deviations in this order of magnitude (100 ms). So, if the controller is fast enough we can correct a potential wrong control action without impact in the overall system. It is the presence of these continuous elements that allow the implementation of the fail-bounded approach to fault-tolerance since they provide the grace-time to the system.

3.2 System Behavior Classification

In our testbed the controller outputs are generated with the execution of a Petri net with timed transitions. Each Petri net place has associated one control code. A transition is enabled when its input places are all marked and the transition time vanishes. An enabled transition is immediately fired. The new control action is formed by combining the control codes of the new marked places. The controller application is run for seven light sequences cycles (42 different outputs).

For each injected fault the system behavior is classified based on value and time dimensions of controller outputs. Each control action, CA^i, is compared with its reference value, CA^i_{ref}, and the time it stays active, CA^i_t, must be within $CA^i_{Tref} \pm \Delta CA^i_T$, the reference time ($CA^i_{Tref}$) and the design time tolerance (ΔCA^i_T) for this control action.

Each control action is allowed to stay in a 'out-of-control state' for up to 80 milliseconds, CA^i_{slack}. Therefore the system behavior can be classified as:

1. *Correct* – if every control action is correct in value and time:
   $(CA^i = CA^i_{ref}) \wedge |CA^i_t - CA^i_{Tref}| < \Delta CA_T^i,\ 1 \leq i \leq 42$.

2. *Failure-lazy* – if the control actions are correct in value but at least one control action remains active too long, greater than its reference time plus design time tolerance: $(Ca^i = CA^i_{ref}) \wedge CA^i_t > (CA^i_{Tref} + \Delta CA_T^i)$ for some i.

3. *Failure-premature* – If a correct control action has a time length too short we have an untimely transition: $(CA^i = CA^i_{ref}) \wedge CA^i_t < (CA^i_{Tref} - \Delta CA_T^i)$ for some i.
   The system behavior is thus further classified based on the next control action(s) as:

   a) *Then-lazy* – if the next control action is wrong and stays active for too long, i.e. greater than the allowed grace-time $(CA^{i+1} \neq CA^i_{ref} \wedge (CA^{i+1} > CA^i_{Tslack})$.

   b) *Transient error* (but failure avoided) – if the wrong control action is a transient; it stays active with the wrong value during only a short time tolerated by the application.
   $(CA_t^{i+1} < CA^i_{Tslack}) \wedge (CA_t^{i+2} = CA^i_{ref}) \wedge (|CA^i_t + CA^{i+1}_t + CA^{i+2}_t - CA^i_{Tref}| < \Delta CA_T^i)$

4. *Failure-raw* – wrong control action active for too long:
   $(CA^i \neq Ca^i_{ref}) \wedge ((CA_t^{i+1} > CA^i_{Tslack})$

Whenever a wrong control action is active only during a short time interval ($CA^i \neq CA^i_{ref} \wedge CA^{i+1} = CA^i_{ref}$) we need to look ahead to see what happens because we may have a failure or just a transient error such as in case 3.

3.3 The Experimental Testbed

The experiments are controlled by a host computer running the RT-Xception EME (Experiment Management Environment) software for fault-injection experiment management and control. The EME is responsible for fault definition, experiment execution and control, outcome collection, and statistical analysis.

The controller computer is a standard 90MHz Intel Pentium based PC-board with 8M of RAM. The control application is running on top of SMX© (Simple Multitasking Executive) [16], a COTS real-time kernel from Micro Digital, Inc. If any error is detected by the intrinsic error detection mechanisms of the system, such as processor exceptions or operating system checks, the normal procedure is to flag an error and reset the system. A COTS watchdog timer card is used to support the Reset Driven Fault Tolerance (RDFT) technique. The controller computer sends its output using a serial connection, to a third computer that emulates the application. This computer collects the output produced by the controller for later analysis by the EME. This was the same platform used in our previous research on continuous feedback systems [5].

4 Experimental Observations and Discussion

We have injected four series of 2611 faults in four different versions of the target system. These faults were injected in the most sensitive parts of the traffic light controller application: the system constants, the control algorithm and the application code that outputs the control action (initial experiments with faults randomly generated led to so few effective errors that we decided to focus the injection target). Therefore the figures presented below should not be considered as a basis to extract more general dependability metrics, but rather as indicative of the effectiveness of applying these techniques to discrete control applications.

The four fault-injection campaigns envisaged the following four scenarios:

- A baseline system with the control software, without any explicit error detection capability.
- The same system with assertions based on the state-transition model of the application.
- Since we observed a large number of system crashes —thus constraining the effectiveness of software assertions— reset-driven fault-tolerance was added (assertions + RDFT)
- To evaluate the effective contribution of the reset-driven approach, the baseline system without assertions, with RDFT only was also evaluated.

The global figures for the different experiments are presented in Table 2. The columns represent the different outcomes observed: a correct behavior (i.e. outputs followed the reference execution), the occurrence of fail-silent violations (erroneous output without ever being detected as such); this column represents the erroneous behavior presented in section 3.2. Finally, the occurrence of a system failure either with internal detection (triggering a reset) and without (system crash). In the case of unexpected system crash the table also includes the number of erroneous output before crashing (*fsv*). Each field shows the number of faults and the corresponding percent figure. Each series involved the injection of 2611 effective faults (the situation where there was a confirmed change in the internal system state, e.g. a register modified). The last column presents the total number of fail-silent violations (FSV) including those followed by a system crash.

The first relevant observation is that the addition of assertions to the baseline system degraded rather than increased the correct behavior of the system (45,2% instead of 59,9%): the additional complexity increased the probability of failure. Thus, since we are injecting faults focused in the most sensitive parts of the application, the overall dependability decreased. However, the number of erroneous output generated (regardless of a later crash), is significantly reduced from 4% to a marginal 0,7%. This means that, as an error detection technique, the software assertions based on checking the correctness of the state transition were really

Table 2. Global experimental observations

Injection Campaign	Correct Behavior	Fail-Silent Violation (fsv)	System Failure		FSV (total)
			Undetected (crash)	Detected (reset)	
Baseline	1563 59.9%	4 0.2%	1044 40.0% 608 23.3% (101 fsv)	436 16.7%	105 4.0%
Assertions only	1179 45.2%	3 0.1%	1429 54.7% 194 7.4% (16 fsv)	1235 47.3%	19 0.7%
Assertions and RDFT	2492 95.4%	4 0.2%	115 4.4% 97 3.7% (15 fsv)	18 0.7%	19 0.7%
RDFT only	2465 94.4%	5 0.2%	141 5.4% 121 4.6% (31 fsv)	20 0.8%	36 1.4%

effective. However, this effectiveness comes at a high price: the total number of system failures (crashes and forced reset) has grown from 40% to 54.7%. These preliminary observations indicate that an error detection increase may have to be traded by reduced availability (which is, nevertheless, a common trade-off). However, the fail-bounded model for discrete systems mandates that the correct state must be restored as soon as possible, which is prevented by this large number of total system failures.

The following scenario adds reset-driven fault tolerance (RDFT) to the assertion checks, i.e. the controller is continuously performing a hot restart whenever a control action is output and the assertion checks are executed afterwards, when the system state has been flushed from latent transient errors. The observations show a dramatic decrease on the total number of system failures (from 54,7% to 4,4%. This is a direct consequence of using the reset-driven approach since it is based on resetting systematically the system between two consecutive outputs, thus any latent error that would force a system reset or eventually lead to crash is flushed by the programmed reset. In a previous paper we have already demonstrated the impressive effectiveness of this technique [13] and it shows again its potential in this system. The most remarkable effect is the increase in the correct behavior (from 45,2% in the assertion-only system to 95,4%). Interestingly enough, the number of pure fail-silent violations grows slightly (from 0,1% to 0,2%). However, we are now dealing with a very reduced number of faults, thus these figures are not statistically meaningful, only indicative (the 0,1% figure represents 3 out of 2611 faults injected). It must be stressed that these are not median figures, but results derived from a subset of faults injected in the most sensible parts of the system, thus where the presence of the techniques is most visible.

Since the RDFT approach seems so effective, it remains to be understood its raw contribution to the final figures, i.e. whether the dependability increase is due mostly to the RDFT or to the use of assertions. This was the motivation behind the fault-injection campaign experiments involving the baseline case without assertions, using RDFT only. In this scenario we observed a slight decrease on the number of correct outputs generated (from 95,4% to 94,4%) and a similar increase on the system failures (from 4,4% to 5,4%). This indicates that the small variation in the correct outcomes is directly related to the number of failures prevented. Anyway these variations are not conclusive since they fall into the statistical error margin. This result indicates clearly that the RDFT technique is the major responsible for the stability of the system in what concerns correct output generation versus number of failures: the RDFT sets a baseline of around 95% of correct behavior and a remaining 4% to 5% situations where the assertions can show its effectiveness.

Thus, the remaining point is to evaluate the error detection effectiveness of assertions, i.e. whether the controller has output erroneous values before failure whenever it crashed. This is the rationale behind the final column of Table 2. In this column we highlight the total number of FSV observed, including both the 'pure' fail-silent violations (erroneous output without ever being detected) and those followed by crash. As can be seen, the fail-silent violations are lower whenever assertions are used: this is its main contribution to the dependability of the system.

We can now conclude that the global figures indicate clearly that RDFT assures the maximum system stability (preventing crashes) and assertions minimizes the generation of erroneous output (FSV). This combined effect guarantees time-bounded errors thus allowing the extension of the fail-bounded model into the broader field of discrete control applications.

5   Conclusion

In this paper we presented an experimental evaluation showing that the failure bounded model can be extended from continuous feedback applications to discrete systems whenever in the control loop there is a physical system possessing grace time. In such systems the failure boundedness can be applied in the time domain, i.e. *by constraining the duration of an erroneous state-transition*. To support this approach we adopted the reset-driven fault tolerance technique to guarantee that the occurrence of crashes is dramatically reduced, associated to assertions based on the state transitions to prevent the occurrence of erroneous outputs. The experiments presented show a tenfold decrease of controller crashes from 40% to 4,4% and a reduction of erroneous undetected transitions from 4,0% to 0,7% of the 2611 faults injected in the most critical parts of a traffic light control software. These figures support the extension of the fail-bounded model into the broader field of discrete control applications.

Acknowledgments

This work was partially supported by the Group of Networks and Multimedia of the Institute of Telecommunications (IT) Covilhã Lab, Portugal; and by Portuguese Ministry of Education through program Prodep III-Action 5.3-project 185.009.

References

1. Zuberek, W.M.: Timed Petri nets and preliminary performance evaluation. In: 7th Annual Symposium on Computer Architecture, pp. 88–96. ACM Press, New York (1980)
2. Powell, D., Verísimo, P., Bonn, G., Waeselynck, F., Seaton, D.: The Delta-4 Approach to Dependability in Open Distributed Computing Systems. In: 18th Fault-Tolerant Computer Symposium, pp. 246–251. IEEE Press, New York (1988)
3. Avizienis, A.: Building Dependable Systems: How to Keep Up with Complexity. In: 25th Fault-Tolerant Computer Symposium, pp. 4–14. IEEE Press, New York (1995)
4. Somani, A.K., Vaidya, N.H.: Understanding Fault Tolerance and Reliability. IEEE Computer 30(4), 45–50 (1997)
5. Cunha, J.C., Maia, R., Rela, M.Z., Silva, J.G.: A Study on Failure Models in Feedback Control Systems. In: International Conference on Dependable Systems and Networks, pp. 314–323. IEEE Press, New York (2001)
6. Vinter, J., Aidemark, J., Folkesson, P., Karlsson, J.: Reducing Critical Failures for Control Algorithms Using Executable Assertions and Best Effort Recovery. In: International Conference on Dependable Systems and Networks, pp. 347–356. IEEE Press, New York (2001)
7. Kirrman, H.D.: Fault Tolerance in Process Control: An overview and examples of European Products. IEEE Micro 7(5), 27–50 (1987)
8. Silva, J.G., Prata, P., Rela, M.Z., Madeira, H.: Practical Issues in the Use of ABFT and a New Failure Model. In: 28th Fault-Tolerant Computer Symposium, pp. 26–35. IEEE Press, New York (1998)
9. Prata, P., Rela, M.Z., Madeira, H., Silva, J.G: Robust Assertions and Fail-Bounded Behavior. Journal of the Brazilian Computer Society 3(10), 20–32 (2005)
10. Cunha, J.C., Rela, M.Z., Silva, J.G.: Can Software-Implemented Fault-Injection be used on Real-Time Systems? In: Hlavicka, J., Maehle, E., Pataricza, A. (eds.) EDCC 1999. LNCS, vol. 1667, pp. 209–221. Springer, Heidelberg (1999)
11. Carreira, J., Madeira, H., Silva, J.G.: Xception: A Technique for the Experimental Evaluation of Dependability in Modern Computers. IEEE Trans. on Software Engineering 24(2), 125–135 (1998)
12. Madeira, H., Silva, J.G.: Experimental evaluation of the fail-silent behavior in computers without error masking. In: 24th Fault-Tolerant Computer Symposium, pp. 350–359. IEEE Press, New York (1994)
13. Cunha, J.C., Correia, A., Henriques, J., Rela, M.Z.: Reset-Driven Fault Tolerance. In: Bondavalli, A., Thévenod-Fosse, P. (eds.) EDCC 2002. LNCS, vol. 2485, pp. 102–120. Springer, Heidelberg (2002)
14. Libet, B.: Unconscious cerebral initiative and the role of conscious will in voluntary action. Behavioral and brain sciences 8(4), 529–566 (1985)
15. ITS National Architecture, Federal Highway Administration, Technical report, US Department of Transportation (1998)
16. SMX® Simple Multitasking Executive. http://www.smxinfo.com

Designing Fault Injection Experiments Using State-Based Model to Test a Space Software

Ana Maria Ambrosio[1], Fátima Mattiello-Francisco[1],
Valdivino A. Santiago Jr.[1], Wendell P. Silva[1], and Eliane Martins[2]

[1] National Institute for Space Research (INPE)
Av. Dos Astronautas, 1758 - São Jose Campos -12227-010 - Brazil
Phone: +55-12-3945-6586,
{ana,fatima}@dss.inpe.br, {valdivino,wendell}@das.inpe.br
[2] Institute of Computing (IC)
State University of Campinas (UNICAMP)
P.O. Box 6176 - Campinas, 13083-970, SP, Brazil
eliane@ic.unicamp.br

Abstract. Software for space applications requires significant testing. This paper presents an evaluation of the CoFI testing methodology as applied to actual space software, where deterministic fault cases derived from state-based models were executed using the software-implemented fault injection technique. Different models were used to represent the behavior of embedded software in a real satellite computer under the presence of both normal inputs and external faults in communication, processor, and memory. CoFI methodology was used for model construction, the Condado tool for test derivation, and the QSEE-TAS tool for test execution. In total, 8,620% of 471 fault cases detected errors in the software; this is a very large number, and more so considering that the software had already been tested by the company which developed it before being subject the CoFI methodology.

Keywords: deterministic fault injection, software testing method, state-based models.

1 Introduction

The testing phase in software development lifecycle has attracted software engineer attention to answer the question, "how can one test a complex embedded software in a short time without losing testing accuracy?"

Model-based test techniques have been used for protocol conformance testing to complement the ISO practical testing guides, checking the implementation with respect to a specification written in a formal notation [12], from which tests are automatically generated [5], [8], [18].

A set of conformance test cases aims to establish that a given Implementation Under Test (IUT): (i) performs all functions of the original specification over the full range of parameter values and (ii) can properly reject erroneous inputs in such a way that it is consistent with the original specification [11]. These test cases generate a certain number of detected errors, but for dependability assessment, fault injection

A. Bondavalli, F. Brasileiro, and S. Rajsbaum (Eds.): LADC 2007, LNCS 4746, pp. 170–178, 2007.
© Springer-Verlag Berlin Heidelberg 2007

methods are recommended. Fault injection execution is an activity highly dependent on the facilities provided by the test environment [3], [6] and constraints in test execution impose constraints in test generation. The CoFI (Conformance and Fault Injection) testing methodology [1] was designed to help determine which faults to inject using the same principles as model-based techniques "starting from a textual specification towards formal models" [13]. Thus, CoFI reinforces the systematic derivation of test cases that may be executed with software-implemented fault injection (SWIFI).

This article presents the results of the use of CoFI to define which tests should be generated to validate the SWPDC (SoftWare embedded into the Payload Data Handling Computer (PDC)) that is intended to be part of a scientific X-ray instrument onboard of the MIRAX satellite under development at the National Institute for Space Research (INPE), Brazil. This software was developed by a private company and delivered to INPE as part of INPE's Quality of Space Application Embedded Software (QSEE) research project of the [15], [16].

The paper is organized as follows. Section 2 presents an overview of the SWPDC. Section 3 shows the testing tools that were used. Section 4 explains the CoFI methodology applied to the SWPDC. Section 5 discusses the test results. Finally, Section 6 presents pertinent conclusions.

2 Overview of the SWPDC

Figure 1 illustrates the SWPDC software in charge of collecting scientific data from the Event Pre-Processors (EPPs); executing commands from the main on-board computer (OBDH); generating housekeeping data; performing data memory management, loading programs, and detecting external faults that can occur at anytime, as is typical in computer space systems.

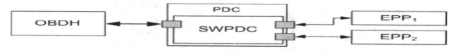

Fig. 1. Context of the SWPDC

Given that the SWPDC is a software embedded in a satellite computer, it is exposed to space radiation, which may cause Single-Event Effects (SEEs) like the Single Event Upset (SEU) and Multiple Bit Upset (MBU). A single bit flip in a digital device is an example of SEU. When several memory bits are upset during the passage of the same particle it is a MBU [10].

The SWPDC also implements error detection mechanisms for Single and Double memory errors, which are "soft" bit errors, in that a reset or rewriting of the device causes normal behavior thereafter.

To detect processor errors the SWPDC is linked to a Watchdog circuit. A watchdog circuit is a computer hardware-timing device that indicates a problem if the software neglects to regularly reset the circuit. Exception handling mechanisms exist to treat communication faults. No complex action to treat such errors is required; however, all errors that occur are reported via housekeeping data transmitted to the Ground System.

3 Test Environment

For the sake of validation, the SWPDC was treated as a black-box whose interactions with the test environment are only through Points of Control and Observation (PCOs). Figure 2 illustrates the test environment where the circles around the SWPDC box indicate the PCO's. The external inputs were all simulated. The dashed arrow from the Watchdog Circuit Simulation and to the Watchdog Error Simulation denotes the SWPDC did not send the watchdog timer signal within the expected period of time. A special circuit triggers Simple and Double memory errors, while another circuit controls the temperature. The EEP Simulator generates the scientific data and the QSEE-TAS (*Automatic Software Testing*) tool [17] simulates the OBDH.

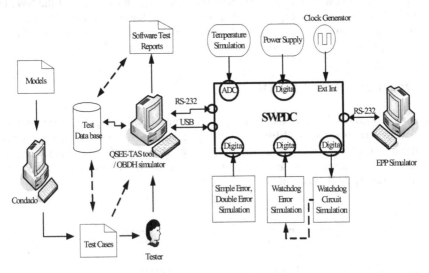

Fig. 2. The Test Environment. Legend: Ext Int = External Interruption; USB = Universal Serial Bus; ADC = Analog-to-Digital Converter.

The QSEE-TAS tool also includes facilities for test configuration, execution, reports, management of the test cases produced by Condado or produced manually, and SWIFI mechanisms that accelerate the occurrence of communication faults in commands produced by the OBDH. This mechanism assigns unspecified and/or incorrect values to fields of the commands to corrupt messages, repeat or delay commands. So far, injection of memory and processor faults has not been automated, so the tester manually interfered in the respective PCO to trigger these types of faults.

The Condado tool [14] automatically derives test cases from state-based models. This tool is based on a theoretical approach of graphs and implements the switch-cover algorithm [7]. Since Condado generates all test cases in the same format: "senddata   (pco,input1)   recdata(pco,output1)   senddata (pco,input2) recdata()...", a converter that takes *specific inputs* (indicating faults to be injected) of the fault cases and produces pre-defined faults was built, thereby permitting QSEE-TAS to execute the test cases produced by Condado directly.

4 CoFI Testing Methodology Applied to the SWPDC Software

CoFI systematizes the creation of partial models of IUT behavior that are employed in automated test methods to generate test cases. In other words, instead of designing a very complex model of software behavior under normal and faulty inputs, which could lead to an explosion of the number of test cases produced from this model, several simpler models are built. The behavior of an IUT is modeled for each service the IUT provides. Scenarios for normal and exceptional behavior are mapped into several state-based models [2], taking into account the *fault types* (or the *fault model*, the term used by the Fault Tolerance community), which describe the way the hardware or software component can fail, an important step for fault injection purposes.

4.1 Creating the SWPDC Models

In this study, we identified the SWPDC inputs that could be executed in the test environment as the commands that characterize the IUT's services. Inputs that could not be executed were not considered, such as duplication and delay in commands coming from an EPP. Next, we defined a syntax for the inputs and outputs used in the models. An **input** carries information on command, channel (the physical representation of the PCO), and faults. Inputs preceded by *Cmd* indicate commands arriving from the OBDH, so the PCO was defined implicitly. The symbol {*badcks*} indicates the injection of a checksum error, while {*sup*} indicates the suppression of a field from the command. Inputs with no faults are all the commands of the PDC-OBDH and PDC-EPP communication protocols (see Figure 1).

Specific inputs indicate the faults to be triggered by the QSEE-TAS tool. The following information may be obtained from such inputs: a) channel-identification; b) number of times the command is repeated; c) delay time (in milliseconds) to wait before sending the command; d) special processing (to calculate checksum or to suppress command fields). Table 1 presents all the fault types accounted for in SWPDC; and sample inputs are also described for each fault type.

Eleven services were identified for the construction of the state-based models. The SWPDC service behavior was represented in scenarios for normal situations (Norm); specified-exceptional situations (SExc); sneak paths (SPat)[1]; the presence of the communication faults such as command corruption, truncated and delay/early commands (Com); and the presence of memory and processor faults (M&Pr).

---

[1] A sneak path [4] is a path in the model that contains unlikely inputs for a given state. To help identify sneak path scenarios the tester creates a state table and completes it with the valid inputs against all states, then, create models that represent out-of-order and duplicated commands, which are two common types of communication faults.

Table 1. Fault types covered by the SWPDC and sample of specific inputs

	Fault Type	Examples of specific inputs	Input description
	Corrupted data field values	CmdTurnOnEPP2,CKS{badcks}	The *Turn On EPP2* command will have an error in checksum field.
		CmdPrepMemoryDumpData,Mem,18,EndI,8000,EndF,FFFF	The *Prepare Memory Dump* command will have an error in the address field.
Communication	Repeated command	CmdTransTestData_2X	The *Transmit Test Data* command will be received twice.Indicates a duplication error.
	Out-of-order commands	-	Commands are sent in an unexpected sequence.
	Truncated – command fields are missing	CmdTurnOffEPP1,NU,{sup}	The third field in *Turn Off EPP1* command will be suppressed.
	Delay/Early – command arriving after/before the specified time	ObsEndT	T time-units will expire. This input is preceded by an action to start a timer in T time-units.
Memory	Simple error	ObsSingleError	A Single Event Upset will occur
	Double error	ObsDoubleError	A Multiple (double) Event Upset will occur
Process	First occurrence of Process-fault	ObsErrorProc1	First indication of the watchdog
	Second occurrence of Process-fault	ObsErrorProc2	Second consecutive indication of the watchdog

Table 2 lists the services and the distribution of the 97 models by services and by scenario type. In general, each set of faults of the same type was mapped in a distinct model, except for memory and processor faults. The grey columns indicate the models that produced fault cases.

The model of the single scenario for M&Pro of the S4-Test Data service is illustrated in Figure 3. This model shows that under the presence of one memory error (represented by the specific input *ObsSingleError*) the SWPDC reacts by correcting

Table 2. Services x models

Services		Models					Total
		Norm	**SExc**	**SPat**	**Com**	**M&Pr**	
S1	Initialization	2	1	1	1	1	6
S2	Scientific data	2	2	1	1	1	7
S3	Housekeeping	3	3	3	1	1	11
S4	Test data	2	4	4	1	1	12
S5	Diagnostics	2	4	4	2	2	14
S6	Memory dump	5	3	5	2	1	16
S7	Change operat mode	1	0	0	0	1	2
S8	Load&execute program	1	5	4	3	2	15
S9	OBDH msg syntax	1	0	0	1	0	2
S10	EPP msg syntax	1	0	0	1	0	2
S11	Special commands	4	0	0	2	4	10
	Total	24	24	22	13	14	97

the error (represented by the *ObsCorrectError* output), reporting the event in housekeeping reports (*ObsWriteHkReport*) and remaining in the same state. But, under a double memory error (*ObsDoubleError*), where SWPDC is not required to correct the error, only a report is produced. In the presence of the first occurrence of a processor error (*ObsErroProc1*), it reports the failure, but in the second occurrence (*ObsErroProc2*), a reset makes the SWPDC return to its initial state (*Standby*).

5 The Fault Injection Experiments

Each model was submitted to the Condado tool. In the IUT models a transition represented an input and the expected corresponding output produced in reaction to that input [11]. This means that the test cases generated by Condado are ordered sets of inputs and outputs, comprising a path from the initial state to a final state. The set of test cases, therefore, covered all branches of each model at least once.

External faults added to the set of inputs normally accepted by the SWPDC define the generation of *fault cases*, which have specific inputs and input data that characterize the fault to be injected, so each fault case is considered a fault injection experiment.

Table 3 shows the distribution of the errors detected by the fault cases in one campaign. In total, 451 fault cases were generated in 770 test cases produced from the models, resulting in 39 detected errors. Processor and memory faults were modeled in a single model (M&Pr), but fault cases and the errors detected were computed separately. There were 2 more processor errors than memory errors detected. The fault cases of communication were derived from the SPat and the Com models. The disproportionate number of communication fault cases reflects the research priority for identifying communication errors.

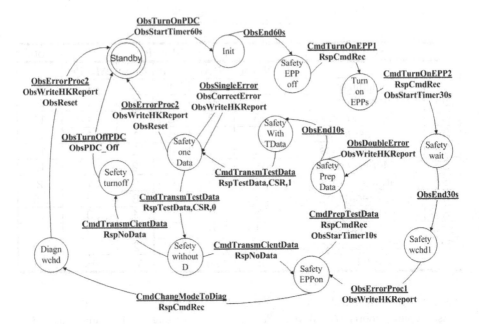

Fig. 3. State-based model representing processor and memory faults

Table 3. Fault type x detected errors

Fault Type	Fault injection experiments	Detected Errors
Communication	283	31
Processor	80	5
Memory	88	3
Total	451	39

The other 319 test cases generated from Norm and SExc models resulted in only 12 errors. Thus, CoFI was able to identify a significant number of errors in a relatively small number of fault cases. This suggests the CoFI methodology identified likely errors successfully when pre-defining which faults to inject, confirming the advantages of deterministic fault injection methods [9].

6 Conclusions

Considering that we were going to validate software supplied by a competent team from a prominent Brazilian Software industry to INPE, which was developed under rigorous quality assurance rules, we expected to find very few errors. The results surprised us as 51 errors were yet found.

Since the models reflected the software behavior based on information obtained from the textual documents such as protocol specification, technical specification, software design, and manual, all non-conformances between code and document were computed as a detected error. These errors were classified as 45% only code errors 33% only document non-conformance errors and 22% code and document non-conformance errors.

The results pointed out that focusing on the faults is more effective than on the normal behavior for validation purposes. Since models were grouped by fault types, the set of automatically generated fault cases were distinguishable by their fault types and statistical calculations on the tests were facilitated.

The INPE test team worked independently of the industrial development team to create the models. Obviously, the greater effort to create the models was compensated by the superior test organization CoFI achieved in comparison with previous ad hoc test designs. The models served as guides to focus the tester's attention to the faults and exceptions that could occur during the software's operation, leading to the design of situations the developers had not thought of. One example is for OBDH to require data during SWPDC initialization service.

Future work is required to verify whether other types of errors are identified when test models are combined. In order to make the CoFI testing methodology applicable to any space application, the adoption of a standardized test language to represent the inputs and outputs seems to be important as well.

Acknowledgments

The authors acknowledge the financial support from Financiadora de Estudos e Projetos (FINEP) to the QSEE research project and all those involved. The authors also thank the reviewers for their insightful comments and constructive suggestions.

References

1. Ambrosio, A.M.: CoFI: uma abordagem combinando teste de conformidade e injeção de falhas para validação de software em aplicações espaciais. INPE-13264-TDI/1031. Instituto Nacional de Pesquisas Espaciais - INPE (2005)
2. Ambrosio, A.M., Martins, E., Vijaykumar, N.L., Carvalho, S.V.: A Methodology for Designing Fault Injection Experiments as an Addition to Communication Systems Conformance Testing. In: Proceedings of the 1st Workshop on Dependable Software - Tools and Methods in the IEEE Conference on Dependable System and Network, Yokohama, Japan, 28 June - 1 July 2005 (2005)
3. Arlat, J., Aguera, M., Amat, L., Crouzet, Y., Fabre, J.-C., Laprie, J.-C., Martins, E., Powell, D.: Fault Injection for Dependability Validation: A Methodology and Some Applications. IEEE Tr on SE 16(2), 166–182 (1990)
4. Binder, R.: Testing Object-Oriented Systems-Models, Patterns and Tools. Addison-Wesley, Reading (2000)
5. Cavalli, A., Gervy, C., Prokopenko, S.: New Approaches for Passive Testing using Extended Finite State Machine Specification. In: WTCS, Canada (2001)
6. Chandra, R., Lefever, R.M., Cukier, M., Sanders, W.H.A: global-state triggered fault injector for distributed system evaluation. IEEE Transaction on Parallel and Distributed Systems 15(7), 593–605 (2004)

7. Chow, T.S.: Testing software design modeled by finite state machines. IEEE Trans on Sw Engineering (TSE) 3, 178–187 (1978)
8. Dssouli, H., Salek, K., Aboulhamid, E., En-Nouaary, A., Bourhfir, C.: Test Development for Comm. Protocols: Towards Automation. Computer Networks 31, 1835–1872 (1999)
9. Echtle, K., Chen, Y.: Evaluation of Deterministic Fault Injection for Fault-Tolerant Protocol Testing. In: IEEE 21th Annual International Symposium on Fault-Tolerant Computing, Montreal, pp. 418–425. IEEE Computer Society Press, Los Alamitos (1991)
10. Goddard Space Flight Center (GSFC) (accessed March 2007), available at: http://radhome.gsfc.nasa.gov/radhome/papers/seeca1.htm
11. Holzmann, G.J.: Design and validation of computer protocols. Prentice-Hall, Englewood Cliffs (1990)
12. International Organization for Standardization ISO/IEC- IS9646 International standard conformance testing methodology and framework. Geneve (1991)
13. Martins, E., Mattiello-Francisco, F.A: Tool for Fault Injection and Conformance Testing of Distributed Systems. LNCS, vol. 2847/2003, pp. 282–302 (2003)
14. Martins, E., Sabião, S.B., Ambrosio, A.M.: ConData: a Tool for Automating Specification-based Test Case Generation for Communication Systems. Software Quality Journal 8(4), 303–319 (1999)
15. Mattiello-Francisco, M.F., Santiago, V.A., Costa, R., Jogaib, L.: Verificação e Validação na terceirização de software embarcado em aplicações espaciais. In: Simpósio Brasiliero de Qualidade de Software - SBQS2006, Villa Velha, ES, Brazil, pp. 368–375 (2006)
16. Santiago, V., Mattiello-Francisco, F., Costa, R., Silva, W.P., Ambrosio, A.M.: QSEE Project: An Experience in Outsourcing Software Development for Space Applications. In: The Nineteenth International Conference on Software Engineering and Knowledge Engineering (SEKE'07), Boston, EUA (2007)
17. Silva, W.P., et al.: QSEE-TAS: Uma Ferramenta para Execução e Relato Automatizados de Testes de Software para Aplicações Espaciais. In: XX Brazilian Symposium on Software Engineering-SBES (2006)

Component-Based Software Certification Based on Experimental Risk Assessment

Regina Moraes[1], João Durães[3], Eliane Martins[1], and Henrique Madeira[2]

[1] State University of Campinas, UNICAMP
São Paulo, Brazil 13.084-971 – Campinas – SP – Brasil
regina@ceset.unicamp.br, eliane@ic.unicamp.br
[2] CISUC, University of Coimbra, Portugal 3030-290 – Coimbra – Portugal
[3] CISUC, ISEC, 3030-290 – Coimbra – Portugal
{jduraes,henrique}@dei.uc.pt

Abstract. Third-party software certification should attest that the software product satisfies the required confidence level according to certification standards such as ISO/IEC 9126, ISO/IEC 14598 or ISO/IEC 25051. In many application areas, especially in mission-critical applications, certification is essential or even mandatory. However, the certification of software products using common off-the-shelf (COTS) components is difficult to attain, as detailed information about COTS is seldom available. Nevertheless, software products are increasingly being based on COTS components, which mean that traditional certification processes should be enhanced to take COTS into account in an effective way. This paper proposes a mean to help in the certification of component-based systems through an experimental risk assessment methodology based on fault injection and statistical analysis. Using the proposed methodology the certification authority or the system integrator can compare among components available the one that best fit for the system that is assembling a component that provides a specific functionality. Based on the results it is also possible to decide whether a software product may be considered certified or not in what concerns the risk of using a COTS into the system. The proposed approach is demonstrated and evaluated using a space application running on top of two alternative COTS real-time operating systems: RTEMS and RTLinux.

Keywords: Component-based system certification, Experimental Risk Assessment, Fault Injection.

1 Introduction

Modern society is highly dependent on computers and software. Currently, software is recognized as the most complex and error-prone part of computer based systems. Thus, software reliability is increasingly important and software products certification is more crucial than ever.

In many cases, software certification is mandatory by law (e.g., software for medical equipment, avionics, telecommunications, etc), and even when certification is

A. Bondavalli, F. Brasileiro, and S. Rajsbaum (Eds.): LADC 2007, LNCS 4746, pp. 179–197, 2007.

merely recommended it still constitutes an important product marketing argument. Traditional quality certification standards are focused on the software development process (e.g., ISO/IEC 12207, Capability Maturity Model - CMM, Capability Maturity Model Integrated - CMMI). However, the certification of software products for safety and business critical application must consider both the development process and the product intrinsic quality. Several certification standards targeting software products have been proposed (e.g., ISO/IEC 12119, ISO/IEC 9126). This trend for software product certification (in addition to software development process certification) is gaining ground. Recent ISO standards are now focusing on component certification, such as the recent draft for software component quality certification ISO/IEC 25051 [21].

Due to the pressure on time and cost, the integration of components that already have been used and tested in other systems (very often, common-off-the-shelf – COTS – components) has become particularly attractive. The objective is to build new software products capitalizing on previously work that can be immediately deployed in new contexts. This software development practice introduces a false sense of safety, as the components have already been used, and constitutes a pragmatic way of coping with the very high complexity of most software products, while it also reduces time to market, cuts development costs, reduces maintenance costs, and potentially improves quality. All these beliefs are based on the assumption that the components have been well tested previously [23]. However, the reuse of COTS in new systems introduces new problems, as software developers (who also assume the role of software integrators) often do not have access to detailed information on the COTS components they use (development and testing methodologies, component architecture and source code). Also, the new operational conditions may differ substantially from those the components were initially designed for, which may expose hidden software faults in the components or originate interoperability problems between components [52]. In short, the use of COTS in new software products represents a risk for the system in which these COTS are integrated and must be specifically addressed in software product certification.

In spite of introducing new risks of failure, component-based software development with intensive reuse of components is a solid trend in the industry and is not likely to disappear, as the alternative would be the much more expensive write-from-scratch approach. Therefore, the choice of the right (i.e., less risky, reliable and robust) COTS components is an essential task and software product certification may be required by acquirers in order to accept software components. Despite the consciousness about its importance, software component certification it is still immature and much research is needed [33].

This paper proposes a methodology to certify software components within a given system and environment. The approach uses software fault injection [10] to measure experimentally the impact of the activation of realistic residual faults in the COTS component on the enclosing system. The proposed methodology combine the use of well established software complexity metrics [28, 47] with statistical analysis to estimate component fault proneness. Combining all measurements, an experimental risk assessment technique is proposed to evaluate the risk represented by the use of a given COTS in the product under certification. The risk is estimated using the classical risk equation that estimates risk as the probability of occurrence of an undesired event and the impact (cost) of the resulting consequences. The proposed risk assessment methodology can help the software evaluation team to reach software system certification. Our proposal integrates the experimental risk assessment methodology in the evaluation process following ISO1/IEC2 14598 standards considering the quality in use metrics as proposed by ISO/IEC 9126 software product standard. The selection of both standards is justified by the complementary characteristics presented by ISO/IEC 9126 and ISO/IEC 14598, which together consider software product and process.

Our goal with this work is the certification of software products that integrate COTS and to enable the comparison of different versions of the software product when competitive COTS that provide the same functionality are integrated in each version allowing the certification of the best version presented.

The proposed approach is demonstrated and evaluated using a satellite data handling application used by the European Space Agency running on top of two alternative COTS real-time operating systems: RTEMS and RTLinux.

The remainder of this paper is organized as follows: the next section presents a survey of software certification, software risk assessment and the related works more relevant to our own. Software certification using experimental risk assessment is presented in Section 3. The case study results are discussed in Section 4. Section 5 concludes this work summing up the main contributions.

2 Software Certification and Risk Assessment: Survey and Related Work

The methodology proposed in this paper is aimed at the certification of a component-based system that has a COTS software product among its components. The proposed certification is based on risk evaluation, which in turn is supported by two research lines: the use of software metrics to estimate component fault density and the injection of software faults to evaluate the cost of component failures.

2.1 Software Certification

Certification is defined as "procedure by which a third-party gives written assurance that a product, process or service conforms to specified requirements" [12]. Certification is the process in which a certification authority issues a certificate document to show that the solicitant abides the principles set out in a specific standard, i.e., certifies that a given entity fulfills a set of quality properties previously established in a given standard. Different standards focus on different sets of properties.

Certification in the software domain can be applied to the software development process (e.g., ISO/IEC 12207, Capability Maturity Model - CMM, Capability Maturity Model Integrated - CMMI) or to the software product (e.g., ISO/IEC 12119, ISO/IEC 9126, ISO/IEC 25051). Our work is focused on the certification of software

---

[1] International Organization for Standardization.
[2] International Electrotechnical Commission.

product and not on the certification of the software development process. Reliability and safety are typical examples of characteristics required in software products certification.

Concerning software component certification, Councill [8] presents set of requirements to guarantee software component quality. That work emphasizes the importance of the estimated risk and the identification, in early software life cycle, the correct implementation of specified requirements among others suggestions to improve software quality. Our work can help in the risk estimation based on early prototype.

The work presented by Stafford and Wallnau [45] proposes a model in which several actors participate in the software component development and receive the responsibilities on the software component quality rather than vesting trust in third-party certification authority. Different actors with distinct roles to play in a component-based development paradigm may interact in a variety of ways to achieve trust. Morris [33] also views the developers' self-certification as a viable alternative to independent certification and proposes a software component certification that developers supply, in a standard portable form with the software package, a way so that the customers are able to manage the certification process they need. Using this standard, the costumers can determine the quality and suitability of the purchased software in their application context. This approach has the disadvantage of requiring the users to build the tests incurring in costs of resources and time.

Following a different approach, Voas [50] suggested that independent agencies such as software certification laboratories should assume the role of software product certification and suggests that the only approach that consumers can trust is the certification provided by agencies that are completely independent from the software product providers. The methodology proposed in that work uses three quality assessment techniques: (i) component black-box testing to verify component quality, (ii) fault injection to determine how well a system tolerates a failing component, and (iii) operational system testing to determine how well the system will tolerate a properly functioning component. The methodology can help developers to decide whether a given component is appropriated for integration in the intended system. Voas [51] also emphasizes that current certification practices are highly process-oriented and suggests that mere best practices guidelines for the development process are not enough to guarantee high-quality software. The work presented by Voas [50] also proposes a high-assurance certification based on desirable-behavior testing (addresses the operational input scenario), abnormal testing (addresses abnormal input scenarios), and fault injection (addresses failures in any subsystem, hardware or external environment). If the software product passes these tests (e.g. the product behaves as expected), then it is certified as high-assurance software. Our work also considers fault injection. However, we use only fault types that are representative of residual faults, according to previous research [10], and derive the probability of fault activation. Additionally, we use complexity metrics to estimate the probability of the component having residual faults [32].

The work presented in [37] focuses on safety certification using the notion of risk assessment of software systems, including systems that use COTS. The proposal includes an iterative process for safety certification focusing on the software product development process. According to that proposal, the safety verifications are done in parallel with software development. That work ([37]) emphasizes the relevance of both static and dynamic characteristics of software evaluation but does not specify how to deal with them. Our work combines static (software complexity metrics and statistical analysis to estimate component fault proneness) and dynamic (fault injection to measure experimentally the impact of fault activation) characteristics of software to estimate the risk that a COTS component can present to the whole software product.

The ISO/IEC 9126 standard [20] defines a software quality model which has been used as a reference for the evaluation of software quality. This standard is composed by the ISO/IEC 9126-1 quality model, the ISO/IEC 9126-2 external metrics, the ISO/IEC 9126-3 internal metrics, and the ISO/IEC 9126-4 quality in use metrics. The main goal of this standard is the identification of the software quality attributes that can be described by suppliers (internal and external attributes) aimed at evaluation/selection of COTS. The ISO/IEC 9126 standard does not describe specific quality requirements for software; instead it defines a quality model that can be applied to any kind of software product. According to ISO/IEC 9126, the quality of a software product is defined by three aspects: the internal quality (internal characteristics such as static models, source code, documen-tation, etc.), the external quality (external characteristics such as the visible effects in the application environment), and the quality in use (considers the customer point of view of the software product and is useful to show the component behavior in different environments) [7]. The ISO/IEC 9126 standard is a generic software quality model and it is very difficult to apply to COTS components.

The ISO/IEC 14598 [19] standard is a complement to ISO/IEC 9126 and provides the guidelines for the evaluation of software products using ISO/IEC 9126. In practice, both standards are used in conjunction. The process can be used to evaluate both finished products and products still under development. ISO/IEC 14598 is composed of six parts: 14598-1 addresses internal metrics, 14598-2 and 14598-6 address support evaluation, 14598-3, 14598-4 and 14598-5 refer to evaluation process. ISO/IEC 14598 suggests that an evaluation module is defined for each measure that is required for the software certification. An evaluation module is "a package of evaluation technology for measuring software quality characteristics, sub-characteristics or attributes" [19]. A package is a set of evaluation methods and techniques, inputs to the evaluation, data to be measured and collected, supporting procedures and tools. The evaluation technology is composed by techniques, tools, metrics, measures and relevant technical information used for evaluation. Through an evaluation module, the detailed information to get the measurements is well documented and represents a mean to obtain a repeatable, reproducible and objective evaluation.

The ISO/IEC 12119 [18] defines quality requirements for software packages and provides guidelines to conduct the tests to assert the conformance of the software to the standard. The ISO/IEC 25051 standard [21] is an improvement of the ISO/IEC 12119. It focuses on COTS software products and specifies quality requirements which address test documentation, test cases and test reporting. ISO/IEC 25051 provides the instructions to evaluate the conformity to the standard. It also includes recommendations for safety of business critical COTS software products. The main goal of this standard is to provide the user with confidence that the COTS software product performs as offered and delivered. This standard does not address the development process quality of the COTS software supplier. Our approach differs from this one as our focus is the COTS software product when it is integrated in the larger system.

2.2 Software Risk Assessment

Many studies have tried to minimize the problems associated to software faults and estimate their risk with particular emphasis on studies on software testing, software reliability modelling and software reliability risk analysis [28, 34, 17, 24].

Risk is often assessed based on heuristics [3] or on rigorous analysis using statistical models such as software reliability modeling to estimate the component failure likelihood [28, 44] and hazard analysis to estimate the consequence of failures [25].

The software risk assessment equation used in most of the literature is basically the same and combine the probability of fault in a given software component and faults impact (or cost). However, the equation is interpreted in different ways, depending on the approach used for risk assessment. Rosenberg works [39] uses CK metrics and threshold values to estimate the fault proneness. The failure cost based on field data and the operational profile is the approach used in [43] and [1] considers the component exposure in the point of view of the customer and in the point of view of the vendor to estimate the system risk.

Complexity metrics have been used in many studies that show the relationship between component complexity and error proneness [36, 24, 11]. The study presented in [4] experimentally validates object-oriented design metrics as quality indicators to predict fault-prone classes and concludes that several of these metrics appear to be useful to predict class fault-proneness. However, the usefulness of complexity metrics to estimate error proneness is not consensual. Fenton [13] shows that the use of static metrics to estimate runtime errors does not hold in some cases and Menzies et al. [30] presents some explanations for this apparent contradiction and reinforces the usefulness of static code metrics as probabilistic predictors when a large amount of data is analyzed in order to generalize the results.

The Failure Mode and Effect Analysis (FMEA) technique [25] is widely used to estimate the impact of component failures (known as severity analysis in the context of FMEA). This technique is widely used in the development of software for highly regulated application areas and is suggested as a systematic method that should be used in nuclear software [48], health software [16], and aircraft systems [46] among others.

Experimental evaluation of the impact (cost) of failures using fault injection and robustness tech-niques is widely used approach that allows the observation of the system behavior in the presence of faults [2, 22, 50] when these faults are artificially inserted into the system under test. Fault injection allows testers to better understand how the system under test behaves in the presence of faults, and thus estimate the consequences of the activation of the unknown residual faults in the system.

Most of the fault injection works actually inject faults that emulate hardware transient faults. Very often, faults are injected using Software Implemented Fault

Injection (SWIFI) tools, but even these tools just emulate hardware transient faults. The problem of injecting representative software faults was proposed in [6] in the context of IBM´s Orthogonal Defect Classification (ODC) [5]. Madeira [29] showed that typical fault injection tools are unable to inject a substantial part of the type of faults proposed in [6] and the method requires the knowledge of previous faults in the target system.

The first practical technique to emulate realistic software faults with acceptable accuracy was proposed in [9]. This technique named Generic Software Fault Injection Technique (G-SWFIT) is based on a field study that analyzed and classified software faults in a variety of open-source programs. We use this technique in our proposal to evaluate the impact of a failure of a given software component in the overall system. Section 3.2 presents some details of this technique.

The use of fault injection to estimate risk has not been addressed in the literature, especially what concerns software risk. To the best of our knowledge, the only work that used fault injection to estimate software risk is our previous work [32]. In the present paper we propose the use of experimental risk assessment in the software certification, including software products based on COTS components that generally complicate the certification process, as COTS characteristics are often not fully available.

3 Software Certification Using Experimental Risk Assessment

To certify a software product a complex process is needed to assure the conformity to software products requirements and a set of documents, general information, test and validation must be prepared following a specific standard. Certification becomes even more difficult when COTS components are part of the software system. Regulations and standards required to certify the software product may not apply to the component that developers intend to use. It is largely accepted that the use of COTS increases the probability of system failure [50, 52, 53] and represents a risk to the overall software system [52]. Thus, risk is one of the most important measures that must be considered to certify software system.

ISO/IEC 9126 [20] considers risk as an attribute of safety (quality in use metrics). The proposed certification strategy can help this particular evaluation and ensure that a software product conforms to a pre-defined level of risk. Other certification requirements are also necessary but we focus only on the aspects related to the risk evaluation.

3.1 Quality Model and Evaluation Process

A quality model consists of a set of quality characteristics, each of which is decomposed into a set of quality sub-characteristics. A set of characteristics and sub-characteristics made ISO/IEC 9126 [20] a quality model that focuses on software product and group these characteristics and sub-characteristics on internal quality, external quality and quality in use.

Our work is focused in metrics of quality in use as we are interesting in the evaluation of the quality of a COTS component when it is integrated in a specific software system. Safety is a quality in use sub-characteristic and considers risk as an attribute. Our work can help to obtain a relative measure of this specific attribute. As a first approach, this relative measure does not represent the real software risk, but it is useful to compare with a threshold that considers its limitation or help in choosing among several COTS components (that provide the same functionality) the best one to compose the specific software.

ISO/IEC 14598 [19] can be used in conjunction with ISO/IEC 9126. ISO/IEC 14598 guides the planning and the execution of a evaluation process of software quality product. According to ISO/IEC 14598 the fundamental characteristics expected in the software products evaluation process are repeatability (same product, with the same evaluation specification as done by the same evaluator, must produce results that can be accepted as identical), reproducibility (repeated evaluation of a given product by different evaluators must produce identical results), impartiality (the evaluation must not be influenced by any result in particular) and objectivity (the results are not influenced by evaluator's feelings or opinions). The Evaluation Process as proposed by ISO/IEC 14598 standard encompasses five activities: Evaluation Requirement Analysis, Evaluation Specification, Evaluation Design, Carrying out Evaluation and Conclusion.

3.1.1 Evaluation Requirement Analysis
This activity presents three sub-activities: (i) to establish the evaluation purpose; (ii) to identify products types to be evaluated; (iii) to specify quality model.

Figure 1 presents a schema that shows these activities for our case and emphasized the quality in use metrics, particularly in safety metrics that are the focus of our quality model.

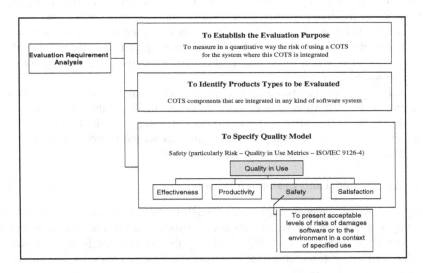

Fig. 1. Evaluation Requirements Analysis Activities

3.1.2 Evaluation Specification

Evaluation Specification activity also presents three sub-activities: (i) to select metrics; (ii) to establish the score level; (iii) to establish the judgment criteria.

The metric chosen was the estimation of the risk represented by use of a given COTS in the software product under certification. Note that the value resulting from the estimation of risk should not be interpreted as an absolute estimation of the probability of failure. Instead it should be understood as a metric on risk mainly intended for comparison purposes. Despite our focus on COTS, the technique can actually be applied to any component of the target system.

Our goal is to provide a quantitative measure of the risk of system **S** having a failure (e.g., to produce erroneous results, or to experience a safety failure, or a timing failure, or a security failure, or become unavailable, etc.) due to a faulty behavior in component **C** caused by the activation of a residual software fault **f** in that component. Equation (1) shows how to estimate the risk.

$$Risk_C = prob(f_C) * cost(f_C) \tag{1}$$

The term *prob(f_C)* represents the likelihood of the existence of residual software faults in component **C**, i.e., corresponds to the component fault-proneness. To estimate this likelihood we propose the use of well-established software complexity metrics [28, 47] and a logistic regression analysis based on these metrics [4]. The term *cost(f_C)* represents the impact of the activation of faults in component **C**, in this work measured by software fault injection. If the injection of faults in a given component shows that a large percentage of faults cause a strong impact in the system (high *cost(f)*) and the likelihood of faults in that component is high (high *prob(f)*), then the component represents a high risk.

A very important aspect in risk assessment is the probability of the activation of the residual faults. This probability is strongly dependent on the workload, the operational profile, and the architecture of the component and cannot be easily modeled by static analysis alone (and details of the component architecture may not be available). In our methodology the fault activation probability is actually evaluated during the fault injection experiments. This is, in fact, an intrinsic aspect of the fault injection experiments: the fault is injected and its activation/non-activation is a consequence of the workload and execution profile and the internal component architecture.

Residual Fault Likelihood Estimation

Our work elaborates from previous proposals [4, 47, 35, 32] to estimate *prob(f)* and follows a model based on logistic regression. Logistic regression [15] was the used statistical analysis to address the relationship between metrics and the fault-proneness of components. Logistic regression gives to each independent variable (e.g. complexity metrics), also called "regressor", an estimated regression coefficient β_i, which measures the regressor contribution to variations in the dependent variable (e.g. the failure likelihood).

To estimate the *prob(f)* we need to identify which metrics are relevant. We also need to select which of them is best suited to the evaluation of the software complexity. We start by considering the cyclomatic complexity (Vg measures the control flow complexity of a program) as regressors for *prob(f)* and we added number of parameters, number of returns, maximum nesting depth, program length and vocabulary size [14]. The accuracy of the results obtained in the experiments was evaluated through the analysis of bug reports available from open software initiatives (see [31]). Halstead's metrics and Vg measure two distinct program attributes [35] leading to a better fault prediction capability [28]. Considering six metrics, the probability that a component has a residual fault is given by equation (2).

$$prob\,(f) = \frac{\exp(\alpha + \beta_1 X_1 + ... + \beta_6 X_6)}{1 + \exp(\alpha + \beta_1 X_1 + ... + \beta_6 X_6)} \qquad (2)$$

In the above equation, X_i represents the product metrics (independent variables) and α and β_i the estimated logistic regression coefficients (see more details in [32]). In the case of a large component composed by sub-components, we have to use the prob(f) combined with the complexity weight of each sub-component in the global component. This is obtained by equation (3), where Metrics$_i$ represents any of the available metrics for each component **i**. The chosen metric can be the one that best represent the system characteristics (for example, maximum nesting depth if the system has several nested structures).

$$prob_g(f) = \sum prob_i(f) * (Metrics_i / \sum Metrics_i) \qquad (3)$$

Failure Cost Estimation

To estimate the cost (or impact) of the activation of faults in component we used G-SWFIT technique [9] to inject software faults. G-SWFIT is based on a set of fault injection operators that reproduce directly in the target executable code the instruction sequences that represent most common types of high-level software faults. These fault injection operators resulted from a field study that analyzed and classified more than 600 real software faults discovered in several programs, identifying the most common (the "top-N") types of software faults [10] that are presented in Table 1 and used in the present paper. The representativeness of the faults injected ensures that the fault injection experiments represent the activation of faults that are likely to exist in the component.

The analysis of the target code is performed by G-SWFIT tool which identifies the places where a realistic software fault could in fact exist. The distribution of the number of fault injected in each component is based in our previous proposal [31] based on column 3 of Table 1.

The evaluation of This impact is translated in the following failure modes: **Hang** – the application is not able to terminate in the pre-determinate time; **Crash** – the application terminates abruptly before the workload complete; **Wrong** – the cost of component failures is done by injecting one fault at the time and the cost is measured as the impact of each fault injected in the component in the whole system. workload terminates but the results are not correct; **Correct** – there are no errors reported and the result is correct.

Table 1. Most frequent fault types found in [10]

Fault types	Description	% of total observed	ODC classes
MIFS	Missing "If (cond) { statement(s) }"	9.96 %	Algorithm
MFC	Missing function call	8.64 %	Algorithm
MLAC	Missing "AND EXPR" in expression used as branch condition	7.89 %	Checking
MIA	Missing "if (cond)" surrounding statement(s)	4.32 %	Checking
MLPC	Missing small and localized part of the algorithm	3.19 %	Algorithm
MVAE	Missing variable assignment using an expression	3.00 %	Assignment
WLEC	Wrong logical expression used as branch condition	3.00 %	Checking
WVAV	Wrong value assigned to a value	2.44 %	Assignment
MVI	Missing variable initialization	2.25 %	Assignment
MVAV	Missing variable assignment using a value	2.25 %	Assignment
WAEP	Wrong arithmetic expression used in parameter of function call	2.25 %	Interface
WPFV	Wrong variable used in parameter of function call	1.50 %	Interface
	Total faults coverage	50.69 %	

When a software fault is injected in a given component, that fault may or may not a cause faulty behavior in the component. Furthermore, only a fraction the faults that cause erroneous behavior in the component will cause the system to fail, as the remaining faults are either tolerated or have no visible effect. This means that the results measured by using fault injection already include the probability of fault activation (and consequent deviation in the component behavior) and the consequence of a failure (for example, the probability that the system crash).

Once we have the estimation of risk computed as showed in equation (1) we need to determine if the component conforms to the desired level of risk (a threshold value that represents the acceptable risk to the system under analysis). The accept threshold of the risk level is strongly dependent on the type of the software product and the context in which this software is used. A general-purpose threshold value is difficult to determine as it is linked to commercial agreements or legal requirements. When users require the assurance (certification) that a specific software product conforms to the requirements for its business or application context, the threshold value (risk level) must be considered as part of the information and agreements firmed between users and evaluators when certification request is done for the competent agency. The risk value computed using equation (1) must be compared with this threshold value. The verdict of the certification is success if risk value is less than the threshold stipulated; otherwise the software product is not certified for the desired level of risk.

Another use of the risk assessment as proposed in this work is the comparison among several versions of the system when the COTS component is replaced with a functionally similar one. In this case, the goal of the certification process is to establish the best COTS for a specific software system. When several COTS component provides the same functionality we can integrate each COTS one at a time and evaluate the software system risk. Based on the results of risk assessment we can determine the best COTS for the specific software system, i.e., we should choose the component that presents the lower risk when integrated in the software system. Figure 2 presents the Evaluation Estimation Activities.

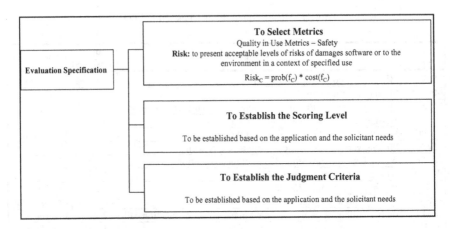

Fig. 2. Evaluation Specification Activities

3.1.3 Evaluation Design

The goal of this activity is to establish the evaluation plan. The plan presents the steps to follow in order to obtain the metrics defined in the evaluation specification. In our case, these steps are presented in Table 2, in order to obtain fault density (first column) and cost (second column).

3.1.4 Performing the Evaluation

This activity presents three sub-activities: (i) to obtain the measurements; (ii) to compare with the established criteria; (iii) to evaluate the results. These sub-activities are demonstrated using the case study in the next section.

Table 2. Steps to assess the Terms of the Risk Equation

Fault Density Likelihood Estimation	Cost (or Impact) Estimation
1. Evaluate the complexity metrics of each component	**1.** Scan each component code in order to define the fault injection local and faults types to be injected (by using GSWFIT tool)
2. Adopt fault density ranges accepted by the industry community as a preliminary estimation of fault densities [38] as a starting estimation for the logistic regression (this preliminary estimation replaces the field observation)	**2.** Plan the faults to be injected in each component, using the faults types and the distribution presented in Table 1 (third column)
3. Use the binomial distribution	**3.** Integrate a component into the software system
4. Apply the regression using the value obtained from natural logarithm of the preliminary fault density and the chosen metrics aim to obtain the coefficients for each component	**4.** Apply the fault injection campaign (one fault at a time) as planned for the specific component
5. Estimate the likelihood of fault of each component by using the computed coefficients in previous step by using the logistic equation presented in equation (4)	**5.** Collect the results of fault injection campaign in accordance of the failure mode presented in Section 3.1.2
6. Estimate the likelihood of fault density for each component as presented in equation (5) when the specific component is composed by several sub-components	**6.** If there is one more component to be integrated return to step 3.

4 Case Study

The software application is a real-time satellite data handling system (DHS) named Command and Data Management System (CDMS). CDMS is responsible for managing all data transactions between ground systems and a spacecraft. The CDMS runs a mission scenario where a space telescope is being controlled and data collected is sent to ground system.

This application is written in C and use a COTS component, which is a real-time operating system (OS). In order to illustrate our proposal in a component-based software, we consider two COTS, with similar functionality but different features: the RTEMS [41] and the RT-Linux[26] real-time OS. The ground control software is hosted in a computer running Linux. To evaluate the software risk, each component is integrated into the system and the methodology is applied. Figure 3 shows the satellite data handling system setup. It also represents the fault injection target, which is the real-time operating system (representing the COTS component: RTEMS or RTLinux, as we have performed two sets of experiments).

The CDMS system is composed by six subsystems (partially shown in Figure 3): Packet Router (PR), Power Conditioning System (PCS), On Board Storage (OBS), Data Handling System (DHS), Reconfiguration Manager (RM), and Payload (PL). The CDMS sends telemetry information for each command sent by the ground control. The timing of the commands and the contents of the telemetry information are used to detect the system correctness/failure.

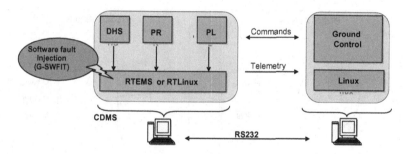

Fig. 3. CDMS Satellite Data Handling setup overview

4.1 Obtaining the Measurements

In order to evaluate the risk of using a COTS into the system two measurements must be obtained: the fault density likelihood estimation and the impact (cost) of fault activation estimation. Both measurements are obtained following the steps presented in Table 2.

4.1.1 Fault Density Likelihood Estimation

RTLinux and RTEMS are composed respectively by 2211 and 1257 modules with a total of 85108 and 63258 lines of code. The regression analysis was applied (as explained in section 3.1.2. See more details in [31] and [32]) and the regression coefficients (βi) were applied in the logistic equation (refer to equation (2) in section 3.1.2.) to obtain the estimated *prob(f)* of each component. The global *probg(f)* estimated for RTLinux is 6.50% and for RTEMS is 7.49% (refer to equation (3) as explained in section 3.1.2).

4.1.2 Cost Estimation

Our current results correspond to 231 faults injected in the RTMES and 341 faults injected in the RTLinux version of CDMS. In both cases, the software faults have been injected in the operating system code (RTMES or RTLinux) using the G-SWFIT technique as explained in section 3.1.2. Table 3 and Figure 4 present the failure modes obtained in the fault injection campaign in the system integrating both operating systems.

Table 3. Failure Modes and Results

Failure Mode Levels	RTEMS		RTLinux	
	#	%	#	%
Correct	170	74	170	50
Wrong	12	5	3	1
Crash	21	9	86	25
Hang	28	12	82	24
Total	231	100	341	100

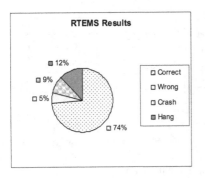
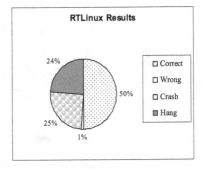

Fig. 4. Fault Injection Results

4.1.3 Risk Evaluation

Table 4 presents the risk evaluation of the system using RTEMS and using RTLinux. The risk was evaluated considering each failure mode that represents erroneous behavior and the combination of all the erroneous failure modes (represented by the column "Incorrect Behavior" in Table 4). Note that this value resulting from the application of the methodology should not be interpreted as an absolute estimation of the probability of failure. Instead it should be understood as a metric on risk mainly intended for comparison.

Table 4. The Risk Evaluation – Failure Mode

Component	prob(f)	Crash		Wrong		Hang		Incorrect Behavior	
		cost(f)	risk	cost(f)	risk	cost(f)	risk	cost(f)	risk
RTEMS	0.0749	0.09	0.67%	0.05	0.37%	0.12	0.89%	0.26	1.94%
RTLinux	0.0650	0.25	1.62%	0.01	0.06%	0.24	1.56%	0.50	3.25%

4.2 Compare with the Established Criteria and Evaluate the Results

To certify a software product in what concerns the risk, we need to compare the risk estimation obtained using our approach with the established threshold. The agreement about the threshold value to certify the software depends on the software product-line. In some areas the threshold value is determined by law (e.g. software for medical equipment, avionics, etc.), other areas that is not too critical, the threshold can be an agreement between solicitant and the certification authority. In addition, our proposal is a metric on risk and a threshold must be established by the solicitant. The threshold value can be a unique value to compare with the incorrect behavior or can be different values to compare with the specific type of incorrect behavior (crash, wrong or hang risk). For example, considering the results presented in Table 4, if the threshold to certify the software would be an estimated risk lower than 2,5%, only the system using RTMS would be certified, as the assessed risk of using RTLinux in the system is higher than the threshold.

Another use of our approach is to compare and choose the best component for a specific software product. When there are several components that provide the same functionality the solicitant should be interested to know which one of them is more appropriated for his system. In this case, the certification must indicate the component that presents the lower risk.

The results presented in this work, for the CDMS system, indicate that RTLinux represents a higher risk than RTEMS for most of the failure modes considered, and thus, RTMES seems to be a better choice for this application, i.e., the CDMS version that integrates RTEMS should be certified. One exception is related to the wrong results, as RTLinux represents a lower risk of wrong results when compared to the RTEMS (i.e., the RTLinux version causes fail silent behavior more frequently).

5 Conclusion and Future Work

This work presents a first proposal to certify a component-based system using experimental risk assessment. Software metrics and software fault injection are combined to provide the software risk evaluation that is the based measurement of the proposed certification, providing a repeatable and reliable metric for software product certification. The cost of the failures of the component is evaluated through the observation of the system behavior due to the injection of realistic and representative faults and fault distribution in the component under evaluation. Several software metrics are considered and logistic regression analysis was used to fit the expression of the fault probability with these metrics. Our risk equation considers the fault probability, the probability of fault activation, the probability of consequent deviation in the component behavior and the consequence of a failure to model the fact that some faults are not activated or tolerated.

Two alternative versions of CDMS that integrate RTEMS and RTLinux (one at each time) were submitted to the proposed certification process. The results showed that it is possible to obtain a metric on risk to be used to certify a component considering static (software metrics) and dynamic aspects (software behavior during runtime) when this component is integrated in a specific software system. Besides the use of the results obtained to verify the component risk based on a threshold values established by the solicitant, the knowledge about this metrics on risk can be used to restruc-tured, wrapping modules or implement new architecture solutions to achieve the desired risk level.

The proposed methodology can also be used to improve the reliability of the target system as it helps system developers/integrator to select the best component (from a pool of alternatives) to integrate in the target system. In our case study, if the proposal is to choose the best component between RTEMS and RT-Linux to integrate into CDMS system, RTEMS should be selected since it presents less risk to CDMS.

Our research group is working to refine the risk evaluation considering other aspects in order to obtain a more realistic measure of software component risk, improve the certification measurement and define threshold value for some product line to improve certification of software system based on risk assessment.

Acknowledgments. The authors thank to CAPES/GRICES, CNPq and FAPESP to partially support this work. We thank also to MSquared Technologies for gracefully providing the full version of RSM tool [40], and Testwell Oy Ltd [49] for CMT++ and CMTjava tools.

References

[1] Amland, S.: Risk-based Testing: Risk analysis fundamentals and metrics for software testing including a financial application case study. The Journal of Systems and Software 53, 287–295 (2000)

[2] Arlat, J., et al.: Fault Injection and Dependability Evaluation of Fault Tolerant Systems. IEEE Transaction on Computers 42(8), 919–923 (1993)

[3] Bach, J.: Heuristic Risk-Based Testing. In: Software Testing and Engineering Magazine (1999)

[4] Basili, V., Briand, L., Melo, W.: Measuring the Impact of Reuse on Quality and Productivity in Object-Oriented Systems. Technical Report, University of Maryland, Dep. Of Computer Science, CS-TR-3395 (1995)

[5] Chillarege, R., Orthogonal Defect Classification, Ch. 9 of Handbook of Software Reliability Engineering, M. Lyu Ed., IEEE Computer Society, McGraw-Hill, (1995).

[6] Christmansson, J., Chillarege, R.: Generation of an Error Set that Emulates Software Faults-Based on Fields Data. In: Proc. of 26th Int. Symp. on Fault-Tolerant Computing, Sendai, Japan, pp. 304–313 (1996)

[7] Colombo, R., Guerra, A.: The Evaluation Method for Software Product. In: Proc. of Int. Conf. on Software \& Systems Engineering \& Applications - ICSSEA '2002, Paris, France (2002)

[8] Councill, B.: Third-Party Certification and Its Required Elements. In: Proc. of The 4th Workshop on Component-Based Software Engineering (CBSE), Springer, Heidelberg, Canada. Lecture Notes in Computer Science (LNCS) (2001)

[9] Durães, J.: Madeira, H. Definition of Software Fault Emulation Operators: A Field Data Study. In: Proc. of The International Conference on Dependable Systems and Networks - DSN2003, pp. 105-114, San Francisco, USA (2003) (William Carter Award for the best student paper)

[10] Durães, J., Madeira, H.: Emulation of Software Faults: A Field Data Study and a Practical Approach. IEEE Transactions on Software Engineering 32(11) (November 2006), ISSN: 0098-558

[11] El Emam, K., Benlarbi, S., Goel, N., Rai, S.: Comparing Case-based Reasoning Classifiers for Predicting High Risk Software Components. Journal of Systems and Software 55(3), 301–320 (2001)

[12] EN 45020 General Terms and Definitions Concerning Standardization and Related Activities. CEN, Brussels (1993)

[13] Fenton, N., Ohlsson, N.: Software Metrics and Risk. In: Proc. of The 2nd European Software Measurement Conference (FESMA 99) (1999)

[14] Halstead, M.: Elements of Software Science. Elsevier Science Inc, New York (1977)

[15] Hosmer, D., Lemeshow, S.: Applied Logistic Regression. John Wiley \& Sons, Chicester (1989)

[16] Health & Safety Commission The use of computers in Safety-critical Applications. Technical Report, UK (1998)

[17] Hudepohl, et al.: EMERALD: A Case Study in Enhancing Software Reliability. Proc. of IEEE Eight Int. Symposium on Software Reliability Engineering - ISSRE98 98, 85–91 (1998)

[18] ISO/IEC 12119. International Organization For Standardization ISO/IEC 12119, Information Technology - Software packages - Quality requirements and testing, p. 16, Geneve (1994)

[19] ISO/IEC 14598-1. International Organization For Standardization ISO/IEC 14598-1 Information Technology - Software product evaluation - Part 1: General Overview; Geneve ISO (1999)

[20] ISO/IEC 9126-1. International Organization For Standardization ISO/IEC 9126-1, Software Engineering - Software product quality - Part 1: Quality Model; Geneve ISO (2001)

[21] ISO/IEC 25051 Software Engineering - Requirements for quality of Commercial Off-The-Shelf (COTS) software product and instructions for testing, Final Draft International Standard (2006)

[22] Iyer, R.: Experimental Evaluation. In: Special Issue FTCS-25 Silver Jubilee, 25th IEEE Symposium on Fault Tolerant Computing, pp. 115–132 (1995)

[23] Jacobson, I., Griss, M., Jonsson, P.: Software Reuse: Architecture, Process and Organization for Business Success. Addison-Wesley, Longman (1997)

[24] Khoshgoftaar, et al.: Process Measures for Predicting Software Quality. In: Proc of High Assurance System Engineering Workshop - HASE'97 (1997)

[25] Leveson, N.: Safeware, System Safety and Computers. Addison-Wesley Publishing Company, Reading (1995)

[26] The linux kernel. Accessed on Feb/06 (2006), http://www.kernel.org

[27] Lyu, M., Chen, J., Avizienis, A.: Experience in Metrics and Measurements for N-Version Programming. Int. Journal of Reliability, Quality and Safety Engineering 1(1), 41–62 (1994)

[28] Lyu, M.: Handbook of Software Reliability Engineering. IEEE omputer Society Press, McGraw-Hill, Los Alamitos (1996)

[29] Madeira, H., Vieira, M., Costa, D.: On the Emulation of Software Faults by Software Fault Injection. In: Proc. of The Int. Conf. on Dependable Systems and Networks, NY, USA (2000)

[30] Menzies, T., Greenwald, J., Frank, A.: Learning Defect Predictors. Journal (submitted, 2006), http://menzies.us/, accessed February/2006

[31] Moraes, R., Durães, J., Martins, E., Madeira, H.: A field data study on the use of software metrics to define representative fault distribution. In: Proc. of The International Conference on Dependable Systems & Networks - DSN2006, IEEE Computer Society Pres, Los Alamitos (2006)

[32] Moraes, R., Durães, J., Barbosa, R., Martins, E., Madeira, H.: Experimental Risk Assessment and Comparison using Software Fault Injection. In: The International Conference on Dependable Systems and Networks - DSN 07, Edimburgo (2007)

[33] Morris, J., Lee, G., Parker, K., Bundell, G., Lam, C.: Software Component Certification. IEEE Computer 34(9), 30–36 (2001)

[34] Musa, J.: Software Reliability Engineering. McGraw-Hill, New York (1996)

[35] Munson, J., Khoshgoftaar, T.: Software Metrics for Reliability Assessment. In: Michael, R. (ed.) Handbook of Software Reliability Engineering, IEEE Comp. Society Press, Los Alamitos (1995)

[36] Kitchenham, B., Pfleeger, S., Fenton, N.: Towards a framework for software measurement validation. IEEE Transactions on Software Engineering 21(12), 929–944 (1995)

[37] Rodríguez-Dapena, P.: Software Safety Certification: A Multidomain Problem. IEEE Software 16(4), 31–38 (1999)

[38] Rome Laboratory (RL). Methodology for Software Reliability Prediction and Assessment. Technical Report RL-TR-92-52, vol. 1 and 2 (1992)

[39] Rosenberg, L., Stapko, R., Gallo, A.: Risk-based Object Oriented Testing. In: Proc of. 13th International Software / Internet Quality Week-QW, San Francisco, California, USA 2 (2000)

[40] Resource Standard Metrics, Version 6.1(2005), http://msquaredtechnologies.com/m2rsm/rsm.htm. Last access

[41] Real-Time Operating System for Multiprocessor Systems. (February 2006) (accessed), http://www.rtems.com

[42] Rushby, John Modular Certification. Langley Research Center. Report Number: NAS 1.26212130, NASA CR-2002-212130, SRI-11003.

[43] Sherer, S.: A Cost-Effective Approach to Testing. IEEE Software 8(2), 34–40 (1991)

[44] Singpurwalla, N.: Statistical Methods in Software Engineering: Reliability and Risk, 1st edn. Springer, Heidelberg (1999)

[45] Stafford, J., Wallnau, K.: Is Third-Party Certification Necessary? In: Proceedings of the 4th ICSE Workshop on Component-Based Software Engineering, Toronto, Canada, May, Toronto, Canada, pp. 13–17 (2001)

[46] Systems Integration Requirements Task Group Certification Considerations for Highly-Integrated or Complex Aircraft Systems, Technical Report AS-1C, ASD, SAE (1996)

[47] Tang, M., Kao, M., Chen, M.: An Empirical Study on Object-Oriented Metrics. In: Proceedings of the Sixth International Software Metrics Symposium, pp. 242-249 (1999)

[48] Nuclear Safety Directorate Computer Based Safety Systems. Technical Assessment Guide T/AST/046, UK, (2000)

[49] Testwell Oy Ltd. Accessed on March/06 (2006), http://www.testwell.fi

[50] Voas, J.: Certifying Off-the-Shelf Software Components. IEEE Computer 31(6), 53–59 (1998)
[51] Voas, J.: Certifying Software for High-Assurance Environments. IEEE Software 16(4), 48–54 (1999)
[52] Weyuker, E.: Testing Component-Based Software: A Cautionary Tale. IEEE Software (1998)
[53] Yang, Y., Boehm, B., Clark, B.: Assessing COTS Integration Risk Using Cost Estimation Inputs. In: Proc. of 28th International Conference on Software Engineering, Shangai, China (2006)

Integrated Intrusion Detection in Databases

José Fonseca, Marco Vieira, and Henrique Madeira

CISUC, Department of Informatics Engineering
University of Coimbra – Portugal
josefonseca@ipg.pt, mvieira@.dei.uc.pt, henrique@dei.uc.pt

Abstract. Database management systems (DBMS), which are the ultimate layer in preventing malicious data access or corruption, implement several security mechanisms to protect data. However these mechanisms cannot always stop malicious users from accessing the data by exploiting system vulnerabilities. In fact, when a malicious user accesses the database there is no effective way to detect and stop the attack in due time. This practical experience report presents a tool that implements concurrent intrusion detection in DBMS. This tool analyses the transactions the users execute and compares them with the profile of the authorized transactions that were previously learned in order to detect potential deviations. The tool was evaluated using the transactions from a standard database benchmark (TPC-W) and a real database application. Results show that the proposed intrusion detection tool can effectively detect SQL-based attacks with no false positives and no overhead to the server.

Keywords: Databases, security, intrusion detection.

1 Introduction

Traditional database security mechanisms offer basic security features such as authentication, authorization, access control, data encryption, and auditing. However, these mechanisms do not assure protection against the exploitation of vulnerabilities in database management systems (DBMS) and are very limited in defending data attacks from the inside of the organization. In fact, as typical database security mechanisms are not primarily designed to detect intrusions (they are designed to avoid the intruder's access to the data), there are many cases where the execution of malicious sequences of SQL[1] commands (transactions) cannot be detected or avoided.

The general lack of intrusion detection features in typical DBMS is an important limitation when it is necessary to assure a strong data security policy. In fact, intrusion detection in DBMS has not been studied much, in a clear contrast to what has happened in operating systems and networking fields, where many intrusion detection approaches have been proposed. However, malicious actions in a database application may not be seen as malicious by existing intrusion detection mechanisms at the network or the operating system levels. Furthermore, inside attacks are particularly difficult to detect and isolate, as the attacks are carried out by legitimate

---

[1] SQL stands for Structured Query Language, the relational language used by relational DBMS [1].

A. Bondavalli, F. Brasileiro, and S. Rajsbaum (Eds.): LADC 2007, LNCS 4746, pp. 198–211, 2007.
© Springer-Verlag Berlin Heidelberg 2007

users that may have access rights to data and system resources. In addition, daily routine and long established habits tend to relax many security procedures. Even simple things such as choosing strong passwords and periodically purging unused database accounts are often neglected in many organizations [2]. This way, a practical tool for intrusion detection in DBMS that detects malicious behavior from applications and users will provide an extra layer of security that cannot be assured by classic security mechanisms.

According to a FBI Computer Crime and Security Survey [3] in 2005, approximately 45% of the inquired entities had reported unauthorized access to information estimating a loss of $31.233.100 and a loss of $30.933.000 due to theft of proprietary information. Up to 56% reported unauthorized use of computer systems and 13% did not know if they had been attacked. Furthermore, 95% of the inquired entities reported more than 10 web site incidents. These figures show the relevance of an intrusion detection mechanism at DBMS level.

Masquerade attacks where people hide their identity by impersonating other people on the computer are one of the most frequent forms of security attacks [4], including in the database domain. Another common database attack is SQL injection in web applications [5], where unchecked input is sent to a back-end database for execution. The attacker can perform this by simply changing the SQL query sent to the server, accessing sensitive data.

The intrusion detection tool presented in this practical experience report adds concurrent intrusion detection to DBMS. This way, data security attacks can be detected and stopped immediately while the mechanism may call the attention of the database administrator (DBA) by sending an email or an SMS message). This tool, named IIDD - Integrated Intrusion Detection in Databases, works in two modes: transactions learning and intrusion detection. During transactions learning, the IIDD extracts the information it needs directly from the network packets sent from client applications to the database server using a network sniffer. The result is the directed graph representing the sequence of SQL commands that composes the authorized transactions. The learned graph is used later on by the concurrent intrusion detection engine. When an intrusion is detected an alarm is raised and, depending on the tool configuration, the database connection between the intruder and the server may be killed. In this case the connection is abruptly broken, and the database automatically performs a rollback of the malicious transaction. An important aspect is that this tool can be easily used in any commercial-off-the-shelf (COTS) DBMS.

The structure of the paper is as follows. Section 2 presents our approach to intrusion detection in DBMS. Section 3 describes the proposed tool. Section 4 presents two examples of utilization of the intrusion detection tool and Section 5 concludes the paper.

2 Intrusion Detection Approach

The main goal of security in DBMS is to protect the system and the data from intrusion and unauthorized accesses, even when the potential intruder gets access to the machine where the DBMS is running. To protect the database from intrusion, the DBA must prevent and remove potential attacks and vulnerabilities. System vulnerabilities are an internal factor related to the set of security mechanisms available (or not available at all) in the system, the correct configuration of those mechanisms, which is a responsibility of the DBA, and the hidden flaws (bugs) in the system implementation. Vulnerability prevention consists of guarantying that the software used has the minimum vulnerabilities possible and this can be achieved by using adequate DBMS software. On the other hand, because the effectiveness of security mechanisms depends on their correct configuration and use, the DBA must correctly configure them by following administration best practices. Vulnerability removal consists in reducing the vulnerabilities found in the system. The DBA must pay attention to the new security patches released by software vendors and install those patches as soon as possible. Furthermore, any configuration problems detected in the security mechanisms must be immediately corrected.

Security attacks are an external factor that mainly depends on the intentionality and capability of humans to maliciously break into the system taking advantage of potential vulnerabilities. The prevention against security attacks includes all the measures needed to minimize (or eliminate) the potential attacks against the system. On the other hand, attack removal is related to the adoption of measures to stop attacks that have occurred before.

General methods for intrusion detection in computer systems are based either on pattern recognition or on anomaly detection. Pattern recognition is the search for known attack signatures in the commands executed. Anomaly detection is the search for deviations from an historical profile of good commands.

Schonlau et al [4] evaluated several anomaly detection approaches and concluded that methods based on the idea that commands not previously seen in the training data may indicate an intrusion attempted, are among the most powerful approaches for intrusion detection. Our intrusion detection approach uses this idea, extending it to a set of SQL commands. However, unlike intrusion detection approaches used in distributed systems that usually rely on sets of predefined commands (normally a small number) or assume the commands are unrelated, in our approach, the SQL commands and their order in each database transaction are relevant.

In spite of all the classical security mechanism developed in the database area, current DBMS are not well prepared for high-assurance privacy and confidentiality [6]. A very important component for the new generation of security aware DBMS is an intrusion detection mechanism [7]. Recent works have addressed concurrent intrusion detection (and attack isolation) in DBMS, and this issue is clearly getting more and more attention.

DEMIDS [8] is a misuse detection system tailored to relational database systems. It uses audit logs to derive user profiles describing typical behavior of users in the DBMS. Chung introduces the notion of distance measure and frequent item sets to capture the working scopes of users using a data mining algorithm. In [9] a real-time intrusion detection mechanism based on the profile of user roles is proposed. An intrusion attack and isolation mechanism was proposed in [10]. This mechanism uses triggers and transaction profiles to keep track of the items read and written by transactions and isolates attacks by rewriting user SQL statements. The use of data dependency relationships and Petri-Nets to model normal data update patterns was proposed in [11] to detect malicious database transactions. DIDAFIT [12] works by matching SQL statements against a known set of valid transactions fingerprints. The algorithm consists in representing SQL as regular expressions using heuristics to assure a low level of false positives. Vieira and Madeira [13] focused on the detection of malicious DBMS transactions by using database audit logs to obtain the sequences of SQL commands executed by users, with the assumption that the transaction profiles was known in advance, and provided manually to the detection mechanism.

Although intrusion detection has already been addressed in the works introduced above, intrusion detection at DBMS level continues to be an open issue. The purpose of the present work is to provide a generic tool that can be used in any database application. This way, the proposed intrusion detection tool is available at [14] for download and public utilization.

2.1 Database Transactions Profiles

In a typical database environment transactions are programmed in the client database applications, which means that the set of transactions remains stable, as long as the application is not changed. For example, in a banking database application users can only perform the operations available at the application interface (e.g., withdraw money, balance check account, etc). No other operation is available for the end-users (e.g., end-users cannot execute ad-hoc SQL commands). This way, it is possible to use transaction profiles for intrusion detection with a reduced risk of false alarms.

Our intrusion detection tool uses the profile of the transactions implemented by the database applications (authorized transactions) to identify user attempts to execute unauthorized SQL commands. A database transaction is represented as a directed graph describing the different execution paths (sequences of selects, inserts, updates, deletes, and stored procedure invocations) from the beginning of the transaction to the commit or rollback commands. The nodes in the graph represent commands and the arcs represent the valid execution sequences. Depending on the data being processed several execution paths may exist for the same transaction and an execution path may include cycles representing the repetitive execution of sets of commands (a typical example of cycles in a transaction is the insertion of a variable number of lines in a customer's order). The transaction ends with a commit or rollback command. The directed graph representing the profile of valid transactions is used to detect unauthorized transactions, which are seen as invalid sequences of SQL commands. This is done by concurrently analyzing the transactions the users execute and comparing them to the profile of the authorized transactions that were previously learned. To learn the profiles and to detect the malicious transactions the following information is required for each command executed:

- **User name:** name of the user who executes the command;
- **Session ID:** identification of the session established when the client application connects to the database server;
- **Action executed:** text of the SQL command. This includes the identification of the end of the transaction (that is the start of a new transaction), which is forced by a commit or a rollback command;
- **Time stamp of the action**: time stamp of the execution of the SQL command.

An important aspect is that the nodes in the graph do not represent concrete commands since these may differ slightly in different executions. For example, consider the following SQL command to select the data from a given employee: "SELECT * from EMP where job like 'CLERK' and SAL >1000". The job and the salary in the select criteria (*job like ?* and *sal* > *?*) depend on the targeted data. This way, instead of considering concrete commands we have to represent those commands in a generic way. The approach consists of parsing the SQL commands and removing all the parts that are not generic (e.g., numbers and strings between quotes are removed). Also, the characters of the command are changed to lowercase.

The proposed intrusion detection technique does not apply to applications that support the execution of ad-hoc queries, as in this case there are no predefined transactions. However, ad-hoc queries normally target decision support system and are not executed in typical database applications, because this type of queries would ruin the performance of the system. The decision support databases are known as data warehouses [15] and are physically separated from typical databases, because the type of queries executed and the data structures used to store data are completely different from typical databases. End-users that process ad-hoc queries represent a small group (managers and decision making personnel) that use a specific type of databases (data warehouses). Data warehouses are periodically loaded with new data that represents the activity of the business since the last load (normally the periodical loads are done on a daily basis). This is part of data warehouses life-cycle and follows a predefined set of rules that are implemented in the loading applications. Our intrusion detection technique is also applicable in this case because it provides the data warehouse server with the capability to detect malicious actions that try to modify the data.

2.2 Learning the Authorized Profiles

Transaction learning consists of identifying the authorized transactions and representing those transactions as a directed graph specifying the sequences of valid commands. The goal is to automatically learn the transaction profiles obtained through the reading of the network packets sent by the client applications to the database server and store them as a directed graph to be used in the detection phase. Obviously, the learning process must be executed in controlled conditions that should cover the different database application functionalities and, at the same time, must be free of intrusion attempts (which would potentially lead to the identification of malicious transactions as authorized ones). It is worth noting that all the database transactions must be executed during the learning phase, which should be achieved in a controlled environment virtually free of intrusion attempts (i.e., without the database fully open to all the users). There are three ways to obtain the transactions profiles:

- **Manual profiling** can be easily performed when the DBA knows the execution profile of the client application and the number and size of the transactions is not too high. The DBA can create manually the graphs describing the authorized transactions.
- **Concurrently** during the normal utilization of the application. In this case special attention must be taken in order to guarantee that the application is free of attacks during the learning period. This procedure can be shortened by manually executing some of the functions of the application.

- **Running application tests.** Database applications are often tested using interface testing tools that generate exhaustive tests that exercise all the application functionalities. In most cases these tests are specified by highly-trained testers, but can also be generated automatically [16, 17].

When an end-user (client) connects to the database a session is established. The session information travels across the network and the relevant information can be captured by a well positioned sniffer application. After establishing the session the user can start executing the client application operations. During execution the application accesses the database through the network sending SQL commands and receiving results. The sniffer reads all that flux of information and retains just what it needs. The capture of information will last until the DBA is confident that all the transactions implemented by the application have been executed at least one time. The sniffer can read the network information that is both encrypted or in clear text. To be able to parse encrypted information, the intrusion detection tool must have access to the decryption function and key. An alternative is to place the intrusion detection tool as a proxy, able to perform secure communication with the database client applications.

One of the key points in the learning phase, and in the detection phase as well, is the detection of the first command and the last command of a transaction. A transaction begins when the previous ends, thus the problem is the detection of the end of a transaction. A transactions is ended explicitly (by a commit or rollback command) or implicitly (by a Data Definition Language (DDL) statement [1]) by the application's code. Fig. 1 shows examples of the graphs generated during transactions learning.

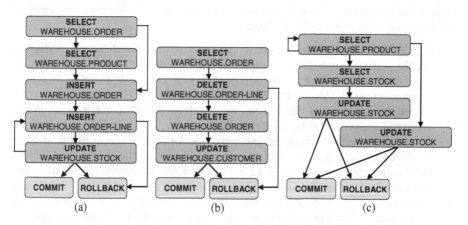

Fig. 1. Examples of typical profiles of database transactions

2.3 Detecting Intrusions

After concluding the learning phase the IIDD tool is able to compare the transactions executed by the users with the authorized profiles described in the transaction graphs. In this phase every command executed must match a profile. When the first command of the transaction is executed the tool searches for all the profiles starting with that same command, which are marked as candidate profiles for the current transaction. The next command executed is then compared with the second command of these candidate profiles. Only those who match remain candidate profiles. This process is executed over and over until the transaction reaches its end or there are no more candidate profiles for that transaction. In this latter case the transaction is identified as malicious. In practice, to detect malicious transactions the IIDD tool implements the following generic algorithm over the transactions graph:

```
while (1) do {
    for each new command executed do {
        if user does not have any active transaction then
            /* command is the 1st command in a new transaction */
            obtain list of authorized trans. starting with
            this command;
        else {
            for each valid (authorized) trans. for the user do {
                if the current command represents a valid successor node
                in the transaction graph then
                    the command is valid;
                else
                    mark the current transaction as a non valid trans.;
            }
            if there are transactions marked as non valid then
                a malicious transaction has been detected;
        }
    }
}
```

When a malicious transaction is detected one or more of the following actions may be executed, depending on the DBA choice:

- Notify the DBA about the intrusion. The database intrusion detection mechanism is able to provide the DBA with relevant information such as the user name, the time stamp, the database objects damaged, etc. It is also possible to send a message (email or SMS) to the DBA to call his immediate attention.
- Immediately disconnect the user session in which the malicious transaction was attempted and prevent it from logging in again.
- Activate a damage confinement and repair mechanism. When available, damage confinement and repair mechanisms are able to confine the damage and recover the database to a consistent state previous to the execution of the malicious transaction. Another possibility is to isolate that transaction from other user transactions (e.g., by creating a virtual database where the malicious transactions are executed to prevent spreading wrong or malicious data to the database [10]).

3   The Intrusion Detection Tool

Fig. 2 presents the typical environment needed to run our intrusion detection tool. The IIDD tool is installed and runs in the Sniffer Computer. The Database Server network cable must connect to a LAN switch port. The Sniffer Computer must be connected to the span port mirroring of the switch. Switches usually prevent promiscuous sniffing, however, most modern switches support span port mirroring, which replicates the data from all ports onto a single port allowing the sniffer to capture the network traffic of the whole LAN.

The IIDD tool is a two tier application with a back end module and a front end interface (Fig. 3). All the heavy processing is done in the back end which is responsible for sniffing the network searching for packets sent to the database, learn the profiles and detect the intrusions. It is named DBSniffer and was written in C++ to be able to access the network using raw sockets and processing them at the highest speed. This program sends messages through the standard output device and creates several files for future analysis. It is organized into three modules: sniffer, learner and detector. The IIDD tool can be run in Windows and Linux operating systems (OS) and can be used in any DBMS as the implementation is generic. Both the learning and the detection modules use a common function that is responsible for the detection of network packets.

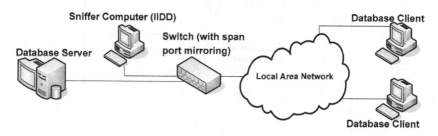

Fig. 2. Architecture setup

The sniffer is the only DBMS specific component and it is responsible for capturing network packets. Because the tool is based on autonomous components that provide well defined interfaces, it is very easy to implement that function for several DBMS and include it in the tool. For this practical experience report we have chosen Oracle 10G R2 [18] since it is one of the most representative DBMS on the market.

The sniffer, learner, and detector modules are executed when they are called by the front end application. The front end is a graphical interface, programmed in Java, whose function is to configure and launch the back end and to show the results. The interface has eight groups with different functions: File, Config, Sniffer, Learner, Detector, Action, Status and Information Panel. A screen shot of the prototype's interface is shown in Fig. 4.

The **Sniffer group** starts and stops the sniffer. The sniffer uses raw sockets and places the network adapter in the promiscuous mode. In this mode the network adapter is able to intercept and read all the packets in the network (recall that in non-promiscuous mode the network adapter reads only the packets aimed to it). The output information is copied to the Information Panel. The sniffer module retains only those packets related to the client database communication and saves that information in two files: one with session information (session.txt) and the other with command data (auditory.txt). A debug file may also be created containing all the packet information captured, before any processing is done to the data.

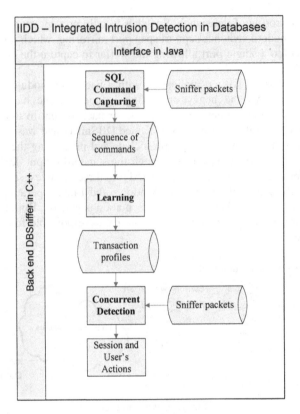

Fig. 3. IIDD tool

The **Learner group** is used to activate the transaction learning mode. Transaction learning includes two steps: parsing and learning. The former uses the auditory.txt file (generated by the sniffer component) and is responsible for cleaning the commands executed by the database users, removing variable numbers, strings, extra spaces and normalizing the case. After that it generates the file aud.txt. Using this file and the session.txt file the learner algorithm can now be executed. In this phase a file is created with all the transaction profiles (profile.txt). The output information is copied to the Information Panel. This ends the learning phase of our mechanism.

The **Detector group** is used to start and stop the online intrusion detector. For the detection the network adapter is again placed in promiscuous mode in order to sniff all the network packets. The packets are filtered to detect malicious commands compared to the transaction profiles previously learned. It also detects deviations from the order of execution of commands inside the transaction. Those suspicious situations raise warnings immediately, which are saved in a debugging file (detect_debug.txt). The output information is copied to the Information Panel.

The **Action group** allows the configuration of the actions to be executed when a malicious transaction is detected or a transaction is found in a misplaced order. The session maybe killed by sending TCP/IP resets. The connection is abruptly broken, and the database performs a rollback of the malicious transaction in this situation. The DBA may be warned by email, SMS or by a siren sound.

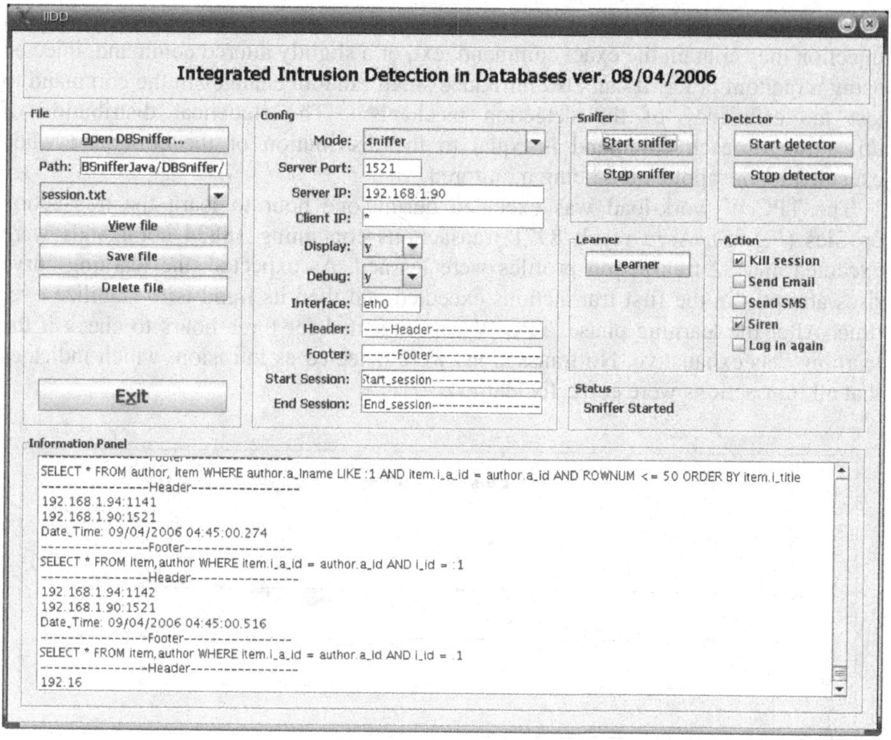

Fig. 4. Interface of the Integrated Intrusion Detection in Databases application

4 Tool Utilization Examples

The well-known TPC-W transactional web benchmark [19] has been used to exemplify the tool utilization. This benchmark provides us with a controlled database environment quite adequate for the evaluation of the learning and detection algorithms. It simulates the activities of an e-commerce business oriented transactional web server. A real database application is also used in the experiments, the SCE (Serviço Central de Esterilização – Central Service of Sterilization). It is an administrative application currently in use in the Hospitals of the University of Coimbra (HUC: http://www.huc.min-saude.pt/) used to manage the whole process of the sterilized material to and from all services in the HUC. This workflow comprises the reception of the material, the selection and the sterilization of the material within a central with steam autoclaves and ethylene oxide, various modes of drying, packaging, sealing, request and delivery.

To obtain the latency and the coverage information we have built a SQL command line tool that records the time stamp of the command request and the time stamp of the server response. It is also capable of some configuration to assist the coverage experiments. This SQL command tool obtains a list of the commands (executed by the client application being monitored) using the text files created by the learner module. With this list we can inject real SQL commands used by the client application into the DBMS while the intrusion detection is active. This command injection may contain the exact command text, or a slightly altered command, injected using a random order. It can also introduce small random changes in the command to test the efficiency of the detection mechanism. The statistical distribution of utilization of each command is equal to the distribution of the command when executed by the application being monitored.

The TPC-W work-load was executed during one hour to learn the transaction profiles (Fig. 5). As a result 8971 transactions containing 18834 commands were executed and 32 transaction profiles were learned. As expected, the learning curve rises abruptly in the first transactions executed and then its trend is to stabilize over time. After the learning phase, TPC-W was executed for three hours to check if the learning was exhaustive. No transactions were detected as intrusion, which indicates that all transactions were correctly learned.

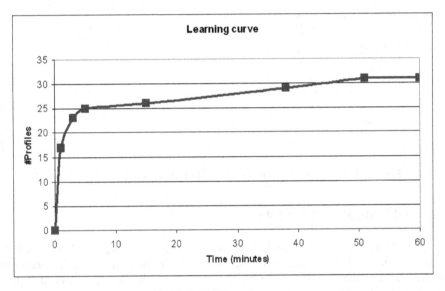

Fig. 5. TPC-W learning curve

As the sniffer is located in a different computer it has no impact on the server performance, thus this mechanism has no performance overhead. Furthermore, the mechanism does not introduce extra packets in the network, causing no negative effect in the network bandwidth.

With our SQL command tool we manually injected 50 malicious commands while the TPC-W was running to produce the load. They were very simple commands to be quickly executed by the server. All these 50 commands were detected as intrusions. The largest latency time obtained was 10 milliseconds and the average latency time was 1.6 milliseconds. However these times may vary with the network setup and usage. All detections were performed before the server had replied to the client, thus before the execution of the next command.

We also performed two additional experiments with extraneous SQL commands injection: in the first we injected the correct commands, but in a random order; and in the second we made a change in one character randomly placed in each command. The distribution of utilization of each command was the real distribution of the command when the TPC-W executes it. For the first experiment 1000 transactions were executed with a total of 2061 commands. For the second experiment 1000 transactions were also executed with a total of 2066 commands. All those transactions were considered malicious resulting in 100% coverage.

Besides the TPC-W benchmark, we performed some experiments with a real database application: the Central Service of Sterilization database mentioned before. The main goal was to evaluate the learning algorithm in a real database scenario, helping us to assess the learning transaction curve and to estimate false positives caused by incomplete learning. We used the information of one working day of real utilization of the database of the SCE, having 8750 commands from 609 sessions and accesses 17 tables. This log was applied to the Learning module and 33 transaction profiles where learned.

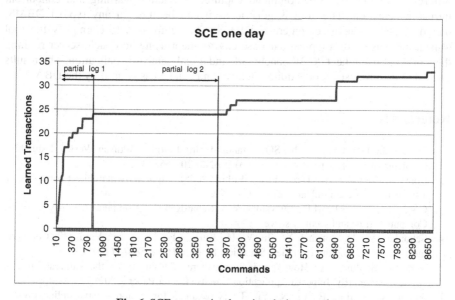

Fig. 6. SCE transaction learning during one day

Fig. 6 shows the learning transaction curve. As we can see, most of the transactions (24 out of 33) were learned very quickly, during the first 858 commands (partial log 1). It is also quite evident that two new groups of database functionalities (and corresponding transactions) were executed around the command number 4000 and command number 6500, corresponding to the two steps in the learning curve. If we had learned only from the partial log 1 or even the partial log 2 it would be necessary to make a conditional detection in those periods of time, as all transactions not learned in log 1 and log 2 would be detected as false positives. In that case, the database administrator would have to add the new transactions to the profile collection, in order to avoid further detection of these transactions as false positives. In a typical database application there are moments in time where some specific procedures are executed (e.g., at the end of the day, at the end of the week, etc) and the time window used to learn the profiles must contain those moments.

An important aspect is that a one day learning period is quite small when we are considering applications that are used during many years (as is the case of SCE). In fact, a larger period is required as some operations are executed in specific moments in time. For the SCE, further experiments showed that a learning period of about a week is required to learn almost all transactions.

5 Conclusions

In this paper we present a new tool for the detection of malicious transactions in DBMS. This database intrusion detection mechanism uses a graph that represents the profile of valid transactions to detect unauthorized transactions and consists of three different components: SQL command capture, transaction learning and concurrent intrusion detection. This tool is generic as it can be used in any typical DBMS, including stat-of-the-art commercial DBMS. The setup used to exemplify the tool utilization consists of a typical database environment using an Oracle server running the workload from the TPC-W benchmark and a real database application. The results show that the proposed tool is quite effective and can be easily used by the DBA.

References

1. Date, C.J., Darwen, H.: The SQL Standard, 3rd Edition, Addison-Wesley Publishing Company, pages 414, paperbound (1993) ISBN 0-201-55822-X
2. Conry-Murray, A.: The Threat From Within (2005), http:// www.itarchitect.com/ shared/ article/showArticle.jhtml?articleId=166400792
3. Gordon, L.A., Loeb, M.P., Lucyshyn, W., Richardson, R.: Computer Security Institute. Computer crime and security survey (2005)
4. Schonlau, M., DuMouchel, W., Ju, W.-H., Karr, A.F., Theus, M., Vardi, Y.: Computer intrusion: Detecting masquerades. Statistical Science 16(1), 58–74 (2001)
5. Surf, M., Shulman, A.: How safe is it out there? Zeroing in on the vulnerabilities of application security, Imperva Application Defense Center Paper (2004)
6. Anton, A., Bertino, E., Li, N., Yu, T.: A roadmap for comprehensive online privacy policies. In: CERIAS Technical Report, 2004-47 (2004)
7. Agrawal, R., Kiernan, J., Srikant, R., Xu, Y.: Hippocratic databases. In: Proceedings of the 28th international conference on Very Large Data Bases. Morgan-Kaufmann, San Francisco (2002)
8. Chung, C.Y., Gertz, M., Levitt, K.: DEMIDS: A Misuse Detection System for Database Systems. In: 3rd IFIP TC-11 WG11.5 Working Conference on Integrity and Internal Control in Information System, pp. 159–178. Kluwer Academic Publishers, Dordrecht (1999)
9. Bertino, E., Kamra, A., Terzi, E., Vakali, A.: Intrusion detection in RBAC-administered databases. In: 21st Annual Computer Security Applications Conference (2005)

10. Liu, P.: DAIS: A Real-time Data Attack Isolation System for Commercial Database Applications. In: Proc. of the 17th Annual Comp. Security Applications Conf. (2001)
11. Hu, Y., Panda, B.: Identification of malicious transactions in database systems. The International Database Engineering and Applications Symposium (2003)
12. Lee, S.Y., Low, W.L., Wong, P.Y.: Learning Fingerprints for a Database Intrusion Detection System. In: 7th European Symp. on Research in Computer Security (2002)
13. Vieira, M., Madeira, H.: Detection of malicious transactions in DBMS. In: The 11th IEEE Intl. Symposium Pacific Rim Dependable Computing, IEEE Computer Society Press, Los Alamitos (2005)
14. Fonseca, J., Vieira, M., Madeira, H.: Tool for Integrated Intrusion Detection in Databases (2007), available at: http://gbd.dei.uc.pt/downloads.php
15. Kimball, R. (ed.): The Data Warehouse Lifecycle Toolkit. Wiley & Sons, Inc., Chichester (1998)
16. Santiago, V., Amaral, A., Vijaykumar, N.L., Mattiello-Francisco, M., Martins, E., Lopes, O.: A Practical Approach for Automated Test Case Generation using Statecharts. In: 30th Annual International Computer Software and Applications Conference, 2006, Chicago (2006)
17. Tsai, W.T., Bai, X., Huang, B., Devaraj, G., Paul, R.: Automatic Test Case Generation for GUI Navigation. In: The Thirteenth International Software & Internet Quality Week (2000)
18. Oracle Corporation, Oracle® Database Concepts 10g Release 1 (10.1) (2003)
19. Transaction Processing Performance Council, TPC Benchmark W (Web Commerce) Specification, Revision 1.8 (2002), available at: http://www.tpc.org/tpcw

Security Rationale for a Cooperative Backup Service for Mobile Devices*

Ludovic Courtès, Marc-Olivier Killijian, and David Powell

LAAS-CNRS, Université de Toulouse, France

Abstract. Mobile devices (e.g., laptops, PDAs, cell phones) are increasingly relied on but are used in contexts that put them at risk of physical damage, loss or theft. This paper discusses security considerations that arise in the design of a cooperative backup service for mobile devices. Participating devices leverage encounters with other devices to temporarily replicate critical data. Anyone is free to participate in the cooperative service, without requiring any prior trust relationship with other participants. In this paper, we identify security threats relevant in this context as well as possible solutions and discuss how they map to low-level security requirements related to identity and trust establishment. We propose self-organized, policy-neutral mechanisms that allow the secure designation and identification of participating devices. We show that they can serve as a building block for a wide range of cooperation policies that address most of the security threats we are concerned with. We conclude on future directions.

1 Introduction

Mobile devices (e.g., laptops, PDAs, cell phones) are increasingly relied on but are used in contexts that put them at risk of physical damage, loss or theft. However, fault-tolerance mechanisms available for these devices often suffer from shortcomings. For instance, replicating data to a storage device (e.g., USB stick or disk drive) carried along with the mobile device is risky: that device could easily be lost or stolen, or it could be damaged precisely when the mobile device itself is damaged. Data "synchronization" mechanisms, which allow one to replicate a mobile device's data on a desktop machine, are an improvement but they usually require that the desktop machine be either physically accessible or reachable *via* the Internet. Use of third-party backup servers typically also requires access to some network infrastructure.

Unfortunately, in many scenarios where devices are carried along in different places, access to a network infrastructure (e.g., *via* a Wi-Fi access point) is at best *intermittent*. Often, access to a network infrastructure may be too costly and/or inefficient energy-wise and performance-wise to be considered viable "just" for backup. In emergency situations and upon disaster recovery, for

---

* This work was partially supported by the MoSAIC project (ACI S&I, French national program for Security and Informatics; see *http://www.laas.fr/mosaic/*), the Hidenets project (EU-IST-FP6-26979), and the ReSIST network (EU-IST-FP6-26764).

A. Bondavalli, F. Brasileiro, and S. Rajsbaum (Eds.): LADC 2007, LNCS 4746, pp. 212–230, 2007.

instance, infrastructure may well be unavailable for an unspecified amount of time. In such cases, data produced on a mobile device while the network is unreachable cannot be replicated using the aforementioned synchronization techniques and could be lost. Similarly, environments with scarce Internet connectivity, such as those targeted by the "One Laptop per Child" project (OLPC, *http://laptop.org/*), can hardly rely on access to an infrastructure for doing data backup.

We aim to address these issues by providing a *cooperative* backup service, called MoSAIC [12,27]. The idea borrows from peer-to-peer cooperative services. The goal of this service is to improve data dependability for mobile devices. It leverages excess storage resources through spontaneous resource sharing among neighboring devices, using short-range wireless communications.

Anyone is free to participate in the service and, therefore, the majority of participants have no prior trust relationship. However, there are also scenarios where owners of a few cooperating devices are personal acquaintances with full trust relationships as far as the backup service is concerned (e.g., colleagues, friends, etc.). In general, an open cooperative service must be able both to account for lack of prior trust relationships among participants and to take advantage of prior trust relationships among device owners when they exist. In addition, services designed for mobile devices and *ad hoc* networks need to meet requirements related to resource constraints (energy, CPU power, network bandwidth) and intermittent or complete lack of access to a fixed network infrastructure. These constraints impose several requirements on the storage layer of our cooperative backup service [12].

In this paper, we focus on security aspects of the cooperative backup service related to secure cooperation and secure interactions between peers. We discuss their integration with the security techniques implemented at the storage layer. We propose *self-organized* security mechanisms that may be used to support behavior accountability and a wide range of cooperation policies. We show how cooperation policies can take advantage of these mechanisms to address some of our security concerns. Our approach differs from earlier work in that it focuses on *policy-neutral* security primitives that do not restrict the user's choice of a policy, rather than focusing on a specific policy.

Section 2 provides an overview of our cooperative backup service. Section 3 presents the security concerns we want to address. Section 4 provides an overview of the storage layer of our cooperative backup service. Section 5 proposes core security mechanisms and shows (i) how they fulfill some of our requirements and (ii) how they can be used as a building block for various cooperation policies. Section 6 deals with implementation considerations. Section 7 summarizes related work. Finally, Section 8 concludes and depicts on-going and future research work.

2   MoSAIC Overview

Our cooperative backup service, which we call MoSAIC, can leverage (i) excess storage resources available on mobile devices and (ii) short-range, high-bandwidth, and relatively energy-efficient wireless communications (Bluetooth,

ZigBee, or Wi-Fi). More importantly, we expect our cooperative backup service to improve long-term availability of data produced by mobile devices. The idea is borrowed from peer-to-peer cooperative services: participating devices offer storage resources and doing so allows them to benefit from the resources provided by other devices in order to replicate their data [27]. Participating devices discover other devices in their vicinity using a suitable service discovery mechanism such as [39] and communicate through single-hop connections, thereby limiting interactions to small physical regions.

Anyone is free to participate in the service and, therefore, participants have no prior trust relationship. In the sequel, we use the term *contributor* when referring to a node acting as a storage provider; we use the term *data owner* when referring to a "client" device, i.e., one that uses storage provided by the contributors to replicate its data. All participating devices may play *both* the owner and the contributor role.

When out of reach of Internet access and network infrastructure, devices meet and spontaneously form *ad hoc* networks which they can use to back-up data. However, it would be unrealistic to rely on chance encounters between devices for recovery. Instead, we require contributing devices to eventually send data stored on behalf of other devices to an agreed-upon Internet-based store accessible by the data owners [12,27]. Once this has been done, the duty of contributing devices has been fulfilled and they can remove the data from their local store. Eventually, data owners may restore their data by querying the Internet-based store. In practice, the implementation of this Internet repository is an orthogonal issue: it could be implemented in a number of different ways ranging from a simple centralized server to a peer-to-peer distributed store.

This way of handling intermittent infrastructure connectivity makes our approach comparable to delay-tolerant networks (DTNs): data blocks that are transmitted by data owners to contributors can be viewed as packets sent to the Internet-based store and where contributors act as relays [42].

MoSAIC's approach to cooperative backup also bears some similarity with earlier work on cooperative data storage [3,26] and caching for mobile devices [22,41]. However, it differs from them in several ways. First, unlike typical distributed file system access patterns, data that is backed up is produced by a single device and may usually not be accessed by other devices. Second, unlike most caching strategies, our approach does not seek to improve locality of data replicas: instead we expect replicas to propagate to the Internet-based store, much like packets in a DTN.

Previous work studied the design of a storage layer for our cooperative backup service and compared the CPU/storage tradeoff of various data encoding schemes [12]. This study led to the storage-layer design outlined in Section 4. We also analytically evaluated the dependability of data carried on a mobile devices participating in the cooperative backup service using generalized stochastic Petri nets (GSPNs) and Markov chains [11]. This paper focuses on primitives enabling cooperation among distrustful participating devices.

3   Security Context and Motivations

This section details security issues that arise in a cooperative backup service among distrustful devices and concludes on security goals.

3.1   Threats to Confidentiality and Privacy

There is an obvious threat to confidentiality when it comes to storing critical data on untrusted devices: A malicious storage contributor may try to access data stored on behalf of other devices. Therefore, confidentiality has to be provided at the storage layer and is achieved through regular encryption techniques, as will be discussed in Section 4. Thus, communication eavesdropping is not a serious additional threat to confidentiality. Since data blocks exchanged between two participating devices are encrypted, an eavesdropper cannot gain any more information about the contents of the data being backed up than the contributor itself. Likewise, data blocks must be named by the data owner in a way that is meaningless to contributors [12] so, again, disclosing such names to a potential eavesdropper does not present an additional threat. Since the storage layer provides end-to-end encryption, the communication layer does not need to provide any additional encryption. This is a fortunate consequence since it allows CPU and energy savings to be made.

However, privacy of the participating users can be threatened. An eavesdropper may be able to know *whether* a device is actively replicating data, and it may be able to estimate the amount of data being replicated. It may also be able to know the parties involved (the physical devices or even their owner), especially when in their physical vicinity. Recent attempts to provide anonymity in MANETs, for instance based on anonymous multi-hop routing [38], appear to be relatively bandwidth-consuming and energy-inefficient. Thus, we do not address threats to privacy in this paper. However, we hope to provide a minimum level of identity privacy by allowing users to use self-managed identifying material (which may not establish any binding with their real-world identity, i.e., *pseudonyms*), rather than compelling the use of identifying material provided by a central authority.

3.2   Threats to Integrity and Authenticity

There are also evident threats to data integrity and authenticity: A malicious contributor could tamper with data stored on behalf of other nodes, or it could inject garbage data that would pass all the integrity checks performed by data owners but would not be of any use to the data owner.

Integrity threats also arise at the communication layer: an intruder may try to tamper with messages exchanged between two devices (essentially storage requests), thereby damaging the data being backed up. Thus, the communication layer must also guarantee the integrity of messages exchanged between participating devices.

3.3 Threats to Availability

Unavailability threats against the cooperative backup service fall into two categories: unavailability resulting from accidental data loss (including accidental failure of contributors holding replicas), and data or service unavailability resulting from *denial of service* (DoS) attacks committed by malicious nodes.

Obviously, data unavailability due to accidental failures of either the owner or contributor devices is the primary concern when building a cooperative backup service.

Malicious participating devices may also try to harm individual users or the service as a whole, denying use of the service by other devices. A straightforward DoS attack is *data retention*: a contributor either refuses to send data items back to their owner when requested or simply claims to store them without actually doing so. DoS attacks targeting the system as a whole include *flooding* (i.e., purposefully exhausting storage resources) and *selfishness* (i.e., using the service while refusing to contribute). These are well-known attacks in Internet-based peer-to-peer backup and file sharing systems [2,13,29] and are also partly addressed in the framework of *ad hoc* routing in mobile networks [5,33]. These threats can be seen as *threats to cooperation*.

3.4 Discussion

Security threats related to the data being backed up, in particular threats to data availability, confidentiality, and integrity are largely addressed by the storage layer of our cooperative backup service. Section 4 provides an overview of the storage layer and how it addresses these issues.

Service availability is also at risk in the presence of intruders and non-cooperative participants. The very possibility of allowing malicious devices to participate in the cooperative service threatens cooperation among participants as a whole. We believe that cooperation can only be leveraged if the cooperative service supports *accountability*. In our view, accountability is a building block upon which users can implement their own higher-level *cooperation policies* defining the set of rules that dictate how they will cooperate. Section 5 proposes core mechanism as a means to provide accountability and discusses cooperation policies that may be implemented on top of it.

4   Architectural Overview of the Storage Layer

The storage layer presented in [12] addresses the efficient storage and indexing of data owners' critical data. It follows a write-once read-many (WORM) or append-only storage model similar to that found in archival storage systems [37], where new versions of files are appended rather than substituted to previously-stored versions. It produces a number of *data blocks*, each of which is bound to a *name* which is used to store/retrieve it to/from contributors. Since participating nodes are mutually suspicious, the storage layer provides guarantees for data confidentiality, integrity and authenticity: it supports data and meta-data encryption as well as integrity and authenticity checks, using an appropriate encoding. The general framework can be summarized as follows:

1. The data owner (rather: the cooperative backup software on the owner-side) chops the data items to be backed up into small blocks and assigns them a *block name*. A block name can be, for instance, a cryptographic hash of the block content, thereby providing *content-addressable storage*[1] [37]. An important requirement is that (i) the naming scheme must be meaningless to contributors and (ii) blocks must be encrypted. In other words, contributors cannot make any assumptions on the block naming scheme used by data owners.

2. The data owner produces meta-data blocks describing, among other things, how data blocks are to be re-assembled to produce the original data. Those meta-data blocks are themselves named in a similar way. Authenticity is achieved by signing just part of the meta-data. For instance, if meta-data blocks are the intermediate nodes of a Merkle tree whose leaves are data blocks [32], then only the root block needs to be signed, which reduces reliance on CPU-intensive cryptography; verifying the root block's signature actually allows the authenticity of the whole tree to be checked.

3. When a contributing device is encountered, the data owner sends it some of its data and meta-data blocks using remote procedure calls (RPCs). This is realized through the invocation put (name, content) which sends data content to the contributor and asks it to bind it to name. Since owners can choose any block naming scheme, contributors must arrange to provide per-owner block name spaces in order to avoid collisions among blocks belonging to different owners. Obviously, in order to increase data availability, data owners may choose to replicate each block [11].

The end result of this backup process is an opaque identifier that names an (encrypted) root meta-data block. We refer to this identifier as the *root block name*.

The root block name is critical since it allows all the user's data to be recovered, so it also needs to be backed up. However, as new versions of the data items (e.g., a single file or a whole file system hierarchy) are backed up, new data and meta-data blocks are created, each having a new name, and thus a new root block name is produced (this issue is not uncommon in the context of peer-to-peer file sharing and archival systems [2,37]). Consequently, data owners should store their latest root block name on contributors *under a fixed block name* to allow restoration to be bootstrapped conveniently. Since it is a critical piece of information, data owners may choose to encrypt it.

When a contributor gains Internet access (rather, when it gets sufficiently cheap or high-bandwidth Internet access), it transfers data blocks stored on behalf of other devices to an Internet-based storage server that data owners can

---

[1] Use of content-addressable storage allows identical data blocks to be identified. Therefore, it permits the implementation of *incremental backup*, where only new blocks are transferred to contributors.

eventually access to restore their data. That Internet store could be implemented in many different ways, ranging from a peer-to-peer distributed store to something as simple as an FTP server. However, it should support the put mechanism or a slightly enhanced version thereof so that both name-block bindings and per-owner block name spaces are preserved.

Restoration of backed up data typically occurs when the data owner device has failed or been lost. In this case, data owners first retrieve the root meta-data block (from the Internet-based store), decrypt it and decode it (which can only be done by its legitimate data owner), and then recursively fetch the blocks it refers to. Fetching blocks upon restoration is achieved through a get (name) RPC that returns the contents of the block designated by name.

Of paramount importance is the inability for arbitrary users to tamper with a data owner's name space on the Internet-based store. For instance, it must be impossible for a malicious user to overwrite a data owner's block associated with a specific name on the Internet repository without this being detected. However, since block encoding is owner-specific, the Internet-based store cannot check the authenticity of incoming data blocks without knowing the exact encoding scheme used by their owner. This can be solved by having the Internet-based store keep a list of all incoming data blocks associated with a given name, should different blocks be put under the same name (collisions). Upon recovery, the data owner can then detect and eliminate invalid data blocks in cases of collisions; invalid data blocks may be readily detected by the data owner using the possibilities offered by its encoding scheme, such as digital signature or hash verification.

It is worth noting that among the mechanisms presented here, only the actual storage protocol (i.e., the put RPCs) is enforced. This leaves users with the ability to choose any *security policy* for their data: they may choose any data availability, confidentiality and integrity mechanism while still conforming to the storage protocol.

5   Leveraging Cooperation

In this section, we present our approach to the design of mechanisms that address the threats to cooperation identified in Section 3. Core mechanisms are proposed to support accountability while being neutral with respect to cooperation policies. We then discuss issues that arise from the self-organized nature of our approach as well as cooperation policies.

5.1   Design Approach

There are essentially two ways to provide security measures against the DoS threats listed earlier in MANETs and loosely connected peer-to-peer backup systems: *via* a *single-authority domain*, where a single authority provides certificates or other security material to participants and/or dictates them a particular policy or mechanism, or through *self-organization*, where no single authority is relied on, at any point in time [9].

In our opinion, reliance on a common authority responsible for applying external *sanctions* to misbehaving participants as in BAR-B [1] falls into the first category. For example, BAR-B contributors *must* provide a proof that they do not have sufficient space when rejecting a storage request; similarly, upon auditing, participants *must* show the list of all blocks stored on their behalf elsewhere and all blocks they store on behalf of other nodes. Failing to do so constitutes a "proof of misbehavior" that may lead to sanctions. This raises fundamental security issues: why would one disclose all this information to some untrusted entity? Does it still qualify as cooperation among *multiple* administrative domains when a single set of rules is enforced through external sanctions? While this approach achieves strong service provision guarantees, it does so at the cost of being authoritarian and seems unsuitable for the kind of open cooperation network we envision.

Likewise, the use of so-called "tamper-resistant security modules" as in [6] can be considered a single-authority domain approach: security modules act as a local representative of an "authority" and *enforce* part of the protocol (in [6], the *nuglet* mechanism) in order to provide protection against malicious users. This leaves the user with no choice but to abide by the rules set forth by the security module and the party that issued it.

In this paper, we only focus on self-organized approaches. First, they are a good match for mobile *ad hoc* networks which *are* self-organized. Second, since we are designing an *open* cooperative service where anyone can participate, self-organization is likely to make the service more readily accessible to everyone; conversely, requiring every user to register with some central authority would be an undesirable burden likely to limit user adoption. Finally, we advocate that reliance on a central authority can in itself be considered as a security threat, to some extent: that authority is in effect a *single point of trust* and its compromise would bring the whole service down. Furthermore, depending on their security policy, users may not be willing to fully trust such an authority just because they have been told it's a "trusted" authority. They may also want to have full control over the actions that can be taken by *their* device, rather than handing over some authority over the device to some possibly unknown third party. Therefore, we prefer to focus on self-organized solutions and do not consider solutions based on a single-authority domain.

As a consequence, we cannot assume that any single cooperation policy is going to be used by *all* devices: each device can, and will, implement its own policy. We believe that the ability to choose a security and cooperation policy is particularly important when using our cooperative backup service for two reasons. First, the goal of this service is to improve the availability of users' critical data. As such, users are likely to be willing to pay attention to the contributors they deal with, and hence, they may be concerned with their cooperation policy. Second, mobile devices being resource-constrained, users are likely to require tight control over their resource usage, and may want to implement a cooperation policy that makes the best use of their resources. This is quite different from, for instance, Internet-based file sharing services where participating devices are typically desktop machines and where, as a result, it is safe to assume that most users will be satisfied with the same default cooperation policy.

Therefore, in this paper we focus on core mechanisms allowing for accountability rather than on actual cooperation policies.

5.2   Providing Secure and Self-Managed Device Designation

Devices must be able to *name* each other (i) to achieve accountability and (ii) to allow contributors to implement per-owner block name spaces, as discussed in Section 4.

To these ends, device names must satisfy the following requirements. First, since we want to build a self-organized service, where no central authority has to be consulted, it must be possible for every device to create its own name or designator. Second, for the naming scheme to be reliable, device names must be *unique* and *context-free* (i.e., their interpretation should be the same in any context). Third, since device names serve as the basis of critical operations, it must be possible to *authenticate* a name-device binding (i.e., assess the legitimacy or "ownership" of a name). Authentication is needed to preclude unauthorized use of a name, as in *spoofing* attacks. Unauthorized uses of device names would effectively hinder the implementation of per-owner block name spaces and accounting mechanisms.

These requirements rule out a number of widespread designation mechanisms. IP addresses, for instance, would obviously be unsuitable to name devices since they have none of these properties (they are not context-free, especially IPv4 link-local addresses, not unique, except for IPv6 addresses, and cannot be authenticated). The designers of Mobile IPv6 (MIPv6) had similar requirements and had made the same observations. This led them to devise "statistically unique and cryptographically verifiable" (SUCV) addresses [36].

The building block for the naming scheme we are interested in (and that of MIPv6 SUCV addresses) is asymmetric cryptography. Public keys have all the desired properties as designators: they are (statistically) unique and context-free, and they provide secure naming (i.e., the name-device binding can be authenticated, thereby precluding spoofing). In practice, public keys can be too large to be used directly as designators, which is why several protocols use cryptographic hashes or fingerprints of the public keys as designators [7,36]. In order to achieve accountability, both contributors and data owners may wish to *identify* the device they are talking to, that is, to authenticate the binding between alleged name of the peer device and the device itself. In other words, *mutual authentication* is required.

It is worth noting that the entities we want to name are instances of the cooperative backup software running on participating devices and *not* people owning the devices, nor even physical devices. Thus, the principals involved in the cooperative backup service are *logical entities* that exist and interact solely through electronic interactions among them. Therefore, authenticating the binding between one of these entities and its name (public key) boils down to verifying that that entity holds the private key corresponding to its name [19].

Doing so is simple and does not require the use of any certification authority whatsoever.

As far as the data restoration bootstrap is concerned, a practical consequence of using public key pairs to identify devices is that a user's key pair is all that is needed to bootstrap restoration, assuming its public key is also used to encrypt the root block name. That means that users must store their key pairs reliably, outside of the cooperative backup service, by copying them on a storage device under their control (USB stick, computer, or even a simple piece of paper stored in a safe place). Obviously, the device where the user's key pair is stored must not be carried along with the mobile device itself, since it could easily be lost, stolen, or damaged along with the mobile device, making it impossible to recover the data. Elliptic curve cryptography (ECC) would be handy for that purpose: it yields keys much smaller than, e.g., "security-equivalent" RSA keys; thus an ECC key pair can be as simple as a pass phrase that may be readily memorized by the user.

5.3   Ensuring Communications Integrity

Once a participating device has authenticated the binding between a peer device and a name, a malicious device may try to send messages and pretend they originate from another device, thereby using resources on behalf of another device. To address this issue, the integrity and authenticity of messages (i.e., RPC invocations) devices exchange must be guaranteed by the communication layer. In particular, once devices have mutually authenticated, using their key pairs, the communication protocol must guarantee that messages received at either end of the communication channel still come from the previously authenticated device. Many well-known cryptographic protocols address this issue, with different security properties.

We believe that non-repudiation is not required in our decentralized, self-managed, cooperative backup system. Non-repudiation could be used, for instance, to make sure that a device cannot deny that it sent a series of storage requests to a certain contributor. That contributor could then *prove* to a third party that it did receive those requests. However, such proofs would likely not be sufficient to be used, for instance, as part of the "history records" maintained by a reputation system (described below): they would concern only individual requests and would consequently fail to provide a sufficiently high-level view of a device's past cooperation. For instance, to prove that a data owner requested 1 GiB of storage, a contributor would need to provide a third party with 1 GiB worth of *put* requests along with the corresponding signatures. Doing so would provide more information that is necessary and would be very bandwidth-consuming, making it impractical. Thus, non-repudiation of individual messages is inappropriate in our context.

Therefore, we plan to use regular message authentication codes (such as HMACs) to provide support for message authenticity checks. HMACs can only be verified by the receiver, and therefore do not provide non-repudiation.

5.4   Thwarting Sybil Attacks

Since key pairs are to be generated in a self-organized way, our system is subject to the Sybil attack [16,30]: devices can change names (i.e., public keys) any time they want, which allows them to escape accountability for their past actions, including misbehavior. This attack defeats the implementation of a proper resource accounting mechanism, and consequently that of resource usage policies. For instance, a data owner can completely circumvent a per-device quota implemented by a contributor by just switching to a new key pair.

The verifiable designation mechanism proposed above cannot by itself prevent Sybil attacks. Instead it is up to cooperation policies to make Sybil attacks less attractive by providing incentives for users to keep using the same name (i.e., the same key pair). In a system where names are managed in a self-organized way, no cooperation policy can *prevent* Sybil attacks: They can only make them less effective, but evidence shows that well-designed policies can make them pretty much worthless [4,30,33].

Naturally, most reasonable cooperation policies have a common denominator: they tend to be reluctant to provide resources to strangers while being more helpful to devices that have already cooperated. However, in order to bootstrap cooperation, many policies may grant at least a small amount of resources to strangers [23]. This means that there is usually (i) a medium- to long-term advantage in keeping the same name and (ii) a short-term advantage in cooperating under a new name. Section 5.5 will show how actual cooperation policies can achieve this.

Fortunately, the impact of Sybil attacks is largely a matter of scale. With Internet-based peer-to-peer cooperative services, any peer can reach thousands of peers in a glimpse. Thus, even if it can only benefit from a small amount of resources from each peer, it may be able to quickly gain a large amount of resources. Conversely, in a cooperative service relying on physical encounters among mobile devices, it may take a long time and a great deal of traveling around before one is able to gain access to a useful amount of resources, which effectively makes selfishness less viable economically. Likewise, the impact of a flooding attack is necessarily limited to physical regions and/or groups of devices.

5.5   Allowing for a Wide Range of Cooperation Policies

User cooperation policies define the set of rules that determine how their device will cooperate. They are usually concerned with the stimulation of cooperation and the establishment of trust with other devices. To that end, cooperation policies can build on the accountability provided by the mechanisms presented above. We can imagine two major classes of cooperation policies: those based on the underlying social network, and those based on past behavioral observations, either private observation or shared reputation [4,23,28,33]. It is our goal to allow users to choose among these cooperation policies.

Cooperation policies based on the relationships already existing in the underlying social network can be as simple as "white lists", where the user only grants resources to devices belonging to personal acquaintances. There can also be more sophisticated policies: a user could also accept storage requests from "friends of friends", and it could accept to dedicate a small amount of resources to strangers as well. It can be argued that such policies do not scale since (i) the number of personal acquaintances of an individual is limited, and (ii) when travelling a lot, these acquaintances may be out of reach. On the other hand, social studies have provided evidence of a "small-world phenomenon" in human relationships [8,34] and algorithms have been proposed to discover chains of acquaintances among arbitrary users [9]. These studies can make cooperation policies based on a social network more relevant. Such policies, were they to insist on being able to verify bindings of keys to real-world identities, would trade privacy for improved resilience to Sybil attacks. However, similar policies may be used with pseudonyms instead of real-world identities.

Cooperation policies based on observations of past device behavior provide an interesting alternative: devices maintain "history records" of each other and make cooperation decisions using them as an input. History records can either be local to a device or they can be shared among devices—the latter is usually referred to as a *reputation* system [4,28,33]. In a reputation system, devices exchange history records and may use them as an additional hint to their cooperation decisions. Simulations have shown that shared history records are usually more efficient than private history records, especially in large networks or in the presence of a high device turnover [4,28]. However, many works that evaluate the outcome of such reputation mechanisms assume that all participating nodes use the *same* cooperation policy [4,33] (e.g., the same node rating algorithm, the same decision-making algorithm, etc.). There is no reason for this to be true. The result of using a reputation mechanism in a world where different policies are in use is, to our knowledge, an open issue. Nevertheless, reputation mechanisms do make Sybil attacks less attractive since few resources can be gained by a stranger. Devising a protocol that would allow trust information to be exchanged among principals potentially using different cooperation strategies is an open issue.

From a privacy viewpoint, maintaining such history records may be a concern when identities are bound to real-world entities, since it would allow one to know where a given person was at a given point in time. However, for users' privacy to be seriously threatened, attackers would need to *physically* track them, which the cooperative backup service could hardly be held accountable for. This is a lesser concern when identities are not bound to real-world entities.

6   Implementation Considerations

This section discusses implementation concerns and in particular the choice of actual protocols to achieve the goals outlined earlier.

6.1   Protocol Choice

While Mobile IPv6 [36] provides some of the features we need, we considered it impractical since its mechanisms are implemented at the network layer, and implementations are not widely available at this time.

Our implementation of the block store (essentially the `put` and `get` requests mentioned earlier) is based on Sun/ONC RPC [40]. ONC RPC defines the so-called "DES authentication mechanism", designed for authentication over a wide-area network; however, the mechanism does not address all our concerns (for example, its naming scheme for peers does not fulfill all the requirements of Section 5.2, and in particular does not allow name-device bindings to be reliably authenticated). The authentication mechanisms for ONC RPC defined in RFC 2695 [10] have similar shortcomings with respect to our goals. The RPCSec bindings for the Generic Security Services Application Programming Interface (GSS-API) [17] were not considered appropriate either (one reason is that most available GSS-API implementations only support Kerberos-based mechanisms, which assumes the availability of such an infrastructure).

Consequently, we decided to use the well-known Transport Layer Security (TLS), a protocol currently widely deployed on the Internet [15]. Although it was not designed with mobile computing and constrained devices in mind, we believe its flexibility makes it a suitable choice. In particular, TLS offers a wide range of *cipher suites*, which allows us to choose cipher suites that meet our resource saving constraints, such as cipher suites with no payload data encryption, as discussed in Section 3.1. TLS provides message authentication guarantees using HMACs, where, again, the HMAC algorithm to be used is negotiated between peers. TLS provides payload compression but this may be disabled (also subject to negotiation between peers). Again, disabling it allows us to save energy, especially since the data that is to be exchanged among peers is already compressed.

As far as mutual authentication is concerned, TLS provides it through *certificate-based authentication mechanisms*. While the main document [15] refers primarily to X.509 certificates, a proposal has been made to extend TLS to support authentication using OpenPGP certificates [31]. This extension is very relevant in our context for a number of reasons. First, OpenPGP certificates can be readily generated using widely available tools (e.g., GnuPG) and they are already familiar to many computer users. Second, OpenPGP certificates are already used in the context of secure electronic communications among individuals. Therefore, the use of OpenPGP certificates also allows users to easily implement cooperation policies based on the underlying social network, as outlined in Section 5.5.

OpenPGP certificates contain a lot more than just a public key. In particular, since they are primarily used to certify a binding between a public key and a real-world person name, they contain information such as the real-world name and email address of the person the public key (allegedly) belongs to (the "user ID packets"), and a list of third-party signatures (certifications) indicating the level of trust put by other people in this name-key binding [7]. This information is only useful when implementing cooperation policies based on the social network.

6.2 Prototype Implementation

We have been working on a prototype implementation of our cooperative backup protocol that uses ONC RPC on top of TLS. Since ONC RPC implementations do not natively support the use of TLS as the underlying protocol, we did our own implementation. This proved to be easy to do, using raw TCP RPC client/server code as a starting point. We use GnuTLS [25] as the underlying TLS implementation since it is the only major implementation supporting the OpenPGP extension [31] as of this writing. GnuTLS is very flexible and has allowed us to actually make various specific trade-offs, such as disabling compression, choosing an encryption-less cipher suite, etc.

Initial measurements show that TLS induces little communication overhead. Handshake itself demands 2 KiB per connection in both directions (when using certificates with no signature packets), most of which stems from the OpenPGP certificate exchange. TLS' record layer incurs little overhead (e.g., less than 30 octets per message with SHA-1-based HMACs), provided messages are at most 16 KiB large—otherwise messages are fragmented, which incurs additional overhead [15]. Although further measurements are needed, these results seem reasonable in our context.

6.3 On-Going and Future Work

We are currently in the process of evaluating the overhead, in terms of network bandwidth and CPU cost, induced by the use of TLS. We have also started implementing a set of cooperation policies, ranging from simplistic policies such as "white lists", to more sophisticated policies that make use of local information of past interactions with other devices. The next step will be the implementation of a reputation system where participating devices can exchange and make use of cooperation certificates.

All these cooperation policies will need to be evaluated and compared, notably in terms of the overall level of cooperation yielded, and in terms of the resilience of the cooperative service to the aforementioned DoS attacks. Different reference scenarios will need to be identified to that end. It is still unclear which method we will choose to achieve this goal. Simulation looks appealing but may be hard to set up to faithfully reflect our system model. On the other hand, we may also try to build on the analytical evaluation of replication strategies that we conducted earlier [11]. Specifically, this evaluation uses a model of interactions among participating devices using Petri nets and Markov chains that could be extended to reflect various cooperation strategies.

7 Related Work

A lot of work has gone into thwarting availability threats due to DoS attacks similar to those described in Section 3.3. Most of this work was done in the area of peer-to-peer storage and cooperative backup. While our cooperative backup scheme with intermittent connectivity to the infrastructure is similar to delay-tolerant networks [42], the security of such networks is still largely an open issue [21,24]. This is partly due to the fact that most applications of DTNs, such as space mission networks, are not expected to be open for anyone to participate, which reduces the incentive to address these issues.

Fall *et al.* did propose security mechanisms permitting DTN routers to detect and eliminate disallowed traffic, and thereby avoid DoS attacks such as flooding against the DTN [20]. However, the proposed solution relies on centralized identity management and authorization: all participants are issued a key pair by an authority, along with a "postage stamp" signed by that authority indicating the allowed "class of service" for that user. Such an approach only addresses specific DoS attacks. Forms of non-cooperation such as refusal to forward a message are not tackled. We also believe that such an approach does not scale and suffers from shortcomings inherent to single-authority domain approaches, as discussed in Section 5.

In general, "trust begets cooperation". In the case of our cooperative backup service, data owners need to trust contributors to provide them the service, while contributors need to trust data owners not to abuse the service (e.g., by flooding it or by being selfish). While both issues have to do with trust establishment between owners and contributors, the literature tends to refer to both aspects using different names, such as *cooperation incentives* and *trust establishment*.

To evaluate the cooperativeness of a peer, one needs to be able to observe both its service usage and its service provision. When the cooperative service is packet forwarding or routing in MANETs, device cooperation can be evaluated almost instantaneously [4,23,33]. However, in cooperative backup services, service usage and service provision call for different evaluation techniques. First, service usage can be balanced using simple strategies such as symmetric trades [29] (i.e., pairwise "tit-for-tat" exchanges), or "storage claims" that may be exchanged among peers [14]. Both approaches assume high connectivity among peers and are therefore unsuitable to MANETs. Second, *periodic auditing* has been proposed to establish trust in contributor service provision [1,13,14,29], but it requires peers to be reachable so that they can be challenged, which is unsuitable to the MANET context. In our cooperative backup service for MANETs, service provision can only realistically be evaluated when gaining Internet access or upon restoration.

Once service provision and usage can be evaluated, self-organized solutions usually make use of "history records" of peer behavior as an aid to cooperation decisions, as mentioned in Section 5.5. Simulations have been made to evaluate the impact on cooperation of such mechanisms when used by all participants, in the context of both private and shared history records [4,28]. In MANETs, reputation mechanisms have been proposed primarily in the context of packet forwarding for multi-hop routing protocols and route discovery [4,33].

Designation issues in a decentralized environment have been studied notably in the context of distributed programming and capability systems [35] as well as in the context of public key infrastructures (PKIs) [18,19]. The provision of guarantees for "address ownership" (i.e., having address-device bindings that can be authenticated) has also been a concern in the design of Mobile IPv6 (MIPv6) [36]. This led the authors to opt for "statistically unique and cryptographically verifiable (SUCV) identifiers". This is similar to one of the mechanisms we propose in this paper, except that we operate at the application level rather than at the network layer, which provides us with more flexibility.

Douceur *et al.* described the Sybil attack as a problem that is inherent to distributed systems using self-managed designators [16]. In [30] the authors showed that a reputation system can efficiently leverage cooperation even when self-managed designators are used.

8 Conclusion

We introduced a cooperative backup service for mobile devices that builds on the peer-to-peer, self-organizing paradigm largely used on the Internet. We identified security threats on such a service and listed subsequent security requirements. We have shown how a reduced set of well-known cryptographic primitives can be used to meet those requirements in a self-organized way. Our approach differs from earlier work in that it focuses on *policy-neutral* security mechanisms, rather than on a specific cooperation policy.

In particular, we advocated the use of public keys as self-managed, secure and unique designators for participating devices and discussed their use as a policy-neutral building block for a variety of cooperation policies, including a reputation system. Systems using self-managed designators are subject to the Sybil attack; therefore, we discussed the impact of this attack in our context and showed how cooperation policies can be implemented that reduce the harm that can be done. Finally, we discussed implementation issues and outlined the foundations of an implementation that uses TLS with OpenPGP certificate-based authentication.

The work presented in this paper is part of a larger design and implementation effort of a cooperative backup service for mobile devices. Our earlier work explored other aspects of the design space, particularly relating to storage tradeoffs and data encoding and compression techniques [12], as well as the evaluation of replication strategies [11]. Future work includes a detailed evaluation of some of the techniques discussed in this paper, as well as the deployment of a prototype cooperative backup service in real-world conditions.

References

1. Aiyer, A.S., Alvisi, L., Clement, A., Dahlin, M., Martin, J.-P., Porth, C.: BAR Fault Tolerance for Cooperative Services. In: Proceedings of the ACM Symposium on Operating Systems Principles, pp. 45–58. ACM Press, New York (2005)
2. Bennett, K., Grothoff, C., Horozov, T., Patrascu, I.: Efficient Sharing of Encrypted Data. In: Batten, L.M., Seberry, J. (eds.) ACISP 2002. LNCS, vol. 2384, pp. 107–120. Springer, Heidelberg (2002)

3. Boulkenafed, M., Issarny, V.: AdHocFS: Sharing Files in WLANs. In: Proceedings of the 2nd International Symposium on Network Computing and Applications (April 2003)
4. Buchegger, S., Le Boudec, J.-Y.: The Effect of Rumor Spreading in Reputation Systems for Mobile Ad-hoc Networks. In: Proceedings of WiOpt '03: Modeling and Optimization in Mobile, Ad Hoc and Wireless Networks (March 2003)
5. Buttyán, L., Hubaux, J.-P.: Stimulating Cooperation in Self-Organizing Mobile Ad Hoc Networks. ACM/Kluwer Mobile Networks and Applications 8(5), 579–592 (2003)
6. Buttyán, L., Hubaux, J.-P.: Enforcing Service Availability in Mobile Ad-Hoc WANs. In: Proceedings of the First ACM International Symposium on Mobile Ad Hoc Networking & Computing, pp. 87–96. IEEE CS Press, Los Alamitos (2000)
7. Callas, J., Donnerhacke, L., Finney, H., Thayer, R.: OpenPGP Message Format (RFC 2440). Internet Engineering Task Force (IETF) (November 1998), http://tools.ietf.org/html/rfc2440
8. Capkun, S., Buttyán, L., Hubaux, J.-P.: Small Worlds in Security Systems an Analysis of the PGP Certificate Graph. In: Proceedings of the Workshop on New Security Paradigms, pp. 28–35. ACM Press, New York (2002)
9. Capkun, S., Buttyán, L., Hubaux, J.-P.: Self-Organized Public-Key Management for Mobile Ad Hoc Networks. IEEE Transactions on Mobile Computing 2(1), 52–64 (2003)
10. Chiu, A.: Authentication Mechanisms for ONC RPC (RFC 2695). Internet Engineering Task Force (IETF) (September 1999), http://tools.ietf.org/html/rfc2695
11. Courtès, L., Hamouda, O., Kaâniche, M., Killijian, M.-O., Powell, D.: Assessment of Cooperative Backup Strategies for Mobile Devices. Technical Report 06817, LAAS-CNRS (December 2006)
12. Courtès, L., Killijian, M.-O., Powell, D.: Storage Tradeoffs in a Collaborative Backup Service for Mobile Devices. In: Proceedings of the Sixth European Dependable Computing Conference, pp. 129–138. IEEE CS Press, Los Alamitos (October 2006)
13. Cox, L.P., Murray, C.D., Noble, B.D.: Pastiche: Making Backup Cheap and Easy. In: Fifth USENIX Symposium on Operating Systems Design and Implementation, pp. 285–298 (December 2002)
14. Cox, L.P., Noble, B.D.: Samsara: Honor Among Thieves in Peer-to-Peer Storage. In: Proceedings 19th ACM Symposium on Operating Systems Principles, pp. 120–132. ACM Press, New York (2003)
15. Dierks, T., Rescorla, E., Teerse, W.: The Transport Layer Security (TLS) Protocol, Version 1.1 (RFC 4346). Internet Engineering Task Force (IETF) (2006), http://tools.ietf.org/html/rfc4346
16. Douceur, J.R.: The Sybil Attack. In: Revised Papers from the First International Workshop on Peer-to-Peer Systems (IPTPS), pp. 251–260. Springer, Heidelberg (2002)
17. Eisler, M., Chiu, A., Ling, L.: RPCSEC_GSS Protocol Specification (RFC 2203). Internet Engineering Task Force (IETF) (September 1997), http://tools.ietf.org/html/rfc2203
18. Ellison, C.M., Frantz, B., Lampson, B., Rivest, R., Thomas, B., Ylonen, T.: SPKI Certificate Theory (RFC 2693). Internet Engineering Task Force (IETF) (September 1999), http://www.ietf.org/rfc/rfc2693.txt
19. Ellison, C.M.: Establishing Identity Without Certification Authorities. In: Proceedings of the Sixth USENIX Security Symposium, pp. 67–76 (1996)

20. Fall, K.: A Delay-Tolerant Network Architecture for Challenged Internets. In: Proceedings of the Conference on Applications, Technologies, Architectures, and Protocols for Computer Communications (SIGCOMM), pp. 27–34 (August 2003)
21. Farrell, S., Cahill, V.: Security Considerations in Space and Delay Tolerant Networks. In: Proceedings of the 2nd IEEE International Conference on Space Mission Challenges for Information Technology, pp. 29–38. IEEE CS Press, Los Alamitos (2006)
22. Flinn, J., Sinnamohideen, S., Tolia, N., Satyanarayanan, M.: Data Staging on Untrusted Surrogates. In: Proceedings of the USENIX Conference on File and Storage Technologies (FAST) (March 2003)
23. Grothoff, C.: An Excess-Based Economic Model for Resource Allocation in Peer-to-Peer Networks. Wirtschaftsinformatik 45(3), 285–292 (2003)
24. Harras, K.A., Wittie, M.P., Almeroth, K.C., Belding, E.M.: ParaNets: A Parallel Network Architecture for Challenged Networks. In: Proceedings of the IEEE Workshop on Mobile Computing Systems and Applications, IEEE Computer Society Press, Los Alamitos (2007)
25. Josefsson, S., Mavrogiannopoulos, N.: The GNU TLS Library (2006), http://gnutls.org/
26. Karypidis, A., Lalis, S.: OmniStore: A System for Ubiquitous Personal Storage Management. In: Proceedings of the Annual IEEE International Conference on Pervasive Computing and Communications (PerCom), pp. 136–147. IEEE CS Press, Los Alamitos (March 2006)
27. Killijian, M.-O., Powell, D., Banâtre, M., Couderc, P., Roudier, Y.: Collaborative Backup for Dependable Mobile Applications. In: Proceedings of 2nd International Workshop on Middleware for Pervasive and Ad-Hoc Computing (Middleware 2004), pp. 146–149. ACM Press, New York (2004)
28. Lai, K., Feldman, M., Chuang, J., Stoica, I.: Incentives for Cooperation in Peer-to-Peer Networks. In: Proceedings of the Workshop on Economics of Peer-to-Peer Systems (2003)
29. Lillibridge, M., Elnikety, S., Birrell, A., Burrows, M., Isard, M.: A Cooperative Internet Backup Scheme. In: Proceedings of the USENIX Annual Technical Conference, pp. 29–42 (June 2003)
30. Marti, S., Garcia-Molina, H.: Identity Crisis: Anonymity vs. Reputation in P2P Systems. In: IEEE Conference on Peer-to-Peer Computing, pp. 134–141. IEEE CS Press, Los Alamitos (September 2003)
31. Mavrogiannopoulos, N.: Using OpenPGP Keys for TLS Authentication (IETF Internet Draft). In: Internet Engineering Task Force (IETF) (July 2006), http://www.ietf.org/internet-drafts/draft-ietf-tls-openpgp-keys-11.txt
32. Merkle, R.C.: Protocols for Public Key Cryptosystems. In: Proceedings of the IEEE Symposium on Security and Privacy, pp. 122–134. IEEE Computer Society Press, Los Alamitos (1980)
33. Michiardi, P., Molva, R.: CORE: A Collaborative Reputation Mechanism to Enforce Node Cooperation in Mobile Ad Hoc Networks. In: Proceedings of the Sixth IFIP TC6/TC11 Joint Conference on Communications and Multimedia Security, pp. 107–121. Kluwer Academic Publishers, Dordrecht (2002)
34. Milgram, S.: The Small World Problem. Psychology Today 2, 60–67 (1967)
35. Miller, M.S.: Robust Composition: Towards a Unified Approach to Access Control and Concurrency Control, PhD Thesis, Johns Hopkins University, Baltimore, MA, USA, (May 2006)

36. Montenegro, G., Castelluccia, C.: Statistically Unique and Cryptographically Verifiable (SUCV) Identifiers and Addresses. In: Proceedings of the Network and Distributed System Security Symposium (NDSS) (2002)
37. Quinlan, S., Dorward, S.: Venti: A New Approach to Archival Storage. In: Proceedings of the First USENIX Conference on File and Storage Technologies, pp. 89–101 (2002)
38. Mizanur Rahman, Sk.Md., Inomata, A., Okamoto, T., Mambo, M., Okamoto, E.: Anonymous Secure Communication in Wireless Mobile Ad-hoc Networks. In: Proceedings of the First International Conference on Ubiquitous Convergence Technology, pp. 131–140. Springer, Heidelberg (2006)
39. Sailhan, F., Issarny, V.: Scalable Service Discovery for MANET. In: Proceedings of the IEEE International Conference on Pervasive Computing and Communication, IEEE Computer Society Press, Los Alamitos (2005)
40. Srinivasan, R.: RPC: Remote Procedure Call Protocol Specification, Version 2 (RFC 1831). In: Internet Engineering Task Force (IETF) (August 1995), http://tools.ietf.org/html/rfc1831
41. Yin, L., Cao, G.: Supporting Cooperative Caching in Ad Hoc Networks. IEEE Transactions on Mobile Computing 5(1), 77–89 (2006)
42. Zhang, Z.: Routing in Intermittently Connected Mobile Ad Hoc Networks and Delay Tolerant Networks: Overview and Challenges. IEEE Communications Surveys & Tutorials 8, 24–37 (2006)

Do You Know… How to Analyze and Share Results from Dependability Evaluation Experiments?

Marco Vieira and Henrique Madeira

CISUC – University of Coimbra
3030 Coimbra, Portugal
{mvieira,henrique}@dei.uc.pt

Abstract. In this tutorial we explore the use of data warehousing and OLAP (On-Line Analytical Processing) technologies to analyze the results from dependability evaluation experiments. The tutorial, intended for researchers working in experimental dependability evaluation, includes a demonstration of the use of these technologies in a concrete example of experimental dependability evaluation.

Keywords: Experimental dependability evaluation, data warehousing, OLAP.

Synopsis

It is well known that the evaluation of dependability features in computer systems is a complex task. Traditional techniques based on analytical and simulation models have to be complemented with experimental approaches based on measurements taken from real systems and prototypes. These experimental techniques, including fault injection, robustness testing, and field measurements, have been extensively used to evaluate specific fault tolerance mechanisms, validate robustness of software components, or to assess the general impact of faults in systems. However, in spite of the effort put on the development of adequate tools and the intensive research devoted to the mitigation of key problems such as experiment representativeness, intrusiveness and portability of tools, two important questions remain largely unanswered:

- How to analyze the usually large amount of raw data produced in dependability evaluation experiments, especially when the analysis is complex and have to take into account many aspects of the experimental setup (e.g., target systems, configurations, workload and programs, faultload, diversity of measures, etc)?
- How to compare results from different experiments or results of similar experiments across different systems if the tools, data formats, and the setup details are different and, often, incompatible?

Data warehousing refers to "a collection of decision support technologies aimed at enabling the knowledge worker (executive, manager, or analyst) to make better and faster decisions" [1]. A data warehouse is a global repository that stores large amounts of data that has been extracted and integrated from heterogeneous systems (operational or legacy systems). OLAP (On-Line Analytical Processing) is the

A. Bondavalli, F. Brasileiro, and S. Rajsbaum (Eds.): LADC 2007, LNCS 4746, pp. 231–232, 2007.

technique of performing complex analysis over the information stored in a data warehouse [2]. The data warehouse coupled with OLAP enable decision makers to creatively analyze and understand business trends since it transforms operational data into strategic decision making information.

The goal of this tutorial is to explore the use of multidimensional analysis and data warehousing & OLAP (On-Line Analytical Processing) technology, to solve the problem of analyzing, sharing, and cross-exploiting results from dependability evaluation experiments. The central idea is to collect the raw data produced in dependability evaluation experiments and store it in a multidimensional data structure (data warehouse). The data analysis is done through the use of commercially available OLAP tools such as the ones traditionally used in business decision support analysis [2] (e.g., Discoverer® from Oracle). That is, instead of following the usual trend of adding data analysis features to fault injectors and robustness testing tools, there is a clear separation between the experimental setup (target specific) and the result analysis setup (general in our approach). Existing tools and experimental setups are used as they are and just export the data obtained in the experiments to a data warehouse, where all the analysis and cross-exploitation of results can be done in an efficient and general way.

The data warehousing approach applied to the analysis of data obtained from dependability evaluation experiments can be used in different scenarios:

- At research team level, to perform the analysis of experimental data in a very efficient way. At the same time, both the data and the OLAP tool needed to analyze the data can be available at the web, allowing a very efficient dissemination of the research results produced by the team.
- At project level (assuming that a project includes several research teams), to allow sharing and cross-exploitation of results obtained by the different teams.
- World wide in the form of common repositories to store and share experimental dependability evaluation results. In fact this is probably the only way to change the current situation, in which many teams are performing experimental dependability evaluation (particularly experiments based on fault injection) and there is no results currently available at the web. The data warehousing approach can change drastically this situation, as it proposes a common format to share the data (the multidimensional model in the form of a star scheme) and a standard type of tool to analyze the results (the OLAP tools) stored in the data warehouses.

The tutorial will start by the problem presentation followed by the discussion of some introductory concepts on building data warehouses, including the following key topics: the steps; the star model; the process of extraction transformation and loading data. Afterwards, we will focus on how to use data warehouses and OLAP to analyze dependability evaluation data. A case study will be presented and discussed before the tutorial closure.

References

1. Chauduri, S., Dayal, U.: An overview of data warehousing and OLAP technology. SIGMOD Record 26(1), 65–74 (1997)
2. Kimball, R., Ross, M.: The Data Warehouse Toolkit: The Complete Guide to Dimensional Modeling, 2nd edn. Wiley & Sons, Inc., Chichester (2002)

Security Patterns and Secure Systems Design

Eduardo B. Fernandez

Dept. of Computer Science and Eng.,
Florida Atlantic University, Boca Raton, FL 33431, USA
ed@cse.fau.edu

Abstract. Analysis and design patterns are well established to build high-quality object-oriented software. Patterns combine experience and good practices to develop basic models that can be used for new designs. Security patterns join the extensive knowledge accumulated about security with the structure provided by patterns to provide guidelines for secure system design and evaluation. They are being adopted by companies such as IBM, Sun, and Microsoft. We show the anatomy of a security pattern, a variety of them, and their use in the construction of secure systems. These patterns include Authentication, Authorization, Role-based Access Control, Firewalls, Web Services Security (SAML, XACML, XML Firewall), and others. We apply these patterns through a secure system development method based on a hierarchical architecture whose layers define the scope of each security mechanism. First, the possible attacks are considered from an analysis of use cases. Then the rights of the users are defined from the use cases using a Role-Based Access Control (RBAC) or other security model. The attacks are used to define the policies that could stop them. The rights are reflected in the conceptual class model. We then define additional security constraints that apply to distribution, interfaces, and components. The patterns are shown using UML models and some examples are taken from my book "Security Patterns" (Wiley 2006).

1 Session Learning Objectives

Attendees should be able to understand the general concept of security patterns as solutions to security problems. We show how the pattern template focuses on specific aspects of security and on the use of the pattern.

We also see how to use security patterns as guidelines to build secure systems. A complete methodology will be presented with some examples.

Finally, we show how to use security patterns to describe a security mechanism. We give several examples of security patterns.

2 Prerequisites

Basic knowledge of UML and object-oriented design is assumed. Understanding of basic security concepts is also needed.

A. Bondavalli, F. Brasileiro, and S. Rajsbaum (Eds.): LADC 2007, LNCS 4746, pp. 233–234, 2007.
© Springer-Verlag Berlin Heidelberg 2007

3 Outline

1. Introduction---Motivation, basic concepts. The context for security. Attacks.
2. The design of secure systems--- Object-oriented design, UML, and patterns, need for good software engineering. Security principles. Security patterns. Standards.
3. Anatomy of a security pattern.
4. Security models and their patterns---policies, access matrix, multilevel models, RBAC
5. Defining authorizations from use cases---nonfunctional aspects of use cases, RBAC and security policies
6. Firewall, IDS, and operating system patterns
7. Authorized conceptual model
8. Secure system architectures---effect of distribution and user interfaces
9. Web application servers and components---mapping RBAC to components, J2EE and .NET
10. Patterns for web services: SAML, XACML, Liberty Alliance, WS-Security. Comparing standards through patterns. Application and XML firewalls
11. Coordination across levels---mapping of authorizations across architectural levels
12. Conclusions---the future

BAR—Where Distributed Computing Meets Game Theory

Lorenzo Alvisi

Laboratory for Advanced Systems Research (LASR)
Department of Computer Sciences
The University of Texas at Austin
lorenzo@cs.utexas.edu

This tutorial describes a general approach for building cooperative services that span multiple administrative domains (MADs). MAD systems are attractive because their diffused control structure may yield services that are potentially less costly and more democratic than their more centralized counterparts. Unfortunately, they are also particularly problematic from a dependability standpoint as they challenge the traditional distinction between correct and faulty nodes.

Nodes in a MAD system can, as always, deviate from their specification because they are *broken*, on account of bugs, errors in software configuration, or even malicious attacks. But MAD systems add a new dimension: without a central administrator to ensure that all unbroken nodes follow faithfully their assigned protocol, nodes may deviate from their specification also because they are *selfish* and are intent on maximizing their own utility. BFT handles the first class of deviations well. However, the Byzantine model classifies all deviations as faults and requires a bound on the number of faults in the system; this bound is not tenable in MAD systems where *all* nodes may benefit from selfish behavior and be motivated to deviate from the protocol. Models based on traditional game theory only account for rational behavior and are therefore brittle: they handle the second class of selfish deviations, but may be vulnerable to arbitrary disruptions if even a single node is broken and deviates from expected rational behavior.

The challenge in developing a solid foundation for constructing MAD services is then (at least) threefold: (1) to develop a model for MAD services in which it is possible to reason and prove properties of MAD services; (2) to understand how to simplify the development of MAD services under the new model, (3) to demonstrate that MAD services developed under this model can be practical by building and deploying useful applications.

This tutorial reports on the initial progress that my colleagues—Mike Dahlin, Allen Clement, Harry Li, Jean-Phippe Martin, Jeff Napper, Edmund Wong—and I have made in addressing these issues:

- It will introduce BAR, a new failure model named after the initial of the three classes of nodes (Byzantine, Altruistic, and Rational) that it explicitly considers. Byzantine nodes can deviate arbitrarily from their specification,

A. Bondavalli, F. Brasileiro, and S. Rajsbaum (Eds.): LADC 2007, LNCS 4746, pp. 235–236, 2007.

even if doing so is against their interest. Altruistic nodes follow their specification faithfully, without consideration of their self interest. Rational nodes behave selfishly and deviate from a given protocol if doing so improves their own utility. We will discuss how BAR can be used to establish a formally sound foundation for modeling realistic MAD services.

– It will present BAR-tolerant protocols for terminating reliable broadcast, state machine replication, and gossip-based multicast
– It will discuss the design and implementation of two BAR-tolerant peer-to-peer systems: BAR-B, a cooperative backup service, and FlightPath, a streaming media application. Both systems provably continue to maintain their properties despite the absence of altruistic peers.

Scaling Dependability and Security in Ad Hoc Networks

Rogério de Lemos

Computing Laboratory
University of Kent, UK
r.delemos@kent.ac.uk

Abstract. The increasing size and complexity of the next generation of large distributed systems will require radical new approaches for guaranteeing certain levels of dependability and security. Current solutions might become brittle in context of new applications, such as pervasive computing, in which there is a large number of components with dynamic interdependencies between them. The inherent complexity of these future systems due to heterogeneity, decentralisation, and emergent technologies also demand scalable and robust solutions. An example of such emergent technologies is ad hoc networks, which are self-configuring networks that enable the connection of thousands of devices in arbitrary topologies. The objective of the panel is to discuss the challenges and the potential solutions when building dependable and secure applications in the context of ad hoc networks. This panel has been organised as a joint event between the Sixth International Conference on Ad-Hoc Networks and Wireless (Ad Hoc NOW 2007) and the Third Latin American Symposium on Dependable Computing (LADC 2007), which are two co-located events of the Mexican International Conference in Computer Science (ENC 2007).

A. Bondavalli, F. Brasileiro, and S. Rajsbaum (Eds.): LADC 2007, LNCS 4746, p. 237, 2007.
© Springer-Verlag Berlin Heidelberg 2007

Assessing, Measuring, and Benchmarking Dependability and Resilience

Henrique Madeira

CISUC - University of Coimbra
3030 Coimbra, Portugal
henrique@dei.uc.pt

Cost pressure, short time to market, and increased complexity are responsible for an evident increase of the failure rate of computing systems, while the cost of failures is growing rapidly, as a result of an unprecedented degree of dependence of our society on computing systems. The combination of these factors has created a dependability and security gap that is often perceived by users as a lack of trustworthiness in computer applications, but that is in fact undermining the network and service infrastructures that constitute the very core of the knowledge-based society.

Assessing resilience is the key stone to improving trustworthiness in computer systems and components. "If you cannot measure something, you cannot really understand it" (Lord Kelvin) - a well-known aphorism which we use to emphasize the need of effective and accurate methods to assess and measure dependability and security in order to understand current risks of network and service infrastructures.

Although considerable efforts have been made, measuring dependability and resilience is still a very difficult problem, especially when the goal is to measure resilience in a standard and comparable way. This panel will discuss the main issues and recent developments on assessing, measuring, and benchmarking resilience, as seen by leading specialists in the field.

A. Bondavalli, F. Brasileiro, and S. Rajsbaum (Eds.): LADC 2007, LNCS 4746, p. 238 2007.
© Springer-Verlag Berlin Heidelberg 2007

Author Index

Lecture Notes in Computer Science

Sublibrary 1: Theoretical Computer Science and General Issues

For information about Vols. 1– 4446
please contact your bookseller or Springer

Vol. 4624: T. Mossakowski, U. Montanari, M. Haveraaen (Eds.), Algebra and Coalgebra in Computer Science. XI, 463 pages. 2007.

Vol. 4621: D. Wagner, R. Wattenhofer (Eds.), Algorithms for Sensor and Ad Hoc Networks. XIII, 415 pages. 2007.

Vol. 4619: F. Dehne, J.-R. Sack, N. Zeh (Eds.), Algorithms and Data Structures. XVI, 662 pages. 2007.

Vol. 4618: S.G. Akl, C.S. Calude, M.J. Dinneen, G. Rozenberg, H.T. Wareham (Eds.), Unconventional Computation. X, 243 pages. 2007.

Vol. 4616: A. Dress, Y. Xu, B. Zhu (Eds.), Combinatorial Optimization and Applications. XI, 390 pages. 2007.

Vol. 4613: F.P. Preparata, Q. Fang (Eds.), Frontiers in Algorithmics. XI, 348 pages. 2007.

Vol. 4600: H. Comon-Lundh, C. Kirchner, H. Kirchner (Eds.), Rewriting, Computation and Proof. XVI, 273 pages. 2007.

Vol. 4599: S. Vassiliadis, M. Berekovic, T.D. Hämäläinen (Eds.), Embedded Computer Systems: Architectures, Modeling, and Simulation. XVIII, 466 pages. 2007.

Vol. 4598: G. Lin (Ed.), Computing and Combinatorics. XII, 570 pages. 2007.

Vol. 4596: L. Arge, C. Cachin, T. Jurdziński, A. Tarlecki (Eds.), Automata, Languages and Programming. XVII, 953 pages. 2007.

Vol. 4595: D. Bošnački, S. Edelkamp (Eds.), Model Checking Software. X, 285 pages. 2007.

Vol. 4590: W. Damm, H. Hermanns (Eds.), Computer Aided Verification. XV, 562 pages. 2007.

Vol. 4588: T. Harju, J. Karhumäki, A. Lepistö (Eds.), Developments in Language Theory. XI, 423 pages. 2007.

Vol. 4583: S.R. Della Rocca (Ed.), Typed Lambda Calculi and Applications. X, 397 pages. 2007.

Vol. 4580: B. Ma, K. Zhang (Eds.), Combinatorial Pattern Matching. XII, 366 pages. 2007.

Vol. 4576: D. Leivant, R. de Queiroz (Eds.), Logic, Language, Information and Computation. X, 363 pages. 2007.

Vol. 4547: C. Carlet, B. Sunar (Eds.), Arithmetic of Finite Fields. XI, 355 pages. 2007.

Vol. 4546: J. Kleijn, A. Yakovlev (Eds.), Petri Nets and Other Models of Concurrency – ICATPN 2007. XI, 515 pages. 2007.

Vol. 4545: H. Anai, K. Horimoto, T. Kutsia (Eds.), Algebraic Biology. XIII, 379 pages. 2007.

Vol. 4533: F. Baader (Ed.), Term Rewriting and Applications. XII, 419 pages. 2007.

Vol. 4528: J. Mira, J.R. Álvarez (Eds.), Nature Inspired Problem-Solving Methods in Knowledge Engineering, Part II. XXII, 650 pages. 2007.

Vol. 4527: J. Mira, J.R. Álvarez (Eds.), Bio-inspired Modeling of Cognitive Tasks, Part I. XXII, 630 pages. 2007.

Vol. 4525: C. Demetrescu (Ed.), Experimental Algorithms. XIII, 448 pages. 2007.

Vol. 4514: S.N. Artemov, A. Nerode (Eds.), Logical Foundations of Computer Science. XI, 513 pages. 2007.

Vol. 4513: M. Fischetti, D.P. Williamson (Eds.), Integer Programming and Combinatorial Optimization. IX, 500 pages. 2007.

Vol. 4510: P. Van Hentenryck, L.A. Wolsey (Eds.), Integration of AI and OR Techniques in Constraint Programming for Combinatorial Optimization Problems. X, 391 pages. 2007.

Vol. 4507: F. Sandoval, A.G. Prieto, J. Cabestany, M. Graña (Eds.), Computational and Ambient Intelligence. XXVI, 1167 pages. 2007.

Vol. 4501: J. Marques-Silva, K.A. Sakallah (Eds.), Theory and Applications of Satisfiability Testing – SAT 2007. XI, 384 pages. 2007.

Vol. 4497: S.B. Cooper, B. Löwe, A. Sorbi (Eds.), Computation and Logic in the Real World. XVIII, 826 pages. 2007.

Vol. 4494: H. Jin, O.F. Rana, Y. Pan, V.K. Prasanna (Eds.), Algorithms and Architectures for Parallel Processing. XIV, 508 pages. 2007.

Vol. 4493: D. Liu, S. Fei, Z. Hou, H. Zhang, C. Sun (Eds.), Advances in Neural Networks – ISNN 2007, Part III. XXVI, 1215 pages. 2007.

Vol. 4492: D. Liu, S. Fei, Z. Hou, H. Zhang, C. Sun (Eds.), Advances in Neural Networks – ISNN 2007, Part II. XXVII, 1321 pages. 2007.

Vol. 4491: D. Liu, S. Fei, Z.-G. Hou, H. Zhang, C. Sun (Eds.), Advances in Neural Networks – ISNN 2007, Part I. LIV, 1365 pages. 2007.

Vol. 4490: Y. Shi, G.D. van Albada, J.J. Dongarra, P.M.A. Sloot (Eds.), Computational Science – ICCS 2007, Part IV. XXXVII, 1211 pages. 2007.

Vol. 4489: Y. Shi, G.D. van Albada, J.J. Dongarra, P.M.A. Sloot (Eds.), Computational Science – ICCS 2007, Part III. XXXVII, 1257 pages. 2007.

Vol. 4488: Y. Shi, G.D. van Albada, J.J. Dongarra, P.M.A. Sloot (Eds.), Computational Science – ICCS 2007, Part II. XXXV, 1251 pages. 2007.

Vol. 4487: Y. Shi, G.D. van Albada, J.J. Dongarra, P.M.A. Sloot (Eds.), Computational Science – ICCS 2007, Part I. LXXXI, 1275 pages. 2007.

Vol. 4484: J.-Y. Cai, S.B. Cooper, H. Zhu (Eds.), Theory and Applications of Models of Computation. XIII, 772 pages. 2007.

Vol. 4475: P. Crescenzi, G. Prencipe, G. Pucci (Eds.), Fun with Algorithms. X, 273 pages. 2007.

Vol. 4474: G. Prencipe, S. Zaks (Eds.), Structural Information and Communication Complexity. XI, 342 pages. 2007.

Vol. 4459: C. Cérin, K.-C. Li (Eds.), Advances in Grid and Pervasive Computing. XVI, 759 pages. 2007.

Vol. 4449: Z. Horváth, V. Zsók, A. Butterfield (Eds.), Implementation and Application of Functional Languages. X, 271 pages. 2007.

Vol. 4448: M. Giacobini (Ed.), Applications of Evolutionary Computing. XXIII, 755 pages. 2007.

Vol. 4447: E. Marchiori, J.H. Moore, J.C. Rajapakse (Eds.), Evolutionary Computation, Machine Learning and Data Mining in Bioinformatics. XI, 302 pages. 2007.